Sin and Grace Apologetics

Defend the Gospel With the Gospel

Robert J. Koester

GWA
Books

SIN AND GRACE APOLOGETICS

GWA Books
gwabooks@midco.net
24-01

ISBN: 978-1-7344319-7-1
Library of Congress Control Number: 2023919971

Contents

Preface

This book is a journey into the world of modern apologetics. Apologetics is the task of answering questions and overcoming doubts about the Christian faith—proving that it's reasonable to believe in Christianity.

In the midst of growing unbelief and skepticism, apologetics is said to hold great promise. This book is written for Lutherans, specifically for Lutherans who believe that the Lutheran Confessions (Luther's Small Catechism, for example) teach Scripture accurately. The purpose of this book is to explore questions Lutherans should be asking when they think about modern apologetics.

Here are the kind of questions we'll try to answer:

- Christians sometimes get the idea that learning apologetics is just a matter of memorizing some standard, easily applied arguments. They also assume that all modern apologists agree on how apologetics should be done. Apologetics, however, is a very complex area of study, and modern apologists have some differing opinions on the best arguments to use. What are those arguments and how important are they?
- *How* should Christians use modern apologetics? Most books on Scripture work to separate truth from error. The author asks, "On the basis of Scripture, is this teaching true or isn't it?" That's not how it is with apologetics. Modern apologetics deals with material that in general is *true*. In this book, the question will be this: *How* should Christians weave this material into their Christian witness?
- Today the vast majority of modern apologists and apologetic ministries find a home in Evangelical/Reformed churches. Do certain teachings of Evangelical/Reformed churches make those churches a more natural fit for apologetics?

  For example, Evangelical/Reformed churches don't clearly define the relationship between Scripture and the Holy Spirit. The concept of Scripture as a "means of grace" is foreign to most members of those churches. Modern apologists believe they must first demonstrate logically that Scripture is reliable before they can use it. Also, in those churches the meaning of the Gospel has to a great extent changed over the years. How do these facts influence their use of apologetics?

This book is also a journey into the basic message of Scripture—human sin and God's grace. We will search God's Word for insights into how its message shapes the role apologetics should play in proclaiming that message.

If you are new to apologetics, by the time you finish this book, you'll have a solid understanding of apologetic arguments and how today's churches are using them. I pray that this book will provide you with a framework to think about when and how to use apologetics in your own life.

Part 1
Introduction to Modern Apologetics

Chapter 1—What Is Modern Apologetics?

This chapter contains a brief history of apologetics and the major arguments used by apologists. If you are new to apologetics, this chapter will help you understand what it is.

Chapter 2—The Different Approaches to Apologetics

Modern apologists practice apologetics in different ways, largely determined by their doctrinal beliefs. This chapter will discuss some of the ways apologetics is practiced and why apologists' beliefs lead them to choose one way or the other

Chapter 1
What is Modern Apologetics?

Many who read this book are familiar with the topic of apologetics. But others might not be, or are just beginning to explore it. If you belong to the second group, this introduction will provide the background you need to understand the subject of apologetics.

Throughout this book, I'll be using the term *modern apologetics*. The word *apologetics* refers to arguments Christians have collected over the years to defend Christianity against attacks from the unbelieving world and to answer various doubts Christians have about their faith. The word *modern* refers to the increased attention apologetics has received in the last 40 or 50 years. During this time it has become a distinct movement within the Christian Church.

So the term *modern apologetics* refers to apologetics in the form that it's used in the Church today. I'll be using this term to anchor us to the present and keep our focus on today's Church.

Apologetics is not new

Apologetics in the early Church

During the first four hundred years of Church history, apologetics referred to defending the Christian Church against false charges, which were often used to justify persecution. Christians were accused of doing hideous things in their "secret" meetings: incest in their love feasts, cannibalism in the Lord's Supper, even killing babies and eating them. Most common was the complaint that Christians had introduced a new religion into the Roman world. During times of difficulty, especially when the empire was threatened by hostile barbarian forces from the north, Christians were often blamed. Supposedly, the Roman gods were jealous of the new Christian God and had withdrawn their support and protection from the empire.

The early Church also had to defend Christianity against attacks by the Jews and against the influence of popular philosophies and religious sects of the day. In the ancient world, it was the job of the philosophers to help people learn how to live wisely. Christians countered by saying that true wisdom is found in Christ alone. Various "gnostic" sects offered a hidden wisdom by which people could find release from their temporal, corrupt bodies and draw closer to the true and permanent reality. Christians countered by saying a person can draw near to God only through his Son, Jesus Christ.

After Christianity became legalized in A.D. 313, Christians began developing arguments designed to win people from the pagans and Jews around them. In time they developed arguments to win Muslims, atheists, agnostics, and those indifferent to religion in general.

The Enlightenment and the advent of modern apologetics

Toward the end of the medieval period (roughly A.D. 500–1500), a spirit of secularism began to influence the Western world. Some rejected revelation entirely, and some even denied the existence of God or whether a person can be sure God truly exists. Avery Dulles writes, "For the first time in history, orthodox Christians felt constrained to prove the existence of God and the possibility and fact of revelation."[1] At this point, apologetics began to take on its modern form.

About a hundred years after the Reformation, philosophers in the Western world started promoting a new, non-Christian worldview. At first these philosophers were considered radical, but in a relatively short time, many of their ideas became mainstream. The period came to be called the Enlightenment and it ushered in the modern world.

People were told to shed the doctrines of the past and let human reason guide their search for the truth because truth can be discovered by human reason alone. Reason alone, they claimed, can provide solutions to the problems of life. The Enlightenment created a new climate in the Western world filled with optimism stemming from the power of human reason, but it was also filled with doubt and skepticism—stemming from the same source.

---

[1] Avery Cardinal Dulles, *A History of Apologetics* (Eugene, OR: Wipf & Stock, 1999), p. 206.

Scripture came under attack. It was not completely discarded, but it could not be read in a straightforward way. It had to be subjected to human reason and analyzed like any other book. The accounts in the Old Testament were considered myths. The books of Scripture were rearranged and assigned to different authors than the ones the books themselves named. Scripture was gleaned for ancient wisdom but not for absolute truth. The ancient wisdom found there was always subject to the analysis of the more advanced reasoning power of the modern mind.

Some came to doubt the existence of God—at least the God of Scripture. Believers countered with a variety of arguments as to why believing that God exists is more reasonable than believing that he doesn't exist. English clergyman Joseph Butler (1692–1752) formulated arguments against English Deists, who believed that God exists but that he lives in a remote part of the universe distant from mankind. And they denied he revealed himself in Scripture. Butler's arguments focused "on facts and evidence, and [his] conclusions were couched in terms of probability."[2] Even though Butler himself did not believe that faith should be based on those arguments, he proved that it is, in fact, reasonable to believe that God is near us and has revealed himself in the Bible. One modern writer has called Butler's work "perhaps the ablest and fairest argument for theism that exists."[3]

Another English clergyman, William Paley (1743–1805), wrote what might be the most well-known apologetic piece of all time: *Natural Theology: or, Evidences of the Existence and Attributes of the Deity, Collected From the Appearances of Nature.* Paley said that if while out walking, he struck his foot against a stone, it would be logical to conclude it had been lying there forever. "But," he continued, "suppose I had found a watch upon the ground, and it should be inquired how the watch happened to be in the place. . . . I should hardly think . . . it had always been there." Paley then analyzed the watch and gave an extended description of what human reason must conclude from the evidence: the watch had to have been created by someone who is far greater than the watch. He compared this with what we can learn about God from his creation.[4]

---

[2]Kenneth D. Boa and Robert M. Bowman Jr., *Faith Has Its Reasons,* Second Edition (Downers Grove: InterVarsity, 2005), p. 23.

[3]William Edgar and K. Scott Oliphint, eds., *Christian Apologetics Past & Present: A Primary Source Reader, Vol. 2 (Wheaton: Crossway, 2011), pp.195-196,* quoting C. D. Broad, *Five Types of Ethical Theory* (London: Routledge, 2008), p. 5.

[4]William Paley, *Natural Theology: or, Evidences of the Existence and Attributes of the Deity, Collected From The Appearances of Nature,"* Chapters 1-3, reproduced in William

During the 1700s the theory of evolution began to replace Scripture's teaching of creation. How long did it take for this shoreline to have formed or that rock formation to have been deposited? Where did fossils come from? Human reason must figure this out, it was said. It seems as if this world was not created in a short time but evolved slowly over a long period of time.

Christians resisted evolution largely because they considered human beings to be God's special creation with unique qualities and characteristics that set them apart from the rest of creation. Everything else might have evolved, but because of how human beings are described in Scripture, they had to be exempted from the process. Moreover, many realized that human evolution undermined the Christian faith.

In the mid-1800s, the theory of evolution got a major boost from the work of Charles Darwin (1809–1882). Darwin's ideas about how animals evolved were convincing to many, but if they were true, mankind had to have evolved at the same time. As the theory of evolution became more firmly entrenched, Christian writers opposed it in works that were the precursors of today's *Christian science* literature.

The Enlightenment elevated human reason and Darwinian evolution stripped God of his place as mankind's creator. This opened the door to a wide variety of worldviews, none of which contained God and Scripture as the source of truth. From this point on, the subject of apologetics was included in the curriculum of many Christian colleges and seminaries.

The rise of modern apologetics

Early years

The start of what we're calling the modern apologetics movement can be traced to C. S. Lewis (1898–1963). Lewis was an unbeliever who came to faith later in life. He was a world-class scholar and a brilliant analyst with the ability to write in clear and vivid language easily understood by the common person. He had a way of expressing his faith that continues to give him a place in many current books on apologetics.

Edgar and K. Scott Oliphint, eds., *Christian Apologetics Past and Present,* Vol. 2 (Wheaton: Crossway, 2011), p. 245.

Yet as recent as the 1970s, there was nothing that could be called an apologetic *movement*. In fact, according to Avery Dulles, apologetics was at a low point: "Who would be so foolish, some asked, as to try to justify faith by reason."[5]

But two men began to do just that: Francis Schaeffer and Josh McDowell.

Francis Schaeffer (1912–1984) was a conservative Presbyterian minister. He founded a religious community in Switzerland called L'Abri. It was a place "that welcomed people from every possible background to discuss the virtues of Christian faith."[6]

Schaeffer had a deep concern for people caught up in the ideas and lifestyle of a decadent Western culture. He believed that all people bear the image of God and have an innate understanding of who they are. People realize there is more to human existence than what is offered in the secular, materialistic culture around them.

Schaeffer's apologetic method was to help people face the shallowness of Western culture and realize that only Christianity leads to a workable society and a fulfilled life. Schaeffer "invited non-Christians to test the claims of Christianity to see if it is consistent and livable."[7] Among his most popular books are *How Should We Then Live: The Rise and Decline of Western Thought and Culture* (written as a book in 1976 and produced as a historical documentary film series in 1977) and *Death in the City* (1982).

While Schaeffer argued for Christianity within the framework of culture, a second man, Josh McDowell (1939–), argued for Christianity on the basis of historical evidence. McDowell was an unbeliever who had examined the historical evidence for Christianity in order to disprove it. But in the process, the historical evidence convinced him that Christianity is true and he came to faith.

McDowell's blockbuster book *Evidence That Demands a Verdict* (written in 1972 and updated in 1979) is arguably one of the most influential religious books of the 20th century. This book is an exhaustive presentation of the historical evidence for Christianity, containing evidence from secular history and evidence from Scripture.

---

[5]Dulles, *A History of Apologetics*, p. xxv.
[6]Edgar and Oliphint, *Christian Apologetics, Vol. 2*, p. 546.
[7]Boa and Bowman Jr., *Faith Has Its Reasons*, p. 31.

Schaeffer and McDowell set the pace for modern apologetics. Schaeffer's "life-style" approach to apologetics is used by a number of current apologists. Mc-Dowell's use of evidence is very popular. If we add to their approaches the historic (classical) arguments for the existence of God and arguments showing the superiority of Christianity to non-Christian philosophies and world religions, we have the broad contours of modern apologetics.

Growing popularity

The works of Francis Schaeffer and Josh McDowell brought apologetics to the attention of many Christians in the pew. But there was still no apologetic movement. As late as 1977, well-known apologist Gary Habermas sent two manuscripts on the resurrection to four publishers without success. One managing editor told him that apologetics was just about dead. A few years later, however, a publishing house asked Habermas to write a book on apologetics for them. In just a few years, "apologetics had become the hottest subject in publishing."[8]

The popularity of apologetics can be attributed to two anti-Christian movements that arose suddenly in the late 1970s. Both movements promoted anti-Christian philosophical and spiritual ideas. Both were high profile and quickly found a place in people's thinking. The first is *postmodernism,* so-called because it was an attack on the "modern" Enlightenment's dependence on human reason as the source of truth. Postmodernists claimed that reason does not provide a solid basis for truth. Rather, truth is what an individual thinks is true—at least in areas like philosophy, morality, and religion. Needless to say, this became another enemy of Scripture's statement that it is God's Word and the source of truth.

Another movement, the *New Age Movement,* taught that previously inaccessible spiritual forces were making themselves available to mankind. The "Age of Aquarius" had begun. People could draw on a plethora of forces to find the truth—to discover new ways of thinking about themselves and the world around them. This was when figurines of angels, reinterpreted as guides for a new age, began appearing in retail shops everywhere. Obviously, this movement posed another challenge to the Christian understanding of God and Scripture as mankind's source of truth.

---

[8]Brian G. Chilton, *The Layman's Manual on Christian Apologetics* (Eugene, OR: Wipf & Stock, 2019), p. ix.

Perhaps even more important than the movements themselves was the general effect they had on people's view of Christianity. They created skepticism and doubt. Atheists and agnostics could now express their views much more openly. In addition to this, higher criticism of Scripture, always popular in liberal churches, and the acceptance of evolution began making inroads into conservative Evangelical/Reformed churches.

As a result, Christians were calling for resources to defend their faith. Over the past 40 years, Christian publishing houses have worked to provide these resources. And in the last 20 years, the internet has become a powerful venue for apologists to explain their arguments and promote their ministries.

The ongoing tension

Before we leave this brief history of apologetics, we should note a certain ambivalence, even opposition, on the part of some toward using apologetic arguments. Already in the early Church, one Church leader, Tertullian (160–225), warned against combatting secular philosophy by using a Christianized form of philosophy:

> The Apostle [Paul] testifies expressly in his letter to the Colossians that we should beware of philosophy. "See to it that no one takes you captive by philosophy and empty deceit, according to human tradition" against the providence of the Holy Ghost. He had been at Athens where he had come to grips with the human wisdom which attacks and perverts truth, being itself divided up into its own swarm of heresies by the variety of its mutually antagonistic sects.
>
> *What has Jerusalem to do with Athens, the Church with the Academy, the Christian with the heretic?* Our principles come from the Porch of Solomon,[9] who had himself taught that the Lord is to be sought in simplicity of heart. *I have no use for a Stoic or a Platonic or a dialectic Christianity. After Jesus Christ we have no need of speculation, after the Gospel no need of research.* When we come to believe, we have no desire to believe anything else; for we begin by believing that there is nothing else which we have to believe.[10]

---

[9]Solomon's Porch, where Solomon taught wisdom from God, is contrasted with the Porch of the Stoic philosopher Zeno, who, along with many other philosophers, taught in the city of Athens.

[10]Tertullian, *"Prescription Against Heretics," Chap. 7*, in *Early Latin Theology*, Library of Christian Classics V (1956), trans. and ed. by S. L. Greenslade, http://www.tertullian.

Tertullian himself may not have emphasized the Gospel as strongly as Paul did, but he wanted Christians to base their hope on the message of Scripture alone.

Along those lines, we note a later theologian of the Western Church, Ambrose of Milan (339–397). Ambrose was

> more concerned with the suppression of paganism than with giving reasons in support of Christianity. He had little respect for reason as an instrument of religious knowledge. "You are commanded to believe," he wrote, "not permitted to inquire." [And Ambrose wrote:] "To Abraham it was counted righteousness that he sought not reasons but believed with most ready faith. It is good that faith should go before reason, lest we seem to exact a reason from our Lord God as from a man."[11]

In the 1960s and 1970s, various denominations (including the confessional Wisconsin Synod Lutheran Church) expressed the same concerns about the use of apologetics.

The arguments of modern apologists

In the rest of this chapter, we'll look at the modern apologetic toolbox—that is, the broad range of arguments apologists use to defend Christianity.

General areas of study

Many apologetic arguments are quite specific and can be stated as simple logical points to show that Christianity is true. Such arguments are the bread and butter of modern apologetics, and we'll look at these in a moment.

There is, however, a kind of apologetics that focuses on broad areas of life. It works to show that Christianity is superior to systems devised by non-Christians to shape and make sense of the world: non-Christian religions, philosophies, and cultures based on non-Christian worldviews. By comparing these systems to Christianity, apologists hope to make Christianity stand out as a more rational alternative.

---

org/articles/greenslade_prae/greenslade_prae.htm (accessed June, 2022). Tertullian quoted Colossians 2:8, here quoted from the *English Standard Version* (ESV).

[11]Dulles, *A History of Apologetics,* p. 61, footnote 53: "F. Holmes Dudden illustrates at length that Ambrose 'consistently depreciates the function of reason in relation to Divine things.' *The Life and Times of Ambrose,* 2 Vols. (Oxford, 1935), 2:558." The first quotation is from Ambrose, *De fide,* 1.78. The second is from Ambrose, *De Abraham,* 1.21.

This kind of apologetics demands the study of large amounts of material plus experience in interacting with people who live by those systems. Most modern apologists admit that a mastery of this material is impossible for most. Apologists are content to boil it down to some basic truths a Christian can use when the opportunity presents itself. Even so, working in these areas usually requires a fairly significant commitment of time and thought.

Apologetics aimed at Christian religions

Christians have always lived next door to followers of non-Christian religions. Paul did mission work among people who worshiped Greek and Roman gods. His confrontations in Iconium, Ephesus, and Athens are good examples of the challenges he faced. Paul's world also was home to many "gnostic" sects—religious groups that promised a higher knowledge through which people could be purified and draw closer to God.

It would be hard to find a church that doesn't help its people understand America's homegrown, non-Christian denominations and spiritualist groups. Churches have always been helping their members understand such religions. In the last 50 years or so, this form of apologetics has become more popular as Christians are increasingly rubbing shoulders with Muslim, Buddhists, Hindus, and members of other non-Christian religions. The call to "coexist" and pleas for unity in diversity are leading people to ask, "Why should Christianity be considered the only path to God?"

Some modern apologists focus on defending Christianity against non-Christian religions and sects. Their main argument is that only Christianity is based on historical fact and has a history that can be verified by external sources. By contrast, non-Christian world religions are based on legends often written hundreds of years after their founders died. Boa and Bowman write that its "historical testable character sets Christianity apart from other religions and is its greatest strength."[12]

To master this area of apologetics also calls for a fairly extensive knowledge of these religions and sects, plus personal experience working with people who belong to them.

---

[12]*Boa and Bowman Jr., Faith Has Its Reasons, p. 174.*

Apologetics aimed at non-Christian philosophies

Early Christians lived in a world dominated by philosophy. Luke, the writer of Acts, commented that in Athens "all the Athenians and the foreigners who lived there would spend their time in nothing except telling or hearing something new" (Acts 17:21). In Athens, Paul conversed with formal philosophers—Epicureans and Stoics—and was given a chance to express his beliefs before a meeting of the city's leading thinkers and statesmen.

Today's philosophers are no less involved in trying to understand the world and plot a course for the well-being of its inhabitants. The philosophies that originated during the Enlightenment (late 17th through late 18th centuries) continue to resurface in new forms.

Some modern apologists, often those with ties to academic institutions, carefully study modern philosophies and point out their weaknesses and internal inconsistencies. They establish arguments to help Christians understand how these philosophies run counter not just to Christianity but to the common experiences of living in the world. They demonstrate that Christianity makes better sense of our existence than human philosophies do and can give people the kind of life they are searching for. They point out how secular philosophies are detrimental to that.

Apologetics aimed at secular worldviews and cultures

Boa and Bowman define "worldview" like this: "A worldview is the sum of a person's basic assumptions, held consciously or subconsciously, about life and the nature of reality."[13] When a person becomes a Christian, their view of life and reality changes; they adopt an entirely new worldview. And they find themselves living with people who hold to the secular worldview they once had.

This area of apologetics is similar to arguments apologists use against non-Christian philosophies. Modern worldview apologists prove that Christianity's worldview provides the most coherent and satisfying basis on which to build one's life. They show unbelievers that their non-Christian worldview does not line up with reality. The non-believer's worldview is not congruent with who they are as a human being, with the world around them, and certainly not with Scripture.

---

[13]*Boa and Bowman Jr., Faith Has Its Reasons, p. 91.*

Brian Morely wrote that in worldview apologetics "we judge those beliefs true that make a 'smooth, systematically consistent picture' out of experience."[14] Or as Boa and Bowman put it: "The basic strategy here is to show that these other worldviews are rationally incoherent . . . that such worldviews are logically self-contradictory or self-refuting."[15]

The worldview apologist points out that secular worldviews lead to emotional and spiritual oppression. These worldviews set up expectations no one can achieve and provide shallow resources for achieving those expectations. Leading apologist William Lane Craig explains: "The atheistic worldview is insufficient to maintain a happy and consistent life. . . . Biblical Christianity therefore provides the two conditions necessary for a meaningful, valuable, and purposeful life: God and immortality."[16]

Tim Keller, who built and pastored a large church in New York City, used Christian worldview apologetics to build his church. He exposed the foolishness of secular worldviews and the unreasonable expectations of the prevailing culture in New York. He taught that only Christianity deals with people in the world as it exists under God. Only the teachings of Christ can free people from slavery to themselves and to others. Keller writes, "Therefore, belief in God offers a better empirical fit, it explains and accounts for what we see better than the alternative account of things."[17] Needless to say, to use this approach successfully requires a thorough understanding of the culture in which one is working. This, in turn, requires constant analysis and updating.

Classical proofs for the existence of God

Some modern apologists, called classical apologists, try to prove that it is illogical to deny the existence of God. Logical proofs for the existence of God were developed by Anselm of Canterbury (1033–1109) and especially by Thomas Aquinas (1225–1274). In fact, to prove the existence of the true God, Aquinas went back to the proofs used by the ancient Greek philosopher Aristotle (384–322 B. C.) to prove the existence of a supreme being.

---

[14]Brian K. Morley, *Mapping Apologetics: Comparing Contemporary Approaches* (Downer's Grove: InterVarsity, 2015), p.156, quoting Edward Carnell, *Introduction to Christian Apologetics, p. 56.*

[15]Boa and Bowman Jr., *Faith Has Its Reasons*, p. 93.

[16]William Lane Craig, *On Guard: Defending Your Faith w\With Reason and Precision* (Colorado Springs: David C. Cook, 2010), pp. 45, 49.

[17]Timothy Keller, *The Reason for God* (New York: Penguin Books, 2018), p. 126.

Here are several commonly used classical arguments.

1. *Cosmological proof.* Cosmos is the Greek word for "universe."

>Since the universe exists, something must have caused it to come into be-ing. The argument goes like this: (1) Whatever exists has a cause for its beginning to exist. (2) The universe began to exist. (3) Therefore, the uni-verse has a cause for its existence (God). This argument has a long history among medieval Islamic philosophers. In recent years apologist William Lane Craig has popularized this argument.

>Related to this argument is the argument from motion. On a billiards ta-ble, the pool cue strikes one ball, which strikes another, which strikes yet another. But someone must have started things—a stationary person who used a cue to strike the white ball and got the sequence started. Likewise, all the movement we see in the universe around us must have been started by some "stationary" being (God).

>This argument is also related to the argument from order. (1) Things that exist have relationships with other things, which make them dependent on these other things; therefore, (2) there must be a being who is not depen-dent on anything else, but absolutely independent (God).

>These arguments all rely on "the impossibility of an infinite regress." An infinite regress is the idea that causation stretches back into infinity past, where there was no one—no "unmoved mover," to use the ancient philos-opher Aristotle's phrase—who got things started.

2. *Ontological proof.* Ontos is the Greek word for "being."

>The classical form of the argument, developed by Anselm of Canterbury, goes like this: (1) Mankind has an idea of an infinite and perfect being; (2) if something is perfect, it must exist; otherwise it would not be perfect. (3) Therefore, an infinite and perfect being exists (God). It can be stated in another way: By definition God is the greatest being that can exist. If God exists in a person's mind, that proves that he must exist in reality. Why? Because it is greater to actually exist than to exist only in a person's mind. Some philosophers accept this argument; others don't.

3. *Teleological proof.* Telos in Greek means "purpose."

When we look at the universe, we observe that it is complex and finely tuned, as if made for a purpose. Therefore, the universe must have been designed by a higher power (God).

4. *Moral proof. Moralitas* is the Latin word meaning "morality" or "morals."

People in general share a common understanding of right and wrong, of punishment and reward. This proves the existence of someone with whom the distinction between right and wrong originated and who rewards the right and punishes the wrong (God).

5. *Epistemological proof. Episteme* is the Greek word for "knowledge."

The human mind can make sense of the world. Therefore, the world must be structured in a way that corresponds to the structure of the human mind. This proves the existence of someone who made both the world and the people who live in it (God).

There are other philosophical proofs for the existence of God. There is the *aesthetic* proof, namely, the proof from beauty. It may be the beauty and elegance of the laws of physics and mathematics, for example. Or it might be the beauty of accomplishments in the past or in one's own life. There must be someone who builds such beauty, elegance, and meaning into the world (God).

There is the argument from *religious need*: Since human beings need God, God really exists. There is the *information* proof: There must be a higher power behind the so-called laws of nature or the laws of mathematics. Apologists ask, where did the amazing amount of information in DNA come from if not from an almighty Creator?

There is the proof from *consciousness*: In various ways humans demonstrate that they are more than evolving molecules. Consciousness is a nonphysical side to human existence, which can only have come from God.

Atheists and religious skeptics have developed a variety of counterarguments against these proofs. Some books by modern Christian apologists go into great detail describing these counterarguments and showing how they can be refuted.

Evidentialist Apologetics

The first two kinds of apologetics—arguments against secular philosophies, worldviews, and non-Christian religions, and proofs for the existence of God—have been under development throughout the history of the Christian Church.

Historical evidences from outside the Bible, on the other hand, have a somewhat more recent history. These arguments were developed as a result of Enlightenment thought, the challenges of secular science, and the resulting skepticism toward Christianity in the Western world. Avery Dulles writes, "As the eighteenth century progressed French apologists, like their colleagues in England, showed an increasing tendency to shift their ground from philosophical reasoning to historical evidence."[18]

The types of apologetics we have looked at so far are complex and difficult to master. They call for knowledge of secular cultures, non-Christian religions, and various areas of philosophy. Evidential apologetics is easier. While there is still a very large amount of material to master, it consists of a specific body of facts that can be learned and applied.

Proofs from outside Scripture

Evidentialist apologetics is driven largely by the conviction that the reliability of Scripture cannot be proved by evidence from within Scripture itself. Scripture must be proven reliable by material found *outside* of it.[19]

Josh McDowell, an early leader in evidentialist apologetics, says there is more than enough historical evidence (evidence found outside Scripture itself) to convince any reasonable person that the Bible is a reliable source of truth. He writes, "An intelligent person who is seeking truth would certainly read and consider a book that has the historical qualifications of the Bible. These unique qualifications separate the Scriptures from any book that has ever been written."[20]

We'll follow McDowell's outline of evidences from his book *Evidence That Demands a Verdict*. We'll note why the arguments are important and what an apologist should know in order to use them effectively.

---

[18]Dulles, *A History of Apologetics,* p. 197.
[19]We'll explore this claim in chapter 10.
[20]Josh McDowell, *Evidence That Demands a Verdict, Revised Edition (San Bernadino: Here's Life Publishers, 1979),* p. ix.

Many arguments are based on human observations about Scripture.

1. No other book has enjoyed the wide circulation of the Bible.

> No other book has been translated into as many languages as the Bible. This has happened in spite of the fact that its followers have been persecuted and that the Bible has been denounced and accused of being filled with errors.

> Using this argument calls for a good understanding of the spread of Christianity, often in the face of terrible persecution. It calls for knowing how Christians have defended Scripture against many within the Church who have reduced Scripture to the level of a human book. Doing this calls for a basic understanding of the liberal historical-critical method of interpreting Scripture. It also includes a basic understanding of what languages the Bible has been translated into.

2. Scholars have developed numerous ways to test if a historical document is authentic, and Scripture passes those tests.

> When the Bible is tested against those criteria, the proof of its authenticity is far greater than for any other historical document. For example, the original text of no other book has survived like the text of the Bible.

> Becoming proficient in this argument requires a grasp of a large amount of fairly technical material. It calls for the study of the careful way in which the Bible was hand copied for most of its history and an awareness of the huge number of Bible manuscripts in existence today. It requires the ability to show that the Hebrew and Greek manuscripts we have today are the same as the originals.

3. Early Christians and secular writers who lived soon after Jesus' resurrection sometimes referred to books of Scripture.

> Many claim that Christian teaching gradually developed during the first two or three centuries after Christ. According to this view, the New Testament books record what the early Church believed about Jesus rather than what Jesus actually said and did.

> However, many manuscripts and portions of Scripture have been found that were in existence soon after Jesus died and rose.

4. Numerous secular writers refer to Jesus as a historical person.

There are not a lot of references to Christ in the secular literature of the time, but the references that exist prove that Jesus was a historical person.

5. Archaeology has proven again and again that Scripture's references to people, locations, and historical facts are true.

Many of these discoveries refute claims by skeptics that Scripture is inaccurate.

All these arguments require a large amount of study to use well.

Proofs from inside Scripture

Apologists often use arguments from within Scripture, miracles and fulfilled prophecies, for example. Of course, any argument from within Scripture assumes that the person to whom one is speaking already believes that Scripture is reliable. So technically, what Scripture says should be used only after the reliability of Scripture has been proved by arguments from outside of Scripture. Nevertheless, these arguments are very powerful to those who are willing to accept them.

1. Anyone can observe the remarkable continuity of the Bible.

For example, the Bible is made up of a large number of individual writings composed over a long period of time by multiple authors. But they all contain a common theme: the coming of Christ. The Old Testament prophets foretold many details about Christ's life, death, and resurrection, and the New Testament writers described how Christ fulfilled them all.

To use this argument requires a good understanding of the content of the Bible. One needs to understand how the Old Testament people understood themselves in relation to the promised Savior. One needs to compare what the Old Testament prophets said would happen with how those prophecies were fulfilled in Christ. One also needs to understand the purpose of the Old Testament Law and how the Law kept the Israelites focused on the coming Savior.

2. Scripture clearly testifies to the fact that Jesus is the Son of God.

Because of what Jesus said about himself, if he is not the Son of God, he was either a liar or a lunatic.

This is a relatively simple argument. Anyone who believes that the Gospels accurately record what Jesus said cannot but believe that he was the Son of God. There is no other acceptable conclusion.

3. If the Son of God came to earth, we would expect him to speak like Jesus of Nazareth and do what Jesus did. Jesus fulfilled all the Old Testament prophecies of the Messiah, and Jesus performed miracles.

This conclusion is based on a comparison of how the Old Testament described the coming Savior and the record of Jesus' life as recorded in the New Testament. Modern apologists point out the statistical impossibility of all the Old Testament prophecies being fulfilled by one man, unless he was the Christ. The apostles themselves often used this argument to prove that Jesus is the Messiah. They also point out that Jesus' miracles prove that he is God's Son.

4. All the events surrounding Jesus' resurrection as described in Scripture prove that he did, in fact, rise from the dead.

This form of apologetics contains arguments from Scripture that Jesus rose from the dead. For example, it includes how the guards and the religious leaders handled the empty tomb. It includes such topics as the nature of crucifixion as a tool of execution, evidence that Jesus was not removed from the tomb by human beings, and evidence from his post-resurrection appearances. It also includes evidence from the results of Jesus' resurrection, for example, the fact that skeptics were convinced and came to faith in Christ and the willingness of the disciples to die for their faith.

Summary

From its beginning, the Christian Church has been defending itself against false charges, non Christian religions, and secular philosophies. From time to time, the emphasis of its apologetics has changed depending on the world around it. In the last 50 years, the world has become more skeptical of Christianity, which has resulted in a new interest in apologetic arguments.

This movement, which we are calling "modern apologetics," is a vast area of study with many highways and byways to explore. In this chapter we have touched on basic arguments against secular philosophies, non-Christian religions, and current worldviews. We have also touched on arguments for the existence of God and the vast amount of evidence that proves the Bible is reliable.

Chapter 2

The Different Approaches to Apologetics

Apologetics: A matter of doctrine and practice

An apologist stands up at a conference, presents his apologetic insights, and then gives the impression that he is reflecting how everyone uses apologetics.

In truth, however, modern apologetics is a very diverse field. James Beilby observes, "At first blush it might seem surprising that there are so many different and incompatible ways in which apologetics is done."[21] He explains why: Apologists use "many different and incompatible ways" to do apologetics, which stem from certain doctrinal differences within the Evangelical/Reformed world.

Steven Cowan, editor of *Five Views on Apologetics,* writes,

> Although apologists agree on the basic definition and goals of apologetics, they can differ significantly on the proper methodology of apologetics. That is, they disagree about how the apologist goes about his task—about the kinds of arguments that can and should be employed and about the way the apologist should engage the unbelievers in apologetic discourse. . . . No two books classify the various methods in exactly the same way.[22]

---

[21]James K. Beilby, *Thinking About Christian Apologetics* (Downer's Grove: InterVarsity, 2011), p. 87. Note other books that try to classify approaches to doing apologetics: Bernard Ramm, *Varieties of Christian Apologetics*; Brian Morley, *Mapping Apologetics*; Steven Cowan, *Five Views on Apologetics*; and Kenneth Boa and Robert Bowman, *Faith Has Its Reasons,* Second Edition. In general, we will follow the classification of the book *Five Views on Apologetics.* Trying to organize the field of modern apologetics has become a pursuit in itself. All who do this humbly admit the subjective nature of their task. They confess that they could organize the field differently if they changed their criteria. They recognize a great overlap between the various approaches and that to a certain extent all of them draw from the same pool of arguments.

[22]Steven B. Cowan, ed., *Five Views on Apologetics* (Grand Rapids: Zondervan, 2000), p. 9.

Most often, these differences do not stem from a personal preference. Rather, they stem from the apologist's Christian beliefs. Boa and Bowman point out that in the apologetic world "there is significant debate concerning the theological foundation of apologetics. To some extent apologetic methods are related to the way one understands and interprets Christian theology."[23] Boa and Bowman use the example of C. S. Lewis, who is much loved throughout the apologetic world:

> C. S. Lewis clearly wrote from an Anglican theological perspective. However much he might have liked to represent all Christian traditions, in fact his views of a variety of issues were quite specific and came out in his apologetics. Lewis held, for example, to a strong doctrine of free will. *Apologists ignore or gloss over such theological matters to the detriment of their efforts.*[24]

No one can "get into apologetics" without wrestling with the relationship between apologetics and their Christian beliefs. Questions like the following are especially important: Are unbelievers able to understand Christian apologetic arguments and let them shape their worldview? Does the sinful nature make it impossible for unbelievers to understand Christian arguments; if not, then to what extent can they understand and apply them? Since people come to faith through the work of the Holy Spirit, how does the Holy Spirit use modern apologetic arguments in his work of leading people to faith?[25] And if he does, how does he use them?

The vast majority of modern apologists come from the broad Evangelical/ Reformed side of Protestantism—Baptist, Reformed, Methodist churches, for example—along with the many nondenominational church groups that have broken off from them.[26]

---

[23]Boa and Bowman Jr., *Faith Has Its Reasons*, p. 40.

[24]Boa and Bowman Jr., *Faith Has Its Reasons*, p. 327 (emphasis added).

[25]Beilby, *Thinking About Christian Apologetics, p. 87.* He suggests five questions we must ask: "1) What is the relationship between faith and reason? 2) To what extent can humans understand God's nature? 3) What is the role of the Holy Spirit in apologetics? 4) What is the nature of truth? 5) What is the task of apologetics?"

[26]Evangelical/Reformed is a general term used to describe the churches that came out of the Calvinist side of the Reformation. Before the Reformation, there had only been one church, the Catholic Church. Martin Luther took a stand against many of the Catholic Church's teachings, and his followers became known as Lutherans. Another church body developed alongside Lutheranism. Its leader was John Calvin. His teachings gave rise to the Calvinistic, or Reformed, side of the Reformation. So after the Reformation, there were three major church bodies: Catholics, Lutherans, and Reformed. *Evangelical* is a very broad term referring to individuals and churches that focus on

A quick overview of apologetic types

In the last chapter, we looked at the arguments apologists use. In this chapter we will look at various schools of apologetics. These schools differ on *how* and *when* their members believe apologetics should be used. Yet we note that apologists rarely fall cleanly into one school or another. Moreover, some books that analyze apologetics list more schools, some fewer.

The next paragraph is a quick overview of the schools before we look at them in more detail.

Classical apologists believe that a person must at least be a theist if evidential arguments are to make sense, so they first argue for the existence of God. If a person comes to believe that God exists, then they use evidence to prove that Christianity is true. *Evidentialism* is the main type of apologetics in use today. It provides various kinds of evidence to prove the truth of Christianity. *Cumulative Case* apologetics is like evidentialist apologetics. However, because of the volume of the material, Christians should merely learn as many arguments and evidences as they can and let them accumulate in their friend's mind until their friend begins to see the logic of Christianity. *Experientialism* claims that the greatest argument for Christianity is one's own conversion experience. However, because they cannot describe or prove their experience, they use apologetics as one tool the Holy Spirit can use to lead an unbeliever to have the experience of receiving Christ and coming to faith. *Presuppositionalists* reject reliance on evidence because they don't believe unbelievers have the ability to understand it. However, many use evidence and arguments in a limited way. *Reformed* apologists argue that Christianity is a basic belief for a Christian, and there is no need to argue for its truth.

For purposes of this book, we will explore the schools in this order.

---

the Gospel. Modern Evangelicalism took shape in the mid-1900s, a reaction to the more strict Fundamentalism of previous years. Evangelical churches usually practice decision theology and seek a conversion experience by which people can be united with God and made sure of their salvation. Billy Graham's ministry is a good example of evangelicalism as it began in the mid-20th century. The name *Reformed* without the addition of Evangelical denotes churches that remain closer to the teaching of John Calvin. Sometimes, however, all Evangelical and Reformed churches are simply referred to as Reformed churches. Liberal churches and Pentecostal/Charismatic churches are not included in this discussion. Liberal churches engage in many social outreach programs, which in a sense becomes their apologetic. Pentecostal/Charismatic churches offer a heightened experience accompanied by signs and wonders, which in a sense becomes their apologetic.

Classical apologetics

Classical apologists use evidentialist arguments but add a dash of presupposi-tionalism. Boa and Bowman explain, "According to both classical apologists and most Reformed apologists . . . one must first have a worldview before one can interpret the facts in the world."[27] Classical apologists don't teach that one must be a Christian to properly understand evidence for the truth of Christian-ity (as strict presuppositionalists do). Rather, they teach that for the arguments and evidences to be effective, a person must first believe that God exists.

Classical apologist Norman Geisler explains, "It is a vicious circle to argue that a given fact (say, the resuscitation of Christ's body) is evidence of a certain truth claim (say, Christ's claim to be God), unless it can be established that the event comes in the context *of a theistic universe*."[28] Boa and Bowman express Geisler's view: "Arguments for the theistic worldview come logically prior to arguments about historical fact, since our objective knowledge of those facts depends on our considering them within the context of the correct [i.e. the theistic] world-view."[29]

Classical apologetics uses a two-step process: First, they argue that God exists. Second, they use evidence to prove that Christianity alone is the religion estab-lished by God To carry out the first step, classical apologists use "the apologetic thought of Christian theologians and philosophers throughout church histo-ry."[30] This is why they are called "classical." In chapter 1 we noted the various "classical" proofs for the existence of God.

After classical apologists have accomplished the first step—proving the exis-tence of God—they continue with the second step, which is to prove the truth of Christianity. In this step they use "the same facts and approaches used by evidentialists."[31]

Classical apologists find fault with evidentialists. Evidentialists "work with hid-den presuppositions about the nature of reality."[32] In other words, evidentialists are presupposing the existence of God too. Evidentialists would admit that, but

[27]Boa and Bowman Jr., *Faith Has Its Reasons*, p. 214.
[28]Boa and Bowman Jr., *Faith Has Its Reasons*, p. 216 (emphasis added), quoting Norman Geisler, *Christian Apologetics* (Grand Rapids: Baker, 1976), p. 95 (emphasis deleted).
[29]Boa and Bowman Jr., *Faith Has Its Reasons*, p. 85.
[30]Boa and Bowman Jr., *Faith Has Its Reasons*, p. 49.
[31]Morley, *Mapping Apologetics*, p. 23.
[32]Boa and Bowman Jr., *Faith Has Its Reasons*, p. 215.

it doesn't bother them. When working with facts, they say, their own presuppositions are irrelevant. Facts are facts. Anyone can understand them and draw the logical conclusions. If a person accepts the evidence, they will confess both that God exists and that Christianity is true.

Evidentialism

Evidentialists believe that Christian apologetics is best done by "accumulating various historical *evidences* for the truth of Christianity."[33] Boa and Bowman point out that "in the modern period American evangelical apologetics has been dominated by the *evidentialist* approach."[34]

By way of contrast, strict Calvinists (presuppositionalists) believe that evidentialism does a disservice to the Christian faith. They believe that Christians who use human logic to prove Christianity are justifying the unbelieving worldview. Facts are not neutral to an unbeliever, they say. Because of the hardness of their hearts, unbelievers will naturally deny the evidence or distort it to fit their unbelieving worldview.

Evidentialists, however, claim that unbelievers do have the natural ability to recognize and accept the truth. They acknowledge that unbelievers are sinful but that they are not impervious to valid logic and evidence. They can look at the evidence without necessarily rejecting or distorting it, and the evidence can, in fact, convince them that Christianity is true.

In the previous chapter, we outlined the various types of historical evidence used by evidentialists. This included evidence from the miraculous way the text of Scripture has been transmitted, evidence from archaeology that proves the places named in Scripture actually existed, evidence from secular documents of the time that speak about Christ or testify to the accuracy of names and events recorded in Scripture. It also included evidence from Scripture itself—the reports of miracles found there, the many Old Testament prophecies fulfilled in the New, and especially the many ways Scripture proves that Jesus died and rose.

---

[33] Cowan, *Five Views on Apologetics*, p. 92 (emphasis added).

[34] Boa and Bowman Jr., *Faith Has Its Reasons,* p. 139 (emphasis original). Sources for evidentialist arguments are endless. We've mentioned Josh McDowell's 1970s book, *Evidence That Demands a Verdict,* and Lee Strobel's more recent book, *The Case for Christ.* There are many more. A YouTube search on "apologetics" yields a large assortment of evidentialists and their ministries. There you can find hundreds of videos that treat all the evidence apologists use to prove the rationality of the Christian religion.

John Warwick Montgomery (1931–)

Most evidentialists come from the Arminian side of the Evangelical/Reformed church. John Warwick Montgomery has done extensive work in association with evidentialist apologists in those church bodies, and in general his apologetics mirrors theirs. However, he makes his home in Lutheranism. We'll let Montgomery give us a feel for the spirit of evidentialism.

Montgomery might fairly be called the dean of evidentialist apologists. He started his apologetic work even before Josh McDowell wrote *Evidence That Demands a Verdict* in the 1970s.[35]

For Montgomery, "the solution is not presupposing the Christian God and viewing all facts accordingly but the opposite—testing theories, assumptions and biases by the facts—which will point us to the Christian God."[36]

For Montgomery, the legal process and its use of evidence provides the framework for proving the Christian religion.[37] Montgomery writes, "Objective empirical evidence for Jesus Christ and his message is the only truly valid Christian apologetic possible, for it alone is subject to the canons of evidence employed in other fields of endeavor."[38]

Montgomery compares Christian apologists to trial lawyers. They are both trying to determine what happened in the past: Who committed the crime? How and why did they do it? Was Jesus a real, historical person?

Where, then, should the apologist begin? With the message of Scripture, of course. But how can the unbeliever be expected to listen to Scripture unless Scripture is first proven to be reliable. Montgomery explains:

> The Gospel is a matter of fact, and its acceptance will necessarily depend on whether the documentary records of Jesus' ministry are sound,

---

[35]Morley, *Mapping Apologetics*, p. 23. He notes Josh McDowell, who was influenced by John Warwick Montgomery.

[36]Morley, *Mapping Apologetics*, p. 294.

[37]Not all evidentialists are lawyers, but a number of Lutheran evidentialists are. They include lawyers John Montgomery, Craig Parton, and Jason Cross. They seem to like providing proof "beyond reasonable doubt."

[38]John Warwick Montgomery, *Faith Founded on Fact: Essays in Evidential Apologetics* (Irvine, CA: NRP Books, 2015), p. 98.

whether the testimonies to His life and work are accurate, and whether one can accept His claims and His resurrection from the dead.[39]

We are in the business of persuading people to accept Jesus as personal Savior—as the only One who can "save them from their sins." To make this case, there is no way to avoid arguing for the soundness of the New Testament documents, the reliability of the testimony to Jesus contained therein, and the facticity of His resurrection from the dead as the final proof of His claims.[40]

To accomplish this, the apologist can use the same well-defined rules of evidence secular courts use to determine if a document is genuine. In his *Tractatus Logico-Theologicus* Montgomery lists three tests that can be applied to Scripture to prove its reliability. First, the *textual test* asks whether the New Testament books we have today are essentially the same as the ones penned by the original authors. Second, the *internal test* asks what the text claims about itself. Unless there is a more authoritative document to prove otherwise, we should accept the claims of the text. Third, the *external test* asks whether there are sources of information outside the text that prove the text to be reliable.[41] Scripture would pass all these tests in a court of law, he says.

Montgomery admits that these tests never result in absolute proof for Scripture's reliability. "Legal methodology, like scientific and historical method, relies on *probability* in arriving at its judgments."[42] Evidentialists say that the probability (that the Scripture is reliable) is so high that people can confidently base their faith and life on it.

Montgomery explains that the goal of apologetics is to lead people to have no excuse to reject the cross: "Apologetics fulfills its function only when it brings the unbeliever to the 'offense of the cross,' i.e. to the cross as evidentially compelling—able to be resisted only by a deliberate act of egocentric will."[43] He writes, "The 21st century apologist must offer positive, compelling evidence

---

[39]John Warwick Montgomery, *Christ as Centre and Circumference: Essays Theological, Cultural and Polemic* (Bonn, Germany: Verlag fuer Kultur und Wissenschaft, 2009), p. 128.

[40]Montgomery, *Christ as Centre and Circumference*, p. 135.

[41]John Warwick Montgomery, *Tractatus Logico-Theologicus (Eugene, OR: Wipf & Stock, 2013)*, pp. 74-82.

[42]Montgomery, *Tractatus Logico-Theologicus*, p. 69 (emphasis original).

[43]John Warwick Montgomery, *"Once Upon an A Priori"* in E. R. Geehan, ed., *Jerusalem and Athens: Critical Discussions on the Philosophy and Apologetics of Cornelius Van Til* (Phillipsburg, NJ: P&R Publishing, 1974), p. 391.

in support of the Christian claim. . . . Merely preaching the good news or announcing the hope is *never* enough! One must *always* give a *reason* for the hope."[44]

As we will see, presuppositionalist Cornelius Van Til taught that in light of mankind's sinfulness, Christian apologists should not pretend to have the same worldview as unbelievers. Montgomery dismisses this. Rather than discount the unbeliever's presuppositions, the apologist enters the unbeliever's world confident that "facts are facts" and the unbeliever can be shown the truth of Christianity by means of those facts. Montgomery writes, "Non-Christian positions must be destroyed factually and the Christian religion established factually. Any lesser procedure is the abrogation of apologetic responsibility to a fallen world."[45] Everyone, the non-Christian as well as the Christian "employs and must employ inductive procedures to distinguish fact from fiction."[46] He writes, "The starting-point has to be the common rationality (the inductive and deductive procedures) which all men share."[47]

Gary Habermas (1950 –)

Many evidentialists try to carry a full arsenal of arguments. Gary Habermas is an exception. He has become famous for what he calls the "minimal facts approach." In the midst of a mass of apologetic material that could take several lifetimes to master, Habermas offers a streamlined approach that depends on relatively few facts. This approach has become popular because it makes logical sense and is relatively easy to master.

Habermas focuses on one event: Jesus' resurrection. His contention is that if a person can be convinced to believe in the resurrection, that person will accept that Jesus is God. If they accept that Jesus is God, then obviously, God exists. If Jesus is God, then what he says must be true, which includes his claim to be the world's Savior. And since Jesus said that the Old Testament is God's Word, a believer will view that portion of Scripture as true.

---

[44]Montgomery, *Christ as Centre and Circumference,* pp. 134-135 (emphasis added).

[45]Montgomery, "Once Upon an A Priori," in E. R. Geehan, ed., *Jerusalem and Athens,* p. 388.

[46]Montgomery, "Once Upon an A Priori," in E. R. Geehan, ed., *Jerusalem and Athens,* p. 390.

[47]Montgomery, "Once Upon an A Priori," in E. R. Geehan, ed., *Jerusalem and Athens,* p. 391.

To prove that Jesus rose from the dead, Habermas concentrates on historical evidence. The only data he will use is data that is (1) "strongly evidenced" and (2) "granted by virtually all scholars on the subject, even the skeptical ones."[48] When all the data is considered, Habermas contends, five facts emerge as virtually incontestable: Jesus died by crucifixion; Jesus' disciples believed that he rose and that is was Jesus who appeared to them; the church persecutor Paul was suddenly changed; the skeptic James, brother of Jesus, was suddenly changed; and Jesus' tomb was empty.[49]

Although a large amount of scholarship is behind this approach, the average Christian can simply learn to present evidence for the five historical facts noted above, which prove that Jesus rose from the dead. If anyone objects, the Christian can say, "But even unbelieving historians agree that these five facts and the evidence to prove them is true." If a person accepts the facts, there is no reason not to believe in Jesus.

Habermas comments on his use of Scripture: "The point is not that we must avoid using the New Testament when considering Jesus' resurrection. Rather, we simply must approach the New Testament as we would any other book in antiquity."[50]

Cumulative case apologetics

Cumulative case apologetics is a form of evidentialism. Paul Feinberg defines the term: "A cumulative case argument is a broad-based argument involving many elements formulated as an *informal* argument."[51]

The key word in the above quotation is *informal*. It's a shotgun approach. Christians simply learn arguments that interest them and that are best suited for the people they associate with. They then use these arguments in an informal way to build a case for the Christian faith.

Feinberg explains, "I argue for [an] apologetic based on arguments drawn from a variety of elements in our experience that stand in need of explanation." The goal is to show that "a Christian understanding of God and reality best explain

---

[48]Gary R. Habermas and Michael R. Licona, *The Case for the Resurrection of Jesus* (Grand Rapids: Kregel, 2004), p. 47.

[49]Habermas and Licona, *The Case for the Resurrection of Jesus,* pp. 48-77.

[50]Habermas and Licona, *The Case for the Resurrection of Jesus,* p. 45.

[51]Cowan, *Five Views on Apologetics,* p. 346 (emphasis added).

those elements"[52] and "that the preponderance of the evidence . . . points toward the truth of Christianity."[53] The arguments grow in their effectiveness as they accumulate over time in the conversations the believer has with his or her unbelieving friend.

One might describe this approach as "conversational evidentialism." It is easier for those just getting into apologetics. They learn several arguments and weave them into a conversation. They present these arguments with the attitude that it is up to the skeptic to "offer explanations that are at least as good as mine."[54]

Experientialism

Experientialism is not an apologetic method, per se. However, any Lutheran reading books on apologetics—especially those written by evidentialist apologists—must face this topic head-on. Even though experientialism is not a type of apologetics, many Evangelical/Reformed people view it as the highest form of apologetics—something, in fact, that trumps all apologetic arguments.

I'm referring to one's conversion experience. I think it is safe to say that most Evangelical/Reformed apologists simply assume that their believing readers have had a born-again experience and that their apologetic arguments will move a nonbeliever toward a similar experience.

We'll come back to experientialism in chapters 8 and 12.

Presuppositionalism

Historical introduction

Presuppositionalists are usually strict Calvinists. John Calvin (1509–1564) was a younger contemporary of Martin Luther. He was French, grew up Catholic, and in his mid-20s he came to faith in the Gospel uncovered by Martin Luther. Calvin became the leader of what is called the "Swiss Reformation," in contrast to the Lutheran or German Reformation. Calvin spent much of his life in Geneva, Switzerland, where he worked to organize the city around Christian moral principles. He greatly desired to help people understand Scripture. For pastors and church leaders, he wrote a doctrinal book, *The Institutes of the*

---

[52]Cowan, *Five Views on Apologetics*, p. 67.
[53]Cowan, *Five Views on Apologetics*, p. 347.
[54]Cowan, *Five Views on Apologetics*, p. 346.

Christian Religion, as well as commentaries on many books of the Bible. For lay Christians he wrote a catechism, published sermons he preached to his congregation, and encouraged them to read the Bible on their own.

With Scripture, Calvin taught the total depravity of human nature—that people are born spiritually powerless and hostile to God. But along with that, he taught that God does not want everyone to come to faith. God has elected some to believe the gospel and others to reject it (double predestination).

After Calvin died, some Reformed church leaders began to push back against those teachings. Jacob Arminius (1560–1609) reintroduced the truth that God wants all to be saved (which is what Scripture teaches). But he also taught that people are not spiritually dead—that unbelievers have enough spiritual strength to accept Christ's salvation or to reject it (which Scripture does not teach).[55]

The Reformed church has been divided ever since. Some congregations lean toward strict Calvinism and others toward Arminianism. For example, there are two varieties of Baptist churches. General Baptists are Arminian and believe that God wants all people to be saved. Particular Baptists are Calvinistic and believe in double predestination. Modern apologists follow these general contours. Arminians tend to be evidentialists, and strict Calvinists tend to be presuppositionalists.

What is presuppositionalism?

John Frame writes, "Through the history of apologetics, it has been common for Christians to claim some kind of neutral ground, some criteria or standard that both believers and unbelievers can accept without compromising their systems."[56] Vern Poythress explains: "Many people are tempted to picture a discussion in apologetics as a religiously neutral search for truth. Everyone supposedly starts off uncommitted and is trying to find out whether God exists, and which of the world religions might be true. . . . But the Bible indicates that

---

[55] Arminius taught that a Christian comes to faith "by grace alone." But he taught that God has given everyone what is called "prevenient grace." This grace gives a person enough spiritual strength to accept God's Word and Christ as one's Savior.

[56] John M. Frame, *Apologetics: A Justification of Christian Belief* (Phillipsburg, NJ: P&R Publishing, 2015), p. 6.

this picture is completely unrealistic."[57] Presuppositionalism takes the position that people are not engaged in a neutral search for God.[58]

"Most evidentialists are Arminian."[59] They teach that people are sinful and that they will often misinterpret or reject evidence for the truth of Christianity. But their spiritual ability is not completely lost, which results in the belief that unbelievers are, in fact, able to hear and evaluate the evidence objectively. Unbelievers retain the ability to understand and accept an apologist's evidence and logic and, therefore, can do their part in deciding for or against Christianity on that basis.

Strict Calvinist churches tend to be skeptical or at least somewhat guarded about what apologetics can accomplish. After all, they ask, if people by nature are completely sinful, can Christian logic and evidence persuade them to believe in the Christian faith? They answer, no. Christians understand the truth and validity of apologetic arguments for Christianity, but they can't rely on unbelievers to take part in the discussion along with them because they aren't able to.

According to presuppositionalists, unbelievers have their own worldview, and it is impossible for them to relate to the Christian worldview on which apologetic arguments are based. What's more, unbelievers wear colored glasses of hostility toward God that make them not only unable but also unwilling to accept or even to follow an argument for the truth. They will either outright reject the evidence for the truth of Christianity, or they will reinterpret it to support their unbelief.

A Christian's worldview is built on faith that God exists, that he created the world with physical laws and moral absolutes, that God revealed himself in the Bible, and that he will someday judge the world. These beliefs are called presuppositions. Christians will always speak as children of God, that is, presupposing that their Christian faith is true, even when speaking to a child of the world. Their encounter with an unbeliever must never turn into a courtroom process, where both look at the evidence and together determine guilt or innocence.

---

[57]Vern Poythress, forward to *Apologetics: A Justification of Christian Belief,* by John M. Frame, p. xv.

[58]See Siegbert W. Becker, *The Foolishness Of God: The Place of Reason in the Theology of Martin Luther* (Milwaukee: Northwestern, 1982), pp. 59-60 for a good discussion of presuppositionalism and Lutheranism.

[59]Boa and Bowman Jr., *Faith Has Its Reasons,* p. 166.

Presuppositionalist insist that Christians must never put God, the text of Scripture, or Scripture's message on the witness stand and then produce evidence that leads to the verdict that God exists and that Scripture is reliable.

Christians must never attempt to create a neutral space where the debate can take place *on the unbeliever's own terms*. If Christians did that, they would be justifying the unbeliever's naturalistic worldview, which is ultimately based on human authority, with the right to determine whether God exists and his Word is true. John Frame puts it this way: "To tell the unbeliever that we can reason with him on a neutral basis, however that claim might help to attract his attention, is a lie. Indeed, it is a lie of the most serious kind, for it falsifies the very heart of the Gospel—that Jesus Christ is *Lord*."[60] That is, Christians *presuppose* certain truths that God has led them to believe and they pray that God would lead the non-Christian to understand and believe those truths also.

The presuppositionalist point of contact with a non-Christian

But if apologists are unwilling to work with unbelievers on their own terms, unbelievers will have no context—no frame of reference—to understand and believe the message. Their worldview is so different from that of the apologist it's as if the apologist is speaking a different language.

Of course, this creates a problem. There would seem to be no point of contact between the Christian and the unbeliever—no common ground that would allow the Christian to share the truth with the unbeliever.

But there is, in fact, a way apologetic arguments can be used. Although there is no common ground on which Christians can use apologetic arguments *for the truth of Christianity*, as evidentialists do, they can use apologetic arguments *against unbelief*.

The apologist must show the unbeliever that his or her worldview is nonsense. It's a jumble of contradictory ideas and conclusions. The apologist's task is to show that unless God is factored into one's life, every part of their worldview makes no sense and, in some way, leads to guilt, anxiety, and hopelessness. Greg Bahnsen put it like this: "In debating with the unbeliever we will need to show him the irresolvable conflict between his espoused principles and ours, and then argue that apart from the self-attesting Christ of Scripture, his

---

[60]John M. Frame, *Apologetics to the Glory of God: An Introduction* (Phillipsburg, NJ: P&R Publishing, 1994), p. 9 (emphasis original).

thinking—based on his autonomous presuppositions—loses meaning, coherence, and intelligibility."[61]

A presuppositionalist would use the moral proof for the existence of God like this: "If you don't believe in God, then there is no source of right and wrong. Therefore, you must believe that human beings can choose their own definition of right and wrong. Let me ask you this: Does anyone believe it is right to molest children? No, you say? Well, if there is no God, then who led you and everyone else to arrive at that conclusion. You have no answer to that, do you?" Other proofs for the existence of God can be framed in the same way. From that point on, presuppositionalists do nothing more than proclaim what they believe.

Bahnsen explains the apologist's attitude: "Being confident of his ability to challenge apostate thought, the believer must reason, not according to the principles of secular thought, but on the presupposed truth of Christ's word, and looking to the power of His Spirit to bring conviction, conversion, and understanding."[62]

An example of presuppositionalist apologetics

Modern presuppositionalism began with Cornelius Van Til (1895–1947), who explained his views in numerous highly philosophical books. But he also wrote a simple book, *Why I Believe in God*, in which he explains to an unbeliever why he, Van Til, was a believer.

Van Til begins by confessing his faith in Christ as his Savior from sin. He continues by explaining why the unbeliever should accept the Christian religion. His witness, however, is somewhat tentative. This is to be expected. In view of Calvinism's teaching of double predestination and limited atonement, strict Calvinists can never look at an unbeliever and proclaim the good news of Christ's forgiveness: "Jesus died for *you*. God wants *you* in Heaven." A few quotations from *Why I Believe in God* will give us a feel for presuppositionalist apologetics.

Van Til states his position over against evidentialist apologists, who offer proofs for the truth of Christianity under the assumption that unbelievers can draw

---

[61]Greg L. Bahnsen, *Presuppositional Apologetics: Stated and Defended,* ed. Joel McDurmon (Nacogdoches, TX: Covenant Media Press and Powder Springs, GA: American Vision Press, 2008), p. 20.
[62]Bahnsen, *Presuppositional Apologetics,* p. 85.

the same conclusions from the evidence as believers. Van Til apologizes to the unbeliever for the impression evidentialists might have given him in the past:

> I must make an apology to you at this point. We who believe in God have not always made this position plain. Often enough we have talked with you about facts and sound reasons as though we agreed with you on what these really are. In our arguments for the existence of God we have frequently assumed that you and we together have an area of knowledge on which we agree. But we [presuppositionalists] really do not grant that you see any fact in any dimension of life truly.[63]

Van Til describes to the unbeliever what the unbeliever will do if Van Til tries to prove Christianity by using evidence from creation, from fulfilled prophecy, from miracles, or from evidence that God is in control of all things. The unbeliever, he says, will assign a natural cause to all these things, like unbelieving scientists do when they attribute what they observe in nature to evolution.

Van Til says there is only one solution to the unbeliever's problem:

> Only the great Physician through His blood atonement on the Cross and by the gift of His Spirit can take those colored glasses off and make you see facts as they are, facts as evidence, as inherently compelling evidence, for the existence of God.[64]

Van Til describes the emptiness of the unbeliever's life, and then he tells the unbeliever that deep down inside he knows this description is true. (Calvin called this "a sense of the divine.") Van Til explains this to the unbeliever:

> Deep down in your heart you know very well that what I have said about you is true. You know there is no unity in your life. You want no God who by His counsel provides for the unity you need.[65]

But Van Til's Calvinistic witness doesn't give the unbeliever much certainty, which should be at the heart of every Christian witness. He writes about God's grace like this:

> Who by His providence conditioned my youth, making me believe in Him, and who in my later life by His grace still makes me want to be-

---

[63]Cornelius Van Til, *Why I Believe in God* (Phillipsburg, NJ: P&R, 1975; Kindle file, Fig-books, 2012), loc. 184.

[64]Van Til, *Why I Believe in God*, loc. 283.

[65]Van Til, *Why I Believe in God*, loc. 298.

lieve in Him. It is the God who also controlled your youth and so far has apparently not given you His grace that you might believe in Him.[66]

Consistent with this, Van Til ends his little book like this:

> I shall not convert you at the end of my argument. I think the argument is sound. I hold that belief in God is not merely as reasonable as other belief, or even a little or infinitely more probably true than other belief; I hold rather that unless you believe in God you can logically believe in nothing else. But since I believe in such a God, a God who has conditioned you as well as me, I know that you can to your own satisfaction, by the help of the biologists, the psychologists, the logicians, and the Bible critics reduce everything I have said this afternoon and evening to the circular meanderings of a hopeless authoritarian. Well, my meanderings have, to be sure, been circular; they have made everything turn on God. So now I shall leave you with Him, and with His mercy.[67]

This is Van Til's view of an unbeliever, and it reflects the mind of strict Calvinists when they share their faith.

This overview of the kinds of apologetics should help Lutherans see how a person's beliefs naturally shape, even dictate, how that person uses apologetics. It should encourage Lutherans to examine their beliefs and carefully shape their use of apologetics accordingly. In the world of modern apologetics, this is a very reasonable and accepted activity.

John Frame (1939–)

John Frame is a leading thinker on the role of apologetics in evangelism. He is professor of apologetics at the Westminster Seminary's Irvine, California, campus. He was a student of Van Til and has written much to explain Van Til's position. Frame has high regard for Van Til and his approach to apologetics. Yet he gives evidential proofs of Christianity a greater place in apologetics than Van Til did. Boa and Bowman explain, "In his 1987 book *The Doctrine of the Knowledge of God,* Frame presented . . . a systematic refinement of Van Til's position, giving more appreciation to logic and factual evidence while remaining true to Van Til's vision of a thoroughly Reformed, presuppositional apologetic."[68]

---

[66]Van Til, *Why I Believe in God,* loc. 289.

[67]Van Til, *Why I Believe in God,* loc. 329.

[68]Boa and Bowman Jr., *Faith Has Its Reasons,* p. 29 (emphasis added).

Frame gives unbelievers more credit than Van Til did. They *can*, in fact, understand the logic of apologetic arguments and the evidence on which those arguments are based. They *can* conclude from the evidence that Christianity is true.

Some have accused Frame of abandoning the presuppositionalist camp and becoming an evidentialist. But Frame disagrees: "There need be no competition between presuppositions and evidences. Our scriptural presupposition authorizes the use of evidence, and the evidence is nothing more than the application of Scripture to our situation. The use of evidence is not contrary to *sola Scriptura*, but a fulfillment of that principle."[69]

Voddie Baucham (1969–)

Voddie Baucham grew up in a non-Christian home. He came to faith early in his college years. He continued expanding his knowledge of Christianity and subsequently served in various ministries. He is presently dean of theology at African Christian University in Lusaka, Zambia. He confesses his faith in the words of the Second London Baptist Confession of Faith of 1689. This confession of faith was written before most Baptists became Arminian; it is clearly Calvinistic. Baucham is a presuppositionalist.

Baucham's book *Expository Apologetics: Answering Objections With the Power of the Word* integrates apologetics with Scripture. Baucham is not a Lutheran. But his position on the power of God's Word and the role it plays in witnessing to one's faith often leads him to speak about God's Word as a "means of grace" in the way Lutherans use that phrase.

Here is an extended quotation from Baucham's *Expository Apologetics* that gets us to the heart of Baucham's approach to apologetics. It also illustrates the difference between presuppositionalism and evidentialism.

> Practically speaking, this is a matter of perspective. Do we believe that an apologetic encounter is an appeal to the mind of man, or to the Word of God? Do we believe that man is an impartial, all-powerful judge whom we must convince of the rightness and truthfulness of our claims? Or do we believe him to be a fool who suppresses the truth in unrighteousness, and will go on refusing to acknowledge the rightness and truthfulness of our claims "until the day dawn and the morning star rises in [his] heart" (2 Peter 1:19)?

---

[69]Frame, *Apologetics to the Glory of God,* p. 26.

If the former is true, we will lay down our Bibles and try to convince our interlocutor of the rightness and truth of our claims by stepping out of our worldview and into his. We will say things like, "You can't use the Bible with people who don't believe it" and, "You've got to meet people where they are." The irony is that when we assume this posture, we essentially negate our claim to hold to a biblical worldview. We have agreed with our interlocutor that there can be truth apart from God. We agree with him that Scripture is neither sufficient nor necessary. We have answered the fool and become "like him" (Proverbs 24:4).

However, if the latter is true, we will hold on to the Scriptures, believing that God is the fountainhead of all knowledge and Christ is the repository of all wisdom and knowledge (Colossians 2:3). We believe that "faith comes from hearing, and hearing through the word of Christ" (Romans 10:17). As a result, like a warrior whose opponent does not believe in the existence of his sword, we refuse to lay down our arms and argue, opting instead to hack away, knowing that eventually, he will believe . . . or he will perish!

Nor do we simply quote Bible verses and ignore all questions. On the contrary, we answer! We answer just as though we were speaking *for* the Judge not *to* a judge."[70]

Baucham's down-to-earth approach and clear emphasis on God's Word is where all evangelism should begin.

Reformed apologetics

Reformed apologetics is the name given to an apologetic approach developed by Alvin Plantinga (1932–). Plantinga is one of the foremost philosophers of the 20th century, a past chairman of the American Philosophical Association and the Society of Christian Philosophers.

Plantinga rejects the evidentialist claim that "beliefs are rational only as they are justified by appeals to evidence."[71] Brian Morley explains that "Plantinga wants to show that theists are not irrational even if they are unable to demonstrate

---

[70]Voddie Baucham Jr., *Expository Apologetics: Answering Objections With the Power of the Word* (Wheaton: Crossway, 2015), p. 63 (brackets and italics original).

[71]Boa and Bowman Jr., *Faith Has Its Reasons*, p. 31.

their beliefs conclusively from premises accepted by opponents,"[72] that is, by using logical arguments and evidence.

Plantinga's apologetic is actually a theory of how we come to know things, which in philosophy is called *epistemology*. Kelly James Clark writes, "I and other Reformed epistemologists are concerned to eliminate the unjust impression that belief in God requires evidence or argument."[73]

What is Plantinga's argument? He says that belief in God is *basic* to all human beings. In other words, belief in God does not have to be proved; it is a basic fact which all people know is true. Following John Calvin, Plantinga says there is within every human being the "knowledge of the divine" (*sensus divinitatis*), which is part of the image of God that is still in human beings even after the fall into sin.[74] The sinful human nature in people wants to suppress this awareness of God and keep it buried, but people cannot keep it suppressed forever. It surfaces through what people see and experience in the world around them and in the events of their lives.[75]

Plantinga also applies this concept to a believer's knowledge of salvation through God's gift of a Savior. He claims that this and other truths of Scripture are also *basic* (that is, they don't need evidence and argument to prove them true). If it is true that the Holy Spirit leads a person to believe these truths, which he does, then the truth become a *basic* part of a person's knowledge and do not need to be proved true. If this is how God works—and it is, says Plantinga—a person is not being irrational if he or she simply believes what Scripture says about salvation. That person simply *knows* them to be true. Moreover, that person has a right to accept them as *accurate knowledge*, that is, as knowledge gained in a legitimate and honest way, unhindered by human failings. In Plantinga's terms, these beliefs have *warrant* and it is reasonable to believe them.

According to Plantinga, it is modern apologists who are acting irrationally when they try to give the truths of Scripture *warrant* by offering proofs and arguments for them. Here is an extended quotation from Plantinga in which he explains the affect of his ideas on the use of apologetics:

---

[72]Morley, *Mapping Apologetics*, p. 122.

[73]Cowan, *Five Views on Apologetics*, p. 372.

[74]Alvin Plantinga, *Knowledge and Christian Belief* (Grand Rapids: Eerdmans, 2015), p. 47.

[75]See Plantinga, *Knowledge and Christian Belief*, pp. 30-37.

My Christian belief can have warrant, and warrant sufficient for knowledge, even if I don't know of and cannot make a good historical case for the reliability of the biblical writers or for what they teach. I don't *need* a good argument, historical or otherwise, for the resurrection of Jesus Christ, or for his being in fact the divine Son of God, or for the Christian claim that his suffering and death in fact constitutes an atoning sacrifice whereby we can be restored to the right relationship with God. . . . The warrant floats free of such questions. It doesn't require to be validated or proved by some source of belief *other* than faith, such as historical investigation.

Scripture is self-authenticating in the sense that for belief in the great things of the Gospel to be justified, rational, and warranted, no historical evidence and argument for the teaching in question, or for the veracity or reliability or divine character of Scripture (or the part of Scripture in which it is taught), is necessary. The process by which these beliefs have warrant for the believer swings free of those historical and other considerations; these beliefs have warrant in the basic way.[76]

These words do not sound like they should be included in a book on modern apologetics. But the approach to apologetics of men like Plantinga are found in every book that maps modern apologetics. Reformed apologists are considered members of the apologetic community, and their approaches and beliefs are acknowledged as legitimate options.

Summary

In this chapter we have explored the major approaches to apologetics: presuppositionalist, evidentialist, and classical. We have also looked at several subgroups. By meeting a few well-known people in the apologetic world, we've gotten an idea of what Boa and Bowman observe: "Few Christian thinkers exhibit a 'pure' form of any one of the four approaches we have discussed."[77]

Lutherans who are considering using apologetics should know the theology behind each form of apologetics, just as experts in apologetics, people like Boa and Bowman *(Faith Has Its Reasons)*, Steven Cowan *(Five Views on Apologetics)*, and Brian Morley *(Mapping Apologetics)*, are doing. They recognize that modern apologists use methods that are shaped by their doctrinal beliefs.

---

[76]Plantinga, *Knowledge and Christian Belief*, pp. 65-66.
[77]Boa and Bowman Jr., *Faith Has Its Reasons*, p. 425.

One might not be able to thoroughly explain every type of apologetics presented in this chapter. But this chapter has led us to realize that it is legitimate to put apologetics under the microscope of what one believes.

Part 2

Is It Reasonable to Believe in Christianity?

Chapter 3—The Message God Has Given His Church to Preach

Many authors of books on apologetics assume their readers share a common understanding of the Christian religion. But to understand how to defend the Christian religion, we must be sure of what the Christian religion is. This chapter will give an overview of how Scripture describes its message.

Chapter 4—Is Christianity Reasonable? Yes

At this point we come to a major crossroads. If the Christian faith is reasonable, it can be defended by rational arguments. Scripture tells us that human beings can, in fact, reason out certain truths about God. It also relates what role these trutts play in our witness to an unbeliever.

Chapter 5—Is Christianity Reasonable? No

However, God's plan of salvation is not reasonable to human beings. Even when people learn about the salvation God devised, they do not find it rational or reasonable. Therefore, it cannot be "proven" in the traditional way, namely, through human logic.

Chapter 3

The Message God Has Given His Church to Preach

What are we defending?

The word *apologetics* comes from the Greek word *apologeo*, which means "to make a defense," or in a more general sense "to give an answer." Only once in the New Testament does a writer tell his readers to do this (1 Peter 3:15). Otherwise, the word is used to describe what Christians are doing or will be called on to do when on trial for their faith. (We will look closely at the meaning of *apologeo* in chapter 12.)

Being asked to give a reason for their hope forces Christians to think carefully about what they believe. "Why am I a Christian? What is the hope I have as a follower of Jesus?" You would think that every believer would answer those questions in the same way. But that's not the case. There are differences between Catholics, the Reformed, today's Evangelicals, and confessional Lutherans.[78] Those differences are not minor. They extend to the very heart of the faith. So before we think about the role modern apologetics might play in the lives of Christians, we must carefully define the Christian faith on the basis of Scripture.

Sin and grace in the beginning

When people write about an event in history, they usually start at the beginning. No author talks about the beginning of something in chapter 1 of their book and then starts chapter 2 with, "well, that was interesting, but now let's turn to what's really important." The beginning is important because it naturally leads into what follows.

---

[78]"Confessional Lutherans" accept the historic Lutheran Confessions as accurate statements of what the Bible teaches.

Scripture begins with God's creation of the world. After each act of creation, God assessed what he had just made and said it was good. And when everything was done, "God saw everything that he had made, and behold, it was very good" (Genesis 1:31). Adam and Eve had been created in God's image. They were as morally perfect as God was. God had given them a special commandment, not to eat from a certain tree, and it was a joy for them to keep this commandment. They wore no clothing when they were created and felt no shame over their nakedness. Their perfection coincided with God's perfection, and they were happy to be in his company.

But this changed. Moses records the events in Genesis 3.[79] Satan, an angel who had rebelled against God, successfully tempted Adam and Eve to follow suit, which they did. Immediately they knew they deserved to be punished—to die—for their rebellion.

God's perfect creation became imperfect. Terror replaced peace. Lust fostered shame. Self-centeredness replaced the pure love Adam and Eve had for each other. God asked them, "Where are you?" Adam answered, "I heard the sound of you in the garden and I was afraid."

Then each tried to escape guilt by blaming someone else. Adam tried to push the blame on Eve and on God, who created her: "The woman whom you gave to be with me, she gave me fruit of the tree, and I ate." God confronted Eve, "What is this you have done?" Eve also tried to excuse herself by blaming Satan.

Life in a perfect world with a perfect and loving God had been replaced with life in fellowship with Satan, the liar who just ruined everything. There was no possible way Adam and Eve could free themselves from God's judgment. This was guilt at its worst.

No sooner had sin been revealed to a perfect world than God revealed his kindness to a world now filled with sin. God told Satan in Adam and Eve's hearing, "I will put enmity between you and the woman, and between your offspring and her offspring; he shall bruise your head, and you shall bruise his heel." God was saying: "Satan, I will restore hostility to where it belongs, between you and the woman. Your hostility toward her will come to a head in a contest between your offspring and one of the woman's offspring. Her offspring will kill you and free mankind from my judgment and from your control." Adam and Eve had

---

[79]Except as noted, all Scripture references in this section ("Sin and grace in the beginning") are from Genesis 3, the ESV.

done nothing to deserve this promise of God's forgiveness. This was grace at its best.

Out of these events the true "worldview" unfolds. We live in a world created by a perfect and holy God. It's a world filled with sin, guilt, and God's impending judgment. It's a world with people whom God loves and whom he has forgiven. It's a world whose creator had restored peace between himself and mankind by promising them a Savior.

Oddly, it is only at this point that people began to suffer. The suffering described in Genesis 3 was not the natural result of sin. It was suffering God himself imposed. God decreed: "I will surely multiply your pain in childbearing. . . . Cursed is the ground because of you. . . . You are dust and to dust you shall return."

The timing is important. Suffering *followed* the promise. Suffering was not just a matter of God's anger and judgment on sin; he had already forgiven them. Rather, God introduced suffering for Adam and Eve's good, to help them remember their sin and to release their grasp on this world. It helped them concentrate on the coming Savior and yearn for a world to be recreated in its original perfection.

God knew that Adam and Eve would want to hang on to life in this world. And they could have, for the tree of life was still there in the garden. So he removed Adam and Eve from the garden and kept them from ever going back: "Now, lest he reach out his hand and take also of the tree of life and eat, *and live forever*. . . . He drove out the man, and . . . he placed the cherubim and a flaming sword that turned every way to guard the way to the tree of life."

God does not enjoy seeing people suffer, and in many ways, he alleviates the suffering *he* introduced into the world. But the flaming sword and the cherubim will guard Eden's doorway until the end. Then God will recreate this world and give his people new and perfect bodies and spirits. Then the sword will grow cold, the cherubim will depart, and we will once again have access to the tree of life in the new Garden of Eden (Revelation 22:2,3).

This is the Christian hope. And Christians can grasp the meaning of their hope only if they believe God's account of the world's first days—perfection, sin, grace, and a future restoration.

This is the only true "worldview." It's the worldview of Scripture. It's the worldview of all God's people, ancient and modern, no matter in what country or culture they live. Sinful human beings are guilty before God. In Christ, God has freed all people from the guilt of their sin and restored his relationship of peace with them as it was at the beginning. God urges all people to repent of their sins and believe that they are forgiven and that God is reconciled to them. God's people are to be God's mouthpieces to convey this message. God never gave his people another purpose or described their task in any other way.

Sin and grace shaped the subsequent history of the world in the centuries before Christ

God gave the world a wonderful promise. But sin proved more appealing: "The wickedness of man was great in the earth" and "every intention of the thoughts of his heart was only evil continually" (Genesis 6:5). God destroyed the people of the world with a flood. But soon people returned to their evil ways, so God chose a man, Abraham, through whom he would keep this promise alive. He told Abraham to leave his hometown and the idols his family worshiped. He gave him these promises:

> "I will make of you a great nation, and I will bless you and make your name great, so that you will be a blessing. I will bless those who bless you, and him who dishonors you I will curse, and in you all the families of the earth shall be blessed" (Genesis 12:2,3).

Eve's offspring, the world's Savior, would come through Abraham. The blessings God gave to Abraham would always be a gift, just as they had been to Adam and Eve: "And the Scripture, foreseeing that God would justify the Gentiles *by faith*, preached the Gospel beforehand to Abraham, saying, 'In you shall all the nations be blessed.' So then, those who are of faith are blessed along with Abraham, the man of faith" (Galatians 3:8,9). Abraham looked forward to the Savior's arrival and the blessings the Savior would bring, as Jesus said, "Your father Abraham rejoiced that he would see my day. He saw it and was glad" (John 8:56).

Several hundred years later God put Abraham's descendants, the people of Israel, under a comprehensive set of laws. The Law served as a "guardian until Christ came, in order that we might be justified by faith" (Galatians 3:24). The Law served as Israel's guardian in two ways. First, it pointed out the depth of their sin and showed them how much they needed a Savior. Second, through its many symbols, the Law pointed the Israelites ahead to the blessings of the Savior, most prominently the forgiveness of sin through "the Lamb."

For example, once a year the people of Israel were to sacrifice a perfect lamb and eat a special meal. This festival, called Passover, reminded them of how God rescued their forefathers from Egypt—when he put to death the firstborn of every Egyptian household but passed over the homes of the people who had painted the blood of the lamb on their doorposts. This meal contained another powerful symbol. To prepare for the Passover, the Israelites were to rid their homes of leaven. Leaven symbolized sin. God was delivering his people from slavery in Egypt and at the same time he was calling them to live holy lives in fellowship with their holy God.

Paul applied these symbols to us, even though today we are not required to keep the Old Testament Law:

> Cleanse out the old leaven that you may be a new lump, as you really are unleavened. For Christ, our Passover lamb, has been sacrificed. Let us therefore celebrate the festival, not with the old leaven, the leaven of malice and evil, but with the unleavened bread of sincerity and truth. (1 Corinthians 5:7,8)

The Christian's entire life is a celebration of the Lamb's sacrifice and a struggle to put off the leaven of malice and evil.

Years later, Hannah, the mother of the prophet Samuel, expressed a worldview centered on sin and grace. She foresaw God's judgment, and she looked forward to her King, who would destroy evil: "The LORD will judge the ends of the earth; he will give strength to his king and exalt the horn of his anointed" (1 Samuel 2:10).

King David foresaw the Savior's death and resurrection from the dead:

> I have set the LORD always before me; because he is at my right hand, I shall not be shaken. Therefore my heart is glad, and my whole being rejoices; my flesh also dwells secure. For you will not abandon my soul to Sheol, or let your holy one see corruption. (Psalm 16:8-10)

In his sermon at the inauguration of the Christian Church the apostle Peter applied David's words to Jesus (Acts 2:25-27). David's hope in the Savior's resurrection was the foundation on which the New Testament Church was formed.

Space does not permit us to relate the full breadth of the Old Testament message. But it is the same message of God's grace in the face of human sin that Adam and Eve heard in the Garden of Eden. That message was as central to the faith of God's people in the Old Testament as it is to people who live in the New Testament. In the days following Jesus' resurrection, the Lord brought a Christian named Philip into contact with a man from Ethiopia who needed help understanding the Christian faith. God paved the way for Philip by having the Ethiopian man reading from the Old Testament, from Isaiah 53: "Like a sheep he was led to the slaughter and like a lamb before its shearer is silent, so he opens not his mouth" (Acts 8:32). This Old Testament passage gave Philip the perfect place to begin: "Then Philip opened his mouth, and beginning with this Scripture he told him the good news about Jesus" (Acts 8:35).

Jesus tells us that he is the heart of the Old Testament. He rebuked the Jews who did not believe in him: "You search the Scriptures because you think that in them you have eternal life; and it is they that bear witness about me" (John 5:39). And he encouraged those who did believe in him: "Everything written about me in the Law of Moses and the Prophets and the Psalms must be fulfilled" (Luke 24:44).

The heart of the Old Testament is not rules and regulations, commandments and moral advice. It is the message of human sin and God's grace, a promise that we in the New Testament have seen fulfilled.

Jesus came to overcome sin, death, Hell, and the devil and to gain God's forgiveness

Zechariah, the father of John the Baptist, described his son John's work like this:

> And you, child, will be called the prophet of the Most High; for you will go before the LORD to prepare his ways, to give knowledge of salvation to his people in the forgiveness of their sins, because of the tender mercy of our God, whereby the sunrise shall visit us from on high to give light to those who sit in darkness and in the shadow of death, to guide our feet into the way of peace. (Luke 1:76-79)

Jesus defined his ministry in just those terms: "For even the Son of Man came not to be served but to serve, and to give his life as a ransom for many" (Mark 10:45). And Paul defined what Jesus meant by *many*: He "gave himself as a ransom for *all*" (1 Timothy 2:6).

Jesus' sufferings and death established peace between God and the people of the world. Jesus said, "Peace I leave with you; my peace I give to you" (John

14:27). Jesus certainly taught the people God's Law, but he did that only after he gave them forgiving relief for the times they had broken it. He first said, "Do not think that I have come to abolish the Law or the Prophets; I have not come to abolish them but to fulfill them" (Matthew 5:17). Then he could say to the people without crushing them with guilt, "Unless your righteousness exceeds that of the scribes and Pharisees, you will never enter the kingdom of heaven" (Matthew 5:20).

Jesus was filled with compassion over people's suffering. But the people he healed got sick again, and the people he raised from the dead would again lie in their graves. Jesus fed the hungry, but in this world they would hunger again. Jesus cast out demons, but demon possession continued to afflict many who could not be brought to Jesus. However, the forgiveness Jesus won for the world is permanent; it is there for the taking by all who believe, and it can never be taken away.

Satan, who claims the right to accuse us of sin, has been silenced. In the book of Revelation, John heard a loud voice in Heaven proclaim, "Now the salvation and the power and the kingdom of our God and the authority of his Christ have come, for the accuser of our brothers has been thrown down, who accuses them day and night before our God." How was he defeated? "By the blood of the Lamb and by the word of their testimony" (Revelation 12:10,11).

Roughly a third of the gospels is dedicated to the last week of Jesus' life—his betrayal, trials, and crucifixion. That's where Jesus crushed the head of the devil in fulfillment of God's promise to Adam and Eve. Jesus' resurrection is the foundation of the Christian faith. Why? Because it is proof that he won the battle he had been fighting against sin, Satan, and death. Paul put it this way: "He . . . was delivered over *because of* our wrongdoings, and was raised *because of* our justification" (Romans 4:25 New American Standard Bible).[80]

God has always ruled over his creation. But his rule over sinners in rebellion could only end in our being judged and punished. But since sin has been

---

[80]In this verse, the Greek sets up a parallel. Most versions express the parallel like the ESV expresses it: "He was put to death for our sins and raised for our justification." The meaning of the verse becomes somewhat vague when translated that way. It's as if Paul was saying that Jesus was put to death in order to atone for our sins and was raised to life in order that we might be justified. But Scripture does not speak about the resurrection as God's tool to accomplish something, but as proof that something has been accomplished. The NASB 1995 expresses the parallel in grammatically correct and clear terms: "who was delivered over because of our wrongdoings, and was raised because of our justification."

forgiven, God now uses his absolute power to work in all things for the good of his Church and its members. Christ is "far above all rule and authority and power and dominion" and God has "put all things under his feet and gave him as head over all things to the church, which is his body, the fullness of him who fills all in all" (Ephesians 1:21-23).

The message of God's forgiving grace was the heart of the apostles' ministry

In Romans 5 Paul tells us that we will never be ashamed for putting our trust in God's love, for "God's love has been poured into our hearts through the Holy Spirit who has been given to us" (Romans 5:5). This could be interpreted as an infusion of knowledge that God is kind and loving. It could be interpreted as an infusion of power to feel God's love and find inner assurance of it. But it is neither. Rather, it is the Holy Spirit leading sinners to know what God has done for them in Christ. Paul continues in the next sentence and explains what he means by the love of God, which the Spirit has poured into our hearts:

> For while we were still weak, at the right time Christ died for the ungodly. For one will scarcely die for a righteous person—though perhaps for a good person one would dare even to die—but God shows his love for us in that while we were still sinners, Christ died for us. Since, therefore, we have now been justified by his blood, much more shall we be saved by him from the wrath of God. For if while we were enemies we were reconciled to God by the death of his Son, much more, now that we are reconciled, shall we be saved by his life. (Romans 5:5-10)

Paul here emphasizes the timing of God's work on our behalf. God sent his Son to us when we were ungodly sinners who were giving him absolutely no reason to show us mercy. At just that time, when we were sinfully rebelling against God, Christ died for us. Paul's argument goes like this: If God's Son died for our sins and declared us "not guilty" when we were hopeless sinners and if God reconciled himself to us when we were his enemies, can there be any doubt that now—after Christ has died for the sins of all—God wants people to repent of their sins and live in his forgiving grace? The Holy Spirit is pouring out God's love into our hearts by pointing us to God's timing. If God did the hard thing—forgiving us when we were still in rebellion and establishing peace with us when we were still unrepentant enemies, is there any doubt that God will forgive us and save us from his wrath over sin on the Last Day? The hard thing—the impossible thing—has already been done; the rest is easy. The Holy

Spirit is pouring this truth into our hearts, which enables us to know God's love.

In 2 Corinthians 5, Paul defines why "the love of Christ" controls his life. The heart of the Christian "worldview" is summarized in these words:

> For the love of Christ controls us, because we have concluded this: that one has died for all, therefore all have died; and he died for all, that those who live might no longer live for themselves but for him who for their sake died and was raised. (2 Corinthians 5:14-15)

Jesus had said, "And I, when I am lifted up from the earth, will draw all people to myself" (John 12:32). When he suffered and died on a cross, he was not alone. All people—you too—were there with him. The hymn writer asks, "Were you there when they crucified my Lord?" Everyone can answer, "Yes, I was there." That's what Paul means when he says in 2 Corinthians that "all have died." The world died on a cross with Christ, and now the whole world can say, "God's eternal wrath over my sins has been put to rest."

Spreading this "worldview" was Paul's ministry, and it is the ministry of the Christian Church. Through the Church's message, God makes new creations out of fallen sinners: "Therefore, if anyone is in Christ, he is a new creation. The old has passed away; behold, the new has come" (2 Corinthians 5:17).

How did we become new creations? Paul immediately describes how God did this. God made this happen through the ministry of reconciliation." Paul explains what that is:

> All this is from God, who through Christ reconciled us to himself and gave us the ministry of reconciliation; that is, in Christ God was reconciling the world to himself, not counting their trespasses against them, and entrusting to us the message of reconciliation. Therefore, we are ambassadors for Christ, God making his appeal through us. We implore you on behalf of Christ, be reconciled to God. (2 Corinthians 5:18-20)

Through his Son, God reconciled "the world" to himself. In other words, God did away with the hostility between himself and humankind and replaced it with peace. Because Jesus took God's wrath over sin on himself, God now looks at the world with friendship and peace in his heart.

Note carefully that Paul is not referring to God's peace *on believers*. He is referring to the fact that God is at peace *with the world*. Sadly, so much hostility between man and God remains. But the hostility is not on God's side. Even though God is reconciled to all people, those who continue to be afraid of God and live in dread of him remain hostile to him.

It was Paul's job to tell people that God was reconciled to the world and at peace with all people. That is the good news the Christian Church has to give. It's the good news the Church is called on to defend. Knowing that God has reconciled himself to the world, we urge people to be reconciled to God in their own minds. We say, in effect, "Give up your sin and hostility against God. Be at peace with him. You can do that because through the work of his Son, Jesus, he is already at peace with you."

A little later in Romans 5, Paul expresses the same truth in legal terms. In Romans 5:18 Paul writes: "Consequently, just as one trespass resulted in condemnation for all people, so also one righteous act resulted in justification and life for all people" (Romans 5:18 NIV). We chose to quote the NIV translation because it better reflects the parallel between Adam and Christ: Because of Adam's sin, all people stand condemned; because of Christ's act of righteousness, all people are justified (declared "not guilty"). [81]

If that is true, some argue, then all people will go to Heaven and there is no need for the Church "to make disciples of all nations" (Matthew 28:19). But that misses the point. Imagine a rich man opening a bank account for every man, woman, and child on earth with an opening balance of one million dollars. At that point everyone is a millionaire whether they know it or not and whether they use the money or not. But if they don't know about their new bank accounts with a million-dollar balance, they will continue to live as before. Or if they are told what the rich man did for them but scoff at the messenger and refuse to believe him, they will die as paupers even though they are actually millionaires.

The same is true for us, born as spiritual paupers. God is at peace with all people through Jesus' death and resurrection. God has declared all people not

---

[81]The ESV doesn't reproduce the parallel. It translates, "Therefore, as one trespass *led* to condemnation for all men, so one act of righteousness *leads* to justification and life for all men" (Romans 5:18). While this might be understood correctly, the word "leads" gives a tentative feel to the second half of the verse. In other words, Christ's act of righteousness *can* lead to justification and life *if a person has faith*. The passage in Greek does not contain a verb. A very literal translation would be: "So, then, as through one offense to all people to condemnation, so also through one righteous deed to all people to justification of life." The ESV could have reflected the Greek by using the word "led" twice.

guilty because Christ has drawn all people to himself on the cross and suffered for them. But if people don't know this fact, or if they know it and reject it, they will live without God's peace and will die as sinners liable to God's judgment.

John the Baptist proclaimed "a baptism of repentance for the forgiveness of sins" (Luke 3:3). Jesus preached, "Repent, for the kingdom of heaven is at hand" (Matthew 4:17). Because of the life and death of his Son, God can now transfer us "from the dominion of darkness" and bring us "the kingdom of his beloved Son" (Colossians 1:13). For that to happen, people born into the kingdom of darkness must realize where they are headed, straight into the hands of God who will punish every sin. They need to acknowledge their sin, which they *can do* when they learn that God has forgiven their sin and is at peace with them. This is God's gift to us, as Peter said, "God exalted him at his right hand as Leader and Savior, *to give* repentance to Israel and forgiveness of sins" (Acts 5:31).

The Church's ministry is to tell people that God is at peace with them and that the guilt of their sins has been borne by another. The Church's message is never, "You can be saved if you believe." Rather, it is: "you are saved; for goodness sake, believe it. Don't die in your sin and rebellion against God. Repent of your sins. Believe that God, in Christ, has forgiven you. Die in the peace of forgiveness, which is yours in Christ."

This is the meaning of God's grace. This grace lies at the heart of the Christian faith. This is what Christians are called on to proclaim and defend. Faith in this message must be the goal to which all apologetics is designed to lead.

Christians forsake sin and live as forgiven children of God, all to God's glory

Christianity also frees us from self-centered service to God. Some turn to Christianity to help them with day-to-day problems. Some turn to Christianity to find self-esteem or a purpose in life. Some turn to Christianity hoping it will help them become better people or help them find the moral path that leads to God. These reasons are self-centered, and all self-centered service to God keeps people chained to themselves and incapable of truly serving him.

Through his Son, God has created a group of people that belong solely to him for time and for eternity—people who have all they need, who can look outside themselves and serve God and their neighbor free from self-centered ulterior motives.

Paul summarizes the Christian life in these beautiful words:

> For the grace of God has appeared, bringing salvation for all people, training us to renounce ungodliness and worldly passions, and to live self-controlled, upright, and godly lives in the present age, waiting for our blessed hope, the appearing of the glory of our great God and Savior Jesus Christ, *who gave himself for us to redeem us from all lawlessness and to purify for himself a people for his own possession who are zealous for good works.* (Titus 2:11-14)

God's greatest gift is the forgiveness of our sin. Through the death of his Son, he called us away from a life of lawless behavior. He purified us. Through faith in what his Son did for the world, he made us his children—his own possessions—who have a sincere desire to serve him.

Why this discussion is important

This is the hope Christians are called on to defend. It's about sinners repenting of their sin, knowing they are forgiven, and living in hope. We will always want to ask, what is the relationship of apologetics to this hope? Do our apologetic arguments always lead unbelievers in this direction, or do they lead to some other goal?

Summary

The message we are defending is the message of sin and grace, that Jesus paid for the sins of the world and that people are saved entirely through his work. This is the message of Scripture. It is the foundation of the Old Testament. It is the definition of the New Testament Gospel, which Jesus came to establish and which the New Testament writers and evangelists proclaimed and promoted.

Chapter 4

Is Christianity Reasonable? Yes

Introduction

In the last chapter, we explored the heart of Christianity—our problem, the problem God solved, and the way he solved it.

The purpose of modern apologetic arguments is to prove that Christianity is a reasonable religion. People can become Christians without giving up the rational way they think and reasonable way they carry out their lives. So we must ask, is it reasonable to accept the problem Christianity is designed to answer. And is it reasonable to accept God's answer to our problem as Scripture defines it?

Scripture answers these questions with a yes and a no. In this chapter we'll explore the sense in which Scripture says yes.

People are compelled by reason to believe in God

This aspect of Christianity—belief in the existence of God who created the world and everything in it—is a matter of simple logic. Belief in the existence of God is reasonable. Put more strongly, it is unreasonable to deny it.

Paul writes,

> For what can be known about God is plain to them, because God has shown it to them. For his invisible attributes, namely, his eternal power and divine nature, have been clearly perceived, ever since the creation of the world, in the things that have been made. So they are without excuse. (Romans 1:19,20)

God created the world. Ever since that time, the creation has been revealing unseen things about the One who created it. If God created the world, he is not one of the things he created. He must be a divine being, that is, someone in a completely different class from creatures. God must be eternal. Time is an aspect of creation, so it doesn't apply to the One who created it. He must possess unlimited power, for only someone with unlimited power could create a universe with a world like ours, filled with plants, animals, and creatures like mankind.

This is a matter of simple logic. Paul is not teaching the existence and qualities of God. He is saying that creation has already done that for him. From the moment it was finished, creation has been making the existence and invisible qualities of the Creator "plain" to all. And what we learn about God from creation is "clearly perceived." No one is "without excuse" for suppressing the lessons God's creation teaches them.

So why is Paul bringing this up? He tells us why in the first verse of this section: "The wrath of God is revealed from heaven against all ungodliness and unrighteousness of men, who by their unrighteousness suppress the truth" (Romans 1:18).

People are suppressing what they clearly see and understand. The creation reveals a great gulf between the Creator and what he created. Only the Creator deserves mankind's glory. To worship something he created is "ungodly;" that is, it's a rejection of God. To give glory to the creation is "unrighteous;" that is, it's a sin. It's a completely unreasonable thing to do, a sinful error of logic leading to a denial of our God, to whom we owe obedience, honor, and worship.

In this opening section of Romans, Paul is not trying to get people to accept the existence of God. Rather, Paul is condemning idolatry. People suppress what is clear and plain to them in order to justify worshiping gods they themselves have created. Paul's point in Romans 1:19-23 is not "God exists" but "the God—the God *you know* exists—is angry with you for denying him and worshiping what he has created."

How foolish it is to glorify created things rather than the One who created them! Paul says, "Claiming to be wise, they became fools, and exchanged the glory of the immortal God for images resembling mortal man and birds and animals and creeping things" (Romans 1:22,23).

Paul defines this sin a second time: "They exchanged the truth about God for a lie and worshiped and served the creature rather than the Creator, who is blessed forever! Amen" (Romans 1:25). And he defines it a third time: "And since they did not see fit to acknowledge God, God gave them up to a debased mind to do what ought not to be done" (Romans 1:28).

Human reason can distinguish between right and wrong

How does God reveal his anger at the sin of idolatry? He gives people free rein to commit whatever sins please them, and then he lets them go through the suffering these sins bring into their lives.

People also know the difference between right and wrong:

> For when Gentiles, who do not have the Law, by nature do what the Law requires, they are a law to themselves, even though they do not have the Law. They show that the work of the law is written on their hearts, while their conscience also bears witness, and their conflicting thoughts accuse or even excuse them. (Romans 2:14,15)

God had revealed the Law in a special way to the Israelites: He gave them the Ten Commandments written on two tablets of stone. But all people know the work of the law; God has written it on their hearts.

What's more, all people have a conscience, a built-in sense that makes them feel bad when they act against the Law in their hearts and feel good when they act according to that Law.

This aspect of Christian teaching—that we are aware of when we are doing right or wrong—is also a matter of logic. People naturally have everything they need to compare what they are doing with a set standard of right and wrong. To say this is unreasonable.

People know that doing wrong deserves punishment

This third point is a simple matter of putting two and two together. First, the world has a Creator, and it is sinfully illogical to worship what he has created. Second, all people know the Creator's will and that they are not doing it. These two facts can lead to only one conclusion: People are accountable to their Creator for the wrong things they do.

People know they should be punished for their sins, but they suppress that knowledge too. In Romans 1: 24-31 Paul lists the sins people engage in when cut off from God's restraining hand. The physical and emotional damage that comes from unbridled sin should motivate people to quit suppressing what creation reveals about God, to give up idols, to search for the true God (Acts 17:27), and begin serving him. But they don't. Consequently, they suppress what they conclude about God's wrath. Paul writes, "Though they know God's righteous decree that those who practice such things deserve to die, they not only do them but give approval to those who practice them" (Romans 1:32). People *know* that death is a punishment for sin. They *know* it's a punishment from God. They *know* that God is righteous in decreeing this punishment. But they refuse to give up their sin. Not only that, but they urge others to sin along with them.

Sin and grace in Romans 1-3

In an earlier chapter, we listed philosophical arguments for the existence of God. Classical apologists believe that evidence for the truth of Christianity—proofs that Jesus rose and the miraculous transmission of the text of Scripture, for example—make sense only to those who already believe in the existence of God. The existence of God provides the necessary context for the other evidences to make sense. So classical apologists begin their defense of Christianity arguing that there must be a God: everything has a cause, the universe is complex, it is finely tuned, everything exists for a purpose, etc.

When modern apologists argue for the existence of God, they might seem to be doing what Paul is doing here. But the similarity is only on the surface. Paul is not trying to convince his readers to believe that God exists. Rather, he is saying: "God's existence is a matter of simple logic. It is reasonable to glorify him. And it's unreasonable to suppress what you know about God and then glorify things he has made.

Belief in the existence of an eternal, powerful, divine being does not depend on hard-won, deeply thought-out philosophical arguments. Philosophical arguments for God's existence are absolutely true. But it is not scriptural to give people the impression that belief in God is *not* a matter of simple observation and logic. We might ask, might not reliance on arguments for the existence of God actually be counterproductive? In an attempt to stem the tide of skepticism, might not these arguments actually be shoring up the contention of skeptics, namely, that the existence of God is not obvious?

In the opening chapters of Romans, Paul is not teaching natural theology. He is not presenting an argument for a theistic worldview or giving facts on which to build the moral argument for God's existence. That is how most modern apologists use this section of Romans. Doing that, however, masks the real reason why Paul writes these words. He is exposing sin, which deserves eternal punishment:

Now we know that whatever the law says is addressed to those who are under the law, so that every mouth will be silenced and the whole world will be subject to God's judgment. For this reason, no one will be declared righteous in his sight by works of the law, for through the law we become aware of sin. (Romans 3:19,20)

He is leading into what he will talk about beginning in Romans 3:21, the Gospel of God's forgiveness in Christ.

Paul's evangelism starting point in other contexts

When Paul did mission work throughout the Greek and Roman world, he was consistent with what he said in the first chapters of Romans. Paul skillfully took into account the people to whom he was speaking. But he never allowed the cultural beliefs of the people to whom he was speaking to change his basic diagnosis of their problem and their need.

To Jewish people

The apostles proclaimed Christianity to Jewish people by proving that Jesus was the Savior foretold throughout the Old Testament.

In his sermon on Pentecost Sunday, Peter had established the Church's pattern for sharing the Gospel with Jews and converts to Judaism:

Men of Israel, hear these words: Jesus of Nazareth, a man attested to you by God with mighty works and wonders and signs that God did through him in your midst, as you yourselves know—this Jesus, delivered up according to the definite plan and foreknowledge of God, you crucified and killed by the hands of lawless men. God raised him up, loosing the pangs of death, because it was not possible for him to be held by it. For David says concerning him. . . ."You will not abandon my soul to Hades, or let your Holy One see corruption." (Acts 2:24-27)

Paul followed that pattern. After his conversion, Paul "increased all the more in strength, and confounded the Jews who lived in Damascus by proving that Jesus was the Christ" (Acts 9:22). Luke records Paul's full sermon in the synagogue at Antioch in Asia Minor (modern Turkey). Paul reminded the Jews and Gentile converts about God's promises to Israel and proved that those promises were fulfilled in Jesus Christ (Acts 13:16-41). Paul quoted the same Old Testament passage Peter had quoted on Pentecost Sunday, namely, that God would not allow his Holy One to "see corruption" (that is, to decompose in a tomb). Paul concluded his message with a warning of God's judgment on those who refused to believe that Jesus was the Savior: "Beware, therefore, lest what is said in the Prophets should come about: 'Look, you scoffers, be astounded and perish; for I am doing a work in your days, a work that you will not believe, even if one tells it to you'" (Acts 13:40,41).

In the synagogue at the Greek city of Thessalonica, Paul spent three Sabbath days "explaining and proving that it was necessary for Christ to suffer and to rise from the dead, saying, "This Jesus, whom I proclaim to you, is the Christ" (Acts 17:3). He "reasoned with them from the Scriptures, explaining and proving that it was necessary for Christ to suffer and to rise from the dead, and saying, 'This Jesus, whom I proclaim to you, is the Christ'" (Acts 17:2,3). In Corinth, "Paul was occupied with the word, testifying to the Jews that the Christ was Jesus" (Acts 18:5). Paul's coworker Apollos did the same: "He powerfully refuted the Jews in public, showing by the Scriptures that the Christ was Jesus" (Acts 18:28).

The Jewish people were steeped in Moses' Law. The Law was filled with commandments and regulations that impressed on the people that they were sinful. Their sin carried a burden of debt they could not pay. But embedded in those laws were pictures of the sacrifice God would send, who would take on himself the debt they owed.

Paul explained to his hearers what Jesus meant for them: "Let it be known to you therefore, brothers, that through this man forgiveness of sins is proclaimed to you, and by him everyone who believes is freed from everything from which you could not be freed by the Law of Moses" (Acts 13:38,39).

This was how the early Church proclaimed the Gospel to the Jewish people and Gentile converts. It's how they defended the Gospel in the face of Jewish skepticism. Paul and the others appealed exclusively to Scripture to prove that Jesus was the Christ, the promised Savior. If you believe in Scripture, they were saying, it's only logical that you believe that Jesus is the promised Christ.

To Gentiles

God had sent Paul to be his witness to unbelieving Gentiles, most of whom had no knowledge of the Jewish Scriptures. They did not know God's promises, and they were not expecting a Savior. Many found truth in the legends of the Greek and Romans gods and worshiped them. Others found their truth in human reason, debating with one another in order to sort out what made sense and what didn't. Luke, the writer of Acts, described the people of the Greek city of Athens as always on the lookout for new systems of religion and new philosophies: "Now all the Athenians and the foreigners who lived there would spend their time in nothing except telling or hearing something new" (Acts 17:21).

Luke gives us two examples of how Paul preached to Gentile crowds. We'll turn to them now. As we do, remember how in Romans 1 Paul described the Gentiles' sin of suppressing the truth about God and then explained how God was revealing his wrath over their sin of idolatry. The question is: Did Paul use these truths to engage Gentile idolaters and skeptics in his initial attempt to lead them to faith?

At Lystra in Asia Minor (Acts 14:8-20)

At Lystra Paul healed a man crippled from birth. Because of this, the people concluded that he and Barnabas were the Roman gods Zeus and Hermes. The priest of Zeus began to honor them as divine and tried to offer sacrifices to them.

Paul and Barnabas rushed into the crowd. They were not divine, they cried out, but were human beings, no different from the people in the crowd.

Paul immediately began to explain the "good news" he and Barnabas had come to tell them. He began by contrasting the "vain things" these people were worshiping with the "living God" who had created "the heaven and the earth and the sea and all that is in them" (Acts 14:15). It was good news that such a God exists—far different from the fickle and demanding gods they had made for themselves.

In a sense, Paul was telling them about a new God. But actually, the people already knew him. God had revealed himself, his eternal power and divine nature, through his creation (using Paul's words from Romans 1:20).

Paul then pointed to specific ways God had given witness to himself in his creation: "He did not leave himself without witness, for he did good by giving you rains from heaven and fruitful seasons, satisfying your hearts with food and gladness" (Acts 14:15-17).

They had a regular food supply. Rain fell when needed. Sunshine prompted the crops to grow. Each year the people could plan on a time to harvest the ripened grain. The cycle did not happen only if and when the people offered the correct sacrifices to the right gods and made them happy. It was a miraculous act of kindness done by a higher power.

The people also experienced happiness: the joy of work, the satisfaction of family life, the sense of accomplishment from building a house or planting a garden, the pleasure of watching a sunset. The people might have attributed these blessings to their gods. But their reason told them that a higher power was at work. None of their gods had the power or the compassion to bestow these blessings. Legends of their gods' selfish behavior did not make the people confident that their gods would join together for the people's good. It was reasonable to conclude that someone other than their gods and goddesses was at work.

This they knew. But there was something they didn't know, something they could not have reasoned out. In the past, God had not immediately punished their idolatry. But it was a new day, and things were different.

At that point the crowd cut Paul short. They wanted no talk about a divine being greater than the gods they themselves had made. They suppressed the truth about the true God, who had given witness to his existence through his love and care.

They stoned Paul, but God restored him to life. Paul went back into the city and left the next day. We are not told if he made any converts there. But he returned to Lystra on his second missionary journey, and that's where he found his closest fellow-worker, Timothy (Acts 16:1,2).

This is the second of Paul's sermons recorded by Luke. Earlier, when Paul spoke to the Jews in Antioch, he warned them against rejecting Christ as God's fulfillment of the Old Testament prophets. But in Lystra, when he faced priests and worshipers of false gods, he repeated the same truth he had written in Romans 1: God has revealed certain qualities about himself through his creation. And he continues to show undeserved kindness toward mankind and to care for his creation.

This sets the pace for the sermon most often treated in modern apologetic literature, Paul's sermon in Athens. There he faced not only priests and worshipers of idols but also seasoned philosophers.

At Athens in Greece: Acts 17:22-34

On Paul's second missionary journey, God led him into new territory, the country of Greece. While there, he had to spend some time alone in Athens. As was his custom, he went to the Jewish synagogue and talked about Jesus to Jews and Jewish converts. The rest of his time was spent in the public marketplace talking "with those who happened to be there" (Acts 17:17). Among them were philosophers from two schools of thought: Epicureans and Stoics. Some of the philosophers called Paul a babbler.[82] Others seemed interested in the foreign divinities Paul was trying to introduce. Paul had been preaching about Jesus and his resurrection. The philosophers were curious, so they invited Paul to explain his teachings to the Areopagus, a group of leading Athenian statesmen and thinkers.

So on this occasion, Paul was not addressing Jews who knew about the Old Testament promises of a Savior. Nor was he addressing a group of zealous priests intent on doing their civic duty by honoring Paul and Barnabas as gods. Rather, Paul was addressing philosophically minded men who thought carefully about religious matters—men who seriously studied the world around them and worked to understand who or what was the cause of things.

Paul shaped his message to his audience just as he had on the other occasions. But here Paul said nothing other than what he told the Romans: It is a sin to suppress the natural knowledge of God and worship idols. The goal of Paul's sermon was to convict the wise and learned men of the Areopagus of committing this sin. Once he had exposed their sin, which he did using logical argumentation, he could talk about the Man whom God had raised from the dead and who would someday judge all people.

Paul's goal was to expose sin and pave the way for the message of God's forgiveness. He did that in a way appropriate for philosophers, thinkers, and statesmen. But he didn't modify his message to make it more suitable for an audience of thinkers. His message was the same as the one he had been telling the common people in the marketplace. After all, the philosophers who met him in the marketplace were asking him to explain the message he was preaching there, and they would have noticed if his message was altered.

Although Paul was talking to philosophers who tried to discover and define the "first cause" of all things, Paul did not enter into that debate. There was no need

---

[82]This word was used for false teachers in the public market who picked up and passed on scraps of truth or information.

to. His hearers had "read" the book of creation and already knew everything Paul would say to prove it was logically sinful to worship idols. If they continued on their present path, they would be denying the true God and would come under his judgment.

Paul complimented them on their interest in religion. This was not flattery or just a way to get their attention. It was foundational for his argument. The Athenians wanted to learn about the strange new teaching Paul was bringing to their ears. Paul says that his teaching is not really new or strange. The Athenian idol to an unknown god was an acknowledgment that what Paul was about to say was true—there was a God they didn't know. Paul's new God was, therefore, a very old God whose existence the Athenians themselves had sensed. Paul would now tell them about this "unknown" God they worshiped.

Paul's presentation was simple logic. He, just like the Athenians, knew there is a Creator of this world who is Lord of Heaven and earth. It was perfectly reasonable for Paul to worship this God. But it was unreasonable for the Athenians to think that such a God would live in a temple made by those whom he created.[83] What's more, it was illogical to think that the One whose hands "give to all mankind life and breath and everything" needed to have his own needs met "by human hands" (Acts 17:25). After all, God gives everyone "life and breath and everything" (Acts 17:25).

It was also obvious to the Athenians that all human beings were connected, that is, that all people had descended from one person. They could sense that God had created the world for this person, his wife, and their descendants. Simple observation revealed that things don't happen randomly. The Athenians could see the cycle of the seasons, which assured them of a continual food supply. They could deduce that kingdoms rise and fall according to someone's plans, that it was no accident where nations exist and how much land they were allowed to amass. Again, this was all a matter of simple observation and logic.

All of this pointed to a single God who created the world, sustains it, and directs its history. Since they realized these things, they should have taken the only logical course of action: They should have gone looking for this divine

---

[83]In the years before Christ, God chose to live among the people of Israel in a temple at Jerusalem. But note Solomon's prayer at the dedication of the temple. Solomon confessed the same thing Paul was telling the Athenians: "But will God indeed dwell with man on the earth? Behold, heaven and the highest heaven cannot contain you, how much less this house that I have built!" (2 Chronicles 6:18). Then, when Solomon asked God to bless his people who prayed to him at his temple in Jerusalem, he repeatedly asked God to "hear from heaven" (2 Chronicles 6:23) and answer their prayer.

being, who did all these things "in the hope that they might feel their way toward him and find him" (Acts 17:25). They should have rejected all the other gods they were worshiping and begun a search for "the unknown God." And although we don't know what such a search would have looked like, it would not have been in vain, for, as Paul says, "He is actually not far from each one of us" (Acts 17:27).

But could they *really* conclude that there was a divine being who created and sustains the universe? Yes. But what if he was far away and impossible to find? He wasn't. If he directs the lives of the people he created, then he is right here with us: "In him we live and move and have our being" (Acts 17:28). Paul quotes a Greek poet, Aratus, who wrote, "For we are indeed his offspring" (Acts 17:28). We note that Aratus was not confessing the true God. He was an idol worshiper and was saying that people were the offspring of the Greek god Zeus. Paul was not agreeing with that part of Aratus' statement, of course. But Paul could still use Aratus to make his point. If we are offspring of a divine being, we can only conclude that "we ought not to think that the divine being is like gold or silver or stone, an image formed by the art and imagination of man" (Acts 17:29). Richard Balge paraphrases Paul's argument like this: "Since we come from God, how can God come from us? An image made by man's design and skill is man's creation. How can it be his creator?"[84] Once again, Paul is using logic to point out the illogical nature of idol worship.

Paul does not tell the Athenians how they should "feel their way" toward God and "find him." But one thing he made clear. The Athenians were doing the opposite. Instead of searching for the God who clearly revealed himself in the creation around them, they created gods who were limited in power and filled with the same lusts and weaknesses human beings have.

Paul's entire argument was based on logic. But Paul's speech was much more than a display of logic. It was an argument for people who "by their unrighteousness suppress the truth" (Romans 1:18). At verse 30, Paul turns the corner of his address and applies what he had just said: "The times of ignorance God overlooked, but now he commands all people everywhere to repent" (Acts 17:30).

Paul was not engaged in a debate to prove God's existence. The Athenians knew he existed. Their sin was what they did with that knowledge. They chose idols instead, and Paul didn't shrink from calling their idol worship ignorance. In the

---

[84]Richard Balge, *Acts*, of The People's Bible Series (Milwaukee: Northwestern Publishing House, 1988), p. 194.

past God had not condemned people for such idolatry. But it was a different time. The judge of all had appeared, and unless the Athenians repented, forsook their idols, and worshiped him, they would face his judgment.

God will soon judge the world, Paul told them. You can delay no longer. You *must not* delay any longer. God "has fixed a day on which he will judge the world in righteousness by a man whom he has appointed; and of this he has given assurance to all by raising him from the dead" (Acts 17:31).

Paul wasn't given a chance to say more about "the man" through whom God would judge the world. But what he had told the Athenians was enough to get them to "seek God, and perhaps feel their way toward him and find him" (Acts 17:27). And some did just that: "We will hear you again about this." Others "joined him and believed (Acts 17:32,34).

Paul had been asked to explain the faith he was proclaiming in the marketplace. Paul did this tactfully and with a humble spirit. But he never departed from the outline he established in the book of Romans. He preached sin and grace, repentance and faith. "You call the true God 'Unknown,'" Paul was telling the Athenians. "But you do know him. Repent of your willful ignorance. And you *can* repent because the God you know exists is near, and he wants you to know him and his Son."

To be sure, only God's Spirit can lead a person to confess the truth of their sin. Only the Spirit can lead a person to understand its seriousness. Nevertheless, anyone can figure out the truth of God's existence and the sinfulness of idolatry. These truths make perfect sense.

Application to modern apologetics

Paul had resolved to "become all things to all people, that by all means I might save some" (1 Corinthians 9:22). Paul did that in Athens. The people there had asked Paul to give the reason for his hope, which he did. He did not use the logic of philosophy either to speak about Christ or to get a hearing for his message. Paul had a clear understanding of his audience. He spoke tactfully, sincerely, and with love. But he also accused them of suppressing what they already knew about the true God. And he used the pointed word ignorance to describe their entire system of idolatry.

Is the message of Scripture reasonable? Yes—at least certain aspects of it. God's creation puts his power and divine nature on display. So people know God exists. God has embedded the works of the Law in everyone's heart. So people know the meaning of right and wrong. God has also given all people a conscience that tells them if they are doing right or if they are doing wrong. So people know that God is just to punish people for wrong doing. A Christian can talk to an unbeliever confident that the unbeliever knows these truths, and to suppress this knowledge is unreasonable. This was Paul's teaching, whether he was explaining it in doctrinal terms (Romans 1:18-30; 2:13-16) or standing on the front lines preaching to unbelievers (Acts 14:8-20; 17:22-34).

Many modern apologists focus on these truths. They know rational arguments that prove the truth of what Paul said in the sections of Scripture we are looking at. And in the right circumstances and with the right goal in mind, Christians might use these apologetic arguments.

But Paul knew that people were already aware of God's existence, of sin, and of God's judgment. It was not a matter of people not knowing the truth. It was a matter of them suppressing it.

Therefore, is it scriptural to attempt to prove that God exists, which Scripture says needs no proof. Instead of trying to prove the existence of God, a Christian should have the attitude: "You know the truth of what I'm saying. We both see evidence of God's power and divine nature every day. We both define right and wrong in the same way and we know there must be someone who planted that knowledge in us. We all sense that sin is wrong and that sin deserves to be punished. It is illogical to deny these truths."

Paul's reference to the natural knowledge of God was a way to prove what he said in Romans 1:18: "For the wrath of God is revealed from heaven against all ungodliness and unrighteousness of men, who by their unrighteousness suppress the truth." The entire first section of Romans, which includes Paul's words about the natural knowledge of God, ends like this: "No human being will be justified in his sight, since through the law comes knowledge of sin" (Romans 3:20). On that platform, Paul could present God's way out of this dilemma, the Gospel message of forgiveness and salvation.

Summary

People know God exists, that there is such a thing as right and wrong, and that wrongs will be punished. This was Paul's touchpoint with the philosophers of his day. They wanted logic and he gave them truths they already knew and understood, but were suppressing.

This aspect of Christianity is logical. Only the Holy Spirit can stop people's willful suppression of these truths. But human reason must confess they are true. The logic of the Law leads to a horrible end. To be useful, apologetic arguments must have the goal of leading people to know their sin. Only then can they be of service to the good news of Christ, through whom God saved the world.

Chapter 5

Is Christianity Reasonable? No

Introduction

Each day God proves his existence. People look at the world and must conclude that it was created by a powerful divine being. But they suppress that truth and worship created things rather than the Creator. God has implanted his Law in people's hearts, and their consciences tell them when they are doing his will and when they are not. People know they deserve God's judgment. God reveals his anger over this sin by giving people over to their sinful desires and letting them suffer the consequences. All this is reasonable.

Whenever modern apologists warn people that it's not good between them and God as long as they suppress these truths and refuse to search for the true God, they are doing their work. They are teaching people about sin, and that is logical

But, as we will see, apologists want to extend the logic and prove that Christianity is the logical way out of mankind's dilemma It is a path, they believe, that every thinking person can take without jeopardizing human reason.

Yet at this point logic breaks down. In this chapter, we want to explore what Scripture itself says about the reasonableness of God's way out of the dilemma of sin.

1 Corinthians 1:18–2:5

Human wisdom versus God's wisdom

Paul needed to address several problems in the congregation at Corinth. Among them was divisiveness. Some members of the congregation had formed groups, organizing under a particular Christian leader—Paul, Apollos, Peter, or Christ. They were acting like non-Christians who allied themselves with a particular philosophical school and claimed that their leader was closer to the truth than others. Paul worked to correct the problem. In the process, he described the meaning of the Gospel. He also described the only way the Gospel can be taught (or defended) without damaging it.

Paul preached the Gospel "not with words of eloquent wisdom, lest the cross of Christ be emptied of its power" (1 Corinthians 1:17). The successful spread of the Gospel did not depend on any form of human wisdom—either the wise thoughts themselves or the skill with which those thoughts were delivered. It wasn't just that human wisdom was not able to help the spread of the Gospel. The use of human wisdom would actually hinder the spread of the Gospel by robbing the Gospel of its power.[85]

Why is this so? Because the message of Christ crucified, which is God's wisdom for saving the world, is the direct opposite of how the world thinks about salvation. Paul strikes the contrast: "For the word of the cross is folly to those who are perishing, but to us who are being saved it is the power of God" (1 Corinthians 1:18). Believers know that God saves them through the Gospel—the message that Christ died to save the world—and so they know it has great power. To unbelievers, however, the Gospel is foolish.

This is because the world's wisdom and God's wisdom are opposites. In order for people to be saved, God had to "destroy the wisdom of the wise;" he had to "[make] foolish the wisdom of the world" (1 Corinthians 1:19,21). When God looked at the people considered wise by this world—the scribes (among the most learned people of the day), and the debaters (philosophers with impeccable rhetorical abilities)—he saw no one whose wisdom could help people find him. After all, what had the world's wisdom ever accomplished? It had not brought people closer to God. In fact, it had only helped them suppress what they *did* know about him.

---

[85] Apologists sometimes offer ways to define wisdom and foolishness in ways that lessen the contrast between them. Alister McGrath says that in 1 Corinthians 1 Paul is "challenging secular notions of wisdom, not abandoning human notions of rationality." (Alister E. McGrath, *Mere Apologetics: How to Help Seekers & Skeptics Find Faith* [Grand Rapids: Baker, 2012], p. 90.) Paul Gould and Richard Davis interpret Paul's objection to wisdom: "If we're not careful, our love of wisdom can putrefy into a base desire to be publicly recognized as wise. . . . The gospel's content and power take a backseat to how it is communicated. The emphasis becomes the philosopher—the messenger—and not the message." (Paul M. Gould and Richard Davis, eds., "Introduction," in *Four Views on Christianity and Philosophy* [Grand Rapids: Zondervan, 2016], p. 13 [emphasis original]).

So God refused to leverage the world's wisdom, that is, to weave its ideas and concepts into his plan of salvation or even to use rhetorical powers of persuasion to spread it. Rather, "it pleased God through the folly of what we preach to save those who believe" (1 Corinthians 1:21). God's only way to save the world was to completely undermine the world's wisdom and substitute his own wisdom in its place. Only then could people find a clear path to peace and eternal life with him.

Paul repeats this thought in 1 Corinthians 3:

> Let no one deceive himself. If anyone among you thinks that he is wise in this age, let him become a fool that he may become wise. For the wisdom of this world is folly with God. For it is written, "He catches the wise in their craftiness," and again, "The LORD knows the thoughts of the wise, that they are futile." (verses 18-20)

It is difficult to ignore Paul's antithesis in 1 Corinthians 1 between the world's wisdom and God's wisdom. Paul makes the point several times. "Jews demand signs." They wanted miracles to prove that the Gospel message is true. "Greeks seek wisdom." The philosophically minded Gentiles wanted the Gospel to be clad in reason and logic. But God dashed on the rocks the proof of signs and the drawing power of human wisdom:

> We preach Christ crucified, a stumbling block to Jews and folly to Gentiles, but to those who are called, both Jews and Greeks, Christ the power of God and the wisdom of God. For the foolishness of God is wiser than men, and the weakness of God is stronger than men. (1 Corinthians 1:23-25)

God's way of salvation is a turnoff—it's weak, foolish, powerless—to all but those whose eyes God has opened to see the wisdom of putting our salvation in the hands of his Son, whose victory over evil took place on a disgusting tool of execution.

The antithesis between the world's wisdom and God's wisdom can also be seen in the sort of people who accept the "foolishness of God." Paul wrote, "For consider your calling, brothers: not many of you were wise according to worldly standards. . . . God chose what is foolish in the world to shame the wise . . . so that no human being might boast in the presence of God" (1 Corinthians 1:26-29). Those who know they are nothing find their strength in the power of Christ crucified. Those who boast in their strength will be brought to nothing. On the Last Day, the wise and strong people of this world will realize they should have adopted the wisdom of God along with the weak, the lowly, and the despised of this world.

Paul's method of preaching the Gospel

Since people naturally consider God's wisdom—his method for saving the world from the guilt of sin—to be foolish, and since the desire for signs and human wisdom is so embedded in us, why would anyone want to believe the Gospel? The answer is: "*Because of him* you are in Christ Jesus, who became to us wisdom from God, righteousness and sanctification and redemption, so that, as it is written, 'Let the one who boasts, boast in the Lord'" (1 Corinthians 1:30-31). We have accepted God's wisdom for one reason only: God has led us to accept it. He has opened our eyes to see that salvation is found in Christ. In him we find the forgiveness of sins, the power to serve our Creator, and salvation from his judgment on the world.

With all this in mind, Paul lays out the only "logical" method he could use to preach this message. First, before he entered Corinth, he emptied his mind of all "lofty speech" and "wisdom" (1 Corinthians 2:1). Paul was a very learned man and could have presented the Gospel in eloquent terms, using the same methods of philosophical debate the Corinthians were used to hearing. In place of that he substituted the message of "Jesus Christ, and him crucified" (1 Corinthians 2:2). That's all he focused on while working in Corinth. Certainly, Paul would talk with the people of Corinth about the "whole counsel of God" as he did in Ephesus (Acts 20:27). But everything he said would in some way be linked to and flow from God's plan of salvation through the atoning death of Christ.

So when Paul entered Corinth, he was a weak man. He entered the city "in weakness" and "in fear and much trembling" (1 Corinthians 2:3). He had nothing "plausible" to tell them, no "words of wisdom" the unbelievers would find appealing (1 Corinthians 2:4).

Rather, his work among them was a "demonstration of the Spirit and of power" (1 Corinthians 2:4). Here Paul is not talking about miraculous signs and wonders the Holy Spirit often gave him the power to perform. Rather, Paul has in mind what he said at the end of chapter 1: "*Because of him* you are in Christ Jesus" (1 Corinthians 1:30). Paul entered Corinth with a message he knew would be foolish to the people he met there. But he didn't want to enhance his message with human wisdom. He wanted it to be obvious that if people came to faith in his message, it was only because God had brought them to faith.

How vulnerable Paul was! He stood before people with a message he knew was unreasonable, even foolish. Nor would he jump at a demand to perform a miracle to prove it was true. But that's how Paul wanted it. Only then would the Corinthian's faith "not rest in the wisdom of men but in the power of God" (1 Corinthians 2:5). He stripped himself of his own human wisdom and power so that God's wisdom and power could be on full display. Only then could God receive the credit and the glory for bringing people into his kingdom.

How comforting was God's promise when Paul began his work in Corinth: "Do not be afraid, but go on speaking and do not be silent, for I am with you, and no one will attack you to harm you, for I have many in this city who are my people" (Acts 18:9,10). God said this to Paul at the beginning of his work in Corinth. The "people" God was referring to were not people whom Paul had already brought to faith. God had people in that city whom he had chosen to bring into his kingdom, and he would use Paul to speak his Word to them. This is how Paul found the courage to work in Corinth in the midst of his weakness, fear, and trembling.

Application to Modern Apologetics

If a Christian decides to use apologetic arguments, his or her goal must parallel Paul's goal. The goal cannot be to prove the so-called reasonable nature of Christianity. The goal must be to preach the foolishness of the cross.

The existence of God and his will concerning right and wrong are reasonable and can be proven through human logic. But the way God chose to save the world is not reasonable and cannot be discovered or proclaimed through logical argumentation.

That's how it has to be. Human signs and wisdom can only lead away from the truth. So in his wisdom, God put a stop to that. He chose a way to save the world that the world would consider foolish, a way that could not be explained or supported by the world's wisdom. God's methods had to be the opposite of the world's methods. So, "It pleased God through the folly of what we preach to save those who believe" (1 Corinthians 1:21). And Paul shaped his ministry accordingly: "I decided to know nothing among you except Jesus Christ and him crucified" (1 Corinthians 2:2).

R. E. Sproul expresses his hope that Christians would use apologetics "as a reasonable modern response to reasonable modern people who want a reason why they should believe.[86] William Lane Craig said, "Apologetics is therefore vital in fostering a cultural milieu in which the Gospel can be heard as a viable option for thinking people. . . . It will be apologetics which, by making the Gospel a credible option for seeking people, gives them, as it were, the intellectual permission to believe."[87] Would Paul have spoken like that? Everyone who wants to use modern apologetic arguments to proclaim and defend the faith must answer that question.

Summary

Although the law is reasonable, the Gospel is not. God's way of salvation, by Christ alone, seems foolish to human reason. A complete reliance on God's grace to open hearts is not optional, nor is it just one part of a process. A faithful defense of the Gospel will take that fact into consideration.

---

[86]R. C. Sproul, John Gerstner, and Arthur Lindsley, *Classical Apologetics* (Grand Rapids: Zondervan, 1984), p. 1.

[87]Morley, *Mapping Apologetics*, p. 221, quoting William Lane Craig, *Reasonable Faith: Christian Truth and Apologetics* (Wheaton, IL: Crossway, 2008), p. 19.

Part 3
The Christian Faith Made Reasonable

Chapter 6—Making Christianity Reasonable—Up To the Reformation

After the days of the apostles, the meaning of the Gospel shifted. The more the meaning of the Gospel shifted, the more reasonable the Christian religion became and the greater role the logic of apologetic arguments played in defending it.

Chapter 7—Making Christianity Reasonable—After the Reformation

Martin Luther restored the Gospel to the Christian Church. But after the Reformation, Christian churches began to take on many of the ideas that had caused trouble in pre-Reformation times.

Chapter 8—Modern Apologetics Depends On a Reasonable Gospel

Modern apologetics relies on a shifted Gospel and on some of the troublesome teachings we described in the previous two chapters. In this chapter we'll show how they do this.

Chapter 6
Making Christianity Reasonable—Up To the Reformation

Introduction

Why should a person become a Christian? Scripture gives one answer: Human beings sin against God. God graciously sent his Son to take away the guilt of the world's sin by suffering and dying in our place. Jesus' resurrection affirms that God is now at peace with us. God now gives us many blessings because his Son removed the guilt that separated us from him. We have been calling this the *message of sin and grace*.

In this chapter we will explore how the message of sin and grace fared in the days after the apostles. Our conclusion is this: The Christian Church never lost the message of sin and grace. However, in various ways the Christian Church shifted the meaning of the Gospel message—from teaching sin and grace to teaching how people can access God's power to help them change. Therefore, our main concern will not be with formal Church doctrines. Church doctrines eventually reflected, established, and promoted the shift. But here we are focusing on the shift itself.

We will not lose sight of our goal, namely, to evaluate the modern apologetic movement. Here's the conclusion we will arrive at: Modern apologetics finds a home in churches that emphasize a shifted Gospel. On the other hand, they play a lesser role in churches that consider it their purpose to proclaim the message of sin and grace.

In this chapter and the next, through a collection of quotations and anecdotes, we'll highlight various ways the Church shifted its emphasis. We'll use this material in Chapter 8, where we will show the relationship between modern versions of these historical trends and emphases, and modern apologetics.

The history of the shift—apologetics in the early Church

It is impossible to give a hard and fast description of how Paul's doctrine fared among average Christians after his death. Certainly there were many who followed Paul's pattern of doctrine and life—church members and pastors who knew their sin and rested in the good news of God's forgiveness.

However, we can only evaluate the early church by the writings of its most influential spokesmen—Church leaders who were popular enough to have their books copied and passed down through the ages. Since the early Church was a unified body that kept a close watch on what its spokesmen were saying, it is safe to say that in general the spokesmen acknowledged by the early Church reflect what was being taught in most congregations.

Defenses against false accusations of immoral behavior

For the first four hundred years, defending the faith often meant nothing more than refuting false accusations brought against Christians, often made by Roman authorities looking for reasons to persecute them. Christians were accused of doing hideous things in their "secret" meetings: incest in their feasts of Christian love, cannibalism at the Lord's Supper, even killing babies and eating them. Early apologists proved to the Roman authorities that these accusations were simply not true.

A common complaint was that Christians had introduced new gods who were undermining the religion and morals of the Roman Empire. The growing worship of these new gods had prompted the traditional Roman gods to stop protecting the empire. At the end of the fourth century, this charge was used to explain why the empire was falling to German barbarians from the north. The first half of Augustine's *City of God*, the most extensive of all early apologetic works, offers simple, logical reasons why this charge is unfounded and foolish.

Jesus and the apostles defended themselves against various false accusations. So when modern apologists defend Christianity in this way, they are following the pattern laid down in Scripture.

Justin Martyr (100–165)

It was relatively clear-cut when the Church defended itself against false accusations and exposed idol worship for what it was. But challenges facing the early Church came from another source, namely, from secular philosophers.

It was harder for Christians simply to reject what the philosophers around them were teaching. There were a couple reasons for this. Some Greek and Roman philosophers wanted a deeper understanding of truth than that offered by the shallow national religious systems around them, comprising hundreds of idols responsible for this or that aspect of life and the silly legends about their origins and exploits. The ancient philosopher Plato (428–348) came close to teaching a single god with whom all people should become united. For that he was honored by many early Christian teachers.

Philosophers were also concerned about helping people find the best way to live out their lives and achieve happiness. On the surface, early Christian teachers and contemporary philosophers appeared to have the same goal. But similarities between the two were only superficial. Christians who treasured the peace they found in Christ through the forgiveness of sins and served God in the new way of the Spirit could easily see the emptiness of philosophical speculation. What's more, the philosophers of the day taught people what they should *do* to find happiness. Christianity taught that happiness in life and eternity was based on what God's Son *had done for them*. Case closed.

But some Church teachers shifted the meaning of Christianity in such a way that Christianity and philosophy did have the same goal, namely, to discover and promote the best way for people to live. In that context, defending Christianity against philosophy became a different matter. It became a question of which system provided the *best* answer for how one should live.

In their history of apologetics, William Edgar and K. Scott Oliphint observe that in the second century and beyond,

> "We see the apologists going over to the ground of their accusers. They were not, generally speaking, trying to give a systematic exposition of the Christian faith. They were addressing their accusers' assumptions and the contradictions that result."[88]

These apologists did not begin with philosophy's impotence in the face of God's impending judgment on sin. They started on the same "ground" as secular philosophy: the human yearning for truth, morality, fulfillment, and happiness in life. They worked to demonstrate that humans were powerless to fulfill these desires, which could only be satisfied by Christianity. Catholic theologian Avery Dulles puts it this way: The Greek Christian apologists "inspire faith that

---

[88]Edgar and Oliphint, *Christian Apologetics Past & Present*, Vol. 1, p. 37.

the Gospel can engender a wisdom more comprehensive and profound than any rival religion or any philosophy that does not rest on revelation."[89]

The early apologist Justin Martyr was among the first to treat Christianity *as a philosophy*. Edgar and Oliphint relate Justin's conversion to Christianity:

> In his *Dialogue with Trypho,* Justin explains how he studied one philosophical system after another—Stoicism, Aristotelianism, Pythagoreanism, Platonism—before coming to Christianity. One day as he stood near the Aegean Sea, near Ephesus, an old man approached him. "Does philosophy produce happiness?" the old man asked. "Absolutely," Justin replied, "and it alone." The old man then suggested that there were many questions that Plato could not answer, but there is a true philosophy with an explanation for all questions. That philosophy is Christianity."[90]

Justin began to study the Bible. To Justin, Jesus' words had far more power than those of the secular philosophers: "They possess a terrible power in themselves, and are sufficient to inspire those who turn aside from the path of rectitude with awe; while the sweetest rest is afforded those who make a diligent practice of them." [91] Justin came to the conclusion that "Christianity fulfills the highest goals of all pagan philosophers and that it should be seen as the most worthy of all philosophies to be believed."[92]

Most of what the early apologists said in combating secular philosophy was true. But they were too sympathetic with the philosophers' goal, which resulted in a Christianized form of philosophy that strayed from God's goal of gaining pardon for the world through his Son. God's goal shifted to that of the philosophers, namely, to enable a person to lead a truly blessed life.

But this was a shift, not a full-blown abandonment of the message of sin and grace. In his *First Apology*, Justin explains Jacob's prophecy that the Savior would come from the line of Judah. He explains that Jesus was the fulfillment

---

[89]Dulles, *A History of Apologetics,* p. 47. Justin Martyr went so far as to say that the Greek philosophers were "enlightened by the divine Logos (Christ), [and] were in some sense Christians without knowing it" (Dulles, p. 32). Protestants have always puzzled over how the Catholic Church can allow into the Catholic Church certain people who don't know about Christ. The struggle for moral improvement has become so central to Catholicism that anyone who shares in this struggle must be working under God's power and direction. We see that this idea started already in the early church.

[90]Edgar and Oliphint, *Christian Apologetics Past & Present,* Vol. 1, p. 38.

[91]Edgar and Oliphint, *Christian Apologetics Past & Present,* Vol. 1, p. 38.

[92]Edgar and Oliphint, *Christian Apologetics Past & Present,* Vol. 1, p. 41.

of that prophecy: "And after this He was crucified, that the rest of the prophecy might be fulfilled. For this 'washing His robe in the blood of the grape' was predictive of the passion He was to endure, cleansing by His blood those who believe on him."[93]

That's a clear confession of what Jesus did for us. But Justin ended his *First Apology* with nothing more than a warning of God's judgment and a weak statement on how to escape it: "For we forewarn you, that you shall not escape the coming judgment of God, if you continue in your injustice; and we ourselves will invite you to do that which is pleasing to God."[94]

This is an example of what one finds in early Christian apologetic literature. The early apologists boldly defend Christianity. But the shape of their arguments is determined more by secular philosophy than by St. Paul. In Scripture, everything Paul says is saturated with God's salvation in Christ. That cannot be said about the early apologists.

In time, the borderline between God's truth revealed in Scripture and the truths discovered by human philosophy became blurred. When Christianity and philosophy were thought to have the same goal, philosophical ideas could be put to use in Christian theology. Princeton philosophy professor Diogenes Allen wrote a book entitled *Philosophy for Understanding Theology*. The first words of his introduction explain why he thinks an understanding of early Greek philosophy is important: "The two main sources of Christian theology are the Bible and Hellenic culture, especially Greek philosophy."[95] This is a rather jarring statement. Allen is saying that Christians should understand Greek philosophy, not just to understand the world in which early Christians lived and the ideas against which early apologists defended the church. Rather, they should do so because Christian theology gradually included both the truths of Scripture and truths from the Greek philosophers.

Eastern Orthodoxy: Theosis

The shift we are describing—the movement that does not emphasize Scripture's message of sin and grace as much as Christianity's power to promote a moral and happy life—became embedded in the Church.

---

[93]Edgar and Oliphint, *Christian Apologetics Past & Present,* Vol., p. 57.
[94]Edgar and Oliphint, *Christian Apologetics Past & Present,* Vol. 1, p. 63.
[95]Diogenes Allen, *Philosophy for Understanding Theology* (Atlanta: John Knox Press, 1985), p. 1.

In 395 B.C., the Roman Empire divided into two administrative units, one in the east and one in the west. This division also created the boundaries between the Eastern Church, which today we call the Eastern Orthodox Church, and the Western Church, which became known as the Roman Catholic Church.

Most American Christians are more familiar with the history of the Western Church, which includes the development of Roman Catholicism and the Protestant Reformation. The history of the eastern part of Christianity, however, is less well known.

The Eastern Orthodox Church is located in the heartland of Christianity: Israel, Syria, Asia Minor (Turkey), Greece, and countries to their north, east, and south. In the seventh century, the Muslims conquered most of Eastern Orthodox territory and destroyed much of Christianity in that area. Later, Eastern Orthodoxy found a home in Russia, which took on the role of protector of the Eastern Church. Today the Eastern Orthodox Church is the second largest Christian church body, with some 220 million baptized members.

The early Greek-speaking Church fathers—to whom the Eastern Orthodox Church looks for its theology—gave the philosophy of Plato an important role in shaping their discussion of Christianity. Plato taught that all people *emanated* from a "Source" (Plato's god) and that our souls are yearning for reunion with the Source. Plato taught practical methods for achieving this reunion—how to free oneself from the flesh and its self-destructive lusts, which act like chains keeping a person bound to their worldly existence. He taught that as a person does this, his or her soul is released and gradually advances toward the blessedness of the Source.

In their attempt to communicate with the unbelievers around them who thought in platonic terms, early Church teachers shifted how they talked about Christianity. They gave up speaking about the guilt of sin, how God restored us into his favor through the life and death of his Son, and how Christians are renewed in the divine nature as they serve God in righteousness. And they began speaking in Platonic terms—how through Christ a person can draw near to God and can actually *become divine*. The term for this is *theosis*.

Eastern Orthodox Christians (at least those for whom Orthodoxy is more than culture) strive for a degree of *theosis*. For inspiration and direction on their journey, they look to the great mystics who achieved *theosis* in this life. One way church members work toward theosis is by contemplating *icons*, pictures of divinized saints. The people depicted on icons may look odd to those in the

Western Church, but they are purposely painted that way to convey an otherworldly sense of the divine. Members of the Eastern Church see them as a source of great power for divinization.

Orthodox worship services strive for the same thing. Liturgies are filled with elaborate ceremonies, the smell of incense, and the sound of bells. All are designed to give worshipers a foretaste of Heaven and impart power for divinization.

The Word of God is still read and outwardly honored in the Orthodox Church. But there is little about forgiveness to be found there. The short homilies given by modern priests at the end of the liturgy contain little or no talk of hope in Christ; they are primarily encouragements for living based on the law.

Augustine of Hippo (354-430)

As mentioned previously, in A.D. 395 the Roman Empire divided into eastern and western administrative units. The city that had been the capital of the entire Roman Empire, Rome, became the capital of the western part of the empire and would serve as the center of the Western Church. The Bishop of Rome came to be considered the leader of the Western Church.

The writings of the Greek-speaking Eastern Church fathers were gradually lost to the Western Church, largely because the Western Church spoke Latin and lost the ability to read Greek. The Western Church came under the spiritual leadership of Saint Augustine, bishop of the small North African town of Hippo, whose books and letters laid the foundation for the theological development of the Western Church. Alister McGrath describes Augustine's importance in no uncertain terms: "The theology of the medieval period [of the Roman Catholic Church] may be regarded as thoroughly Augustinian, a series of footnotes to Augustine, in that theological speculation was essentially regarded as an attempt to defend, expand, and where necessary modify, the Augustinian legacy."[96]

Augustine lived much of his life as an unbeliever. While still in his teens, following the encouragement of the great Roman statesman and writer Cicero, Augustine decided to give up earthly fame and wealth and search for truth.

---

[96] Alister E. McGrath, *Iustitia Dei: A History of the Christian Doctrine of Justification, Volume I* (Cambridge: Cambridge University Press, 1986), p. 17.

Augustine first tried to find the truth in Manichaeism. Manichaeism was a religious cult that focused on the battle between light and darkness—that the body was darkness and the spirit was light, and with training one could put off the darkness of the body and move toward the light. After nine fruitless years of study, he left Manichaeism and turned to the philosophy of Plato.

As noted previously, ancient philosophy was not only intellectual thinking and debate about the nature of reality. Its goal was to help people find happiness by living in line with reality, as opposed to seeking happiness in false and misleading ideas. Unlike Manichaeism, Plato's reality was that one's body is not bad but is merely farther away from the good than one's spirit is. Platonism taught people how to move closer to the Source, the "highest good." Moving toward the Source was the way to happiness. Nevertheless, platonic philosophy could not help Augustine overcome his desires: the desire for sexual satisfaction and the desire for fame as a teacher of public speaking.

On a trip to Italy, Augustine came to know the Christian bishop of Milan, Ambrose. Under his influence, Augustine came to believe that Christianity and the Catholic Church could provide the truth he was looking for and give him the power to overcome his sinful desires.

Augustine's struggle continued, but now he was under the influence of the Christian Church. He became familiar with people like the hermit Antony, who sold off his large inheritance, went out into the desert, and dedicated himself to a solitary life of self-denial and meditation. Augustine was struck by "the heroic virtue of the monks and virgins who dedicated their lives to God in poverty and chastity, according to the example of Anthony. In their example he found hope and confidence that he himself could be delivered from the enslavement of lust and ambition by embracing the Christian faith with his whole heart."[97]

Finally, in a moment, Augustine received the power to completely overcome his lusts. For many, Augustine's conversion experience has become a model, and in many ways it has shaped how people define Christianity. He describes the event in Book VIII of his *Confessions*. Because of its importance to the history of Christianity, we include a lengthier quotation.

> I hesitated to die to death and live to life; inveterate evil had more power over me than the novelty of good, and as that very moment of time in which I was to become something else drew nearer and nearer, it struck me with more and more horror. Toys and trifles, utter vanities had been

---

[97]Dulles, *A History of Apologetics,* p. 78.

my mistresses, and now they were holding me back, pulling me by the garment of my flesh and softly murmuring in my ear: "Are you getting rid of us?" and "From this moment shall we never be with you again for all eternity?" My God, what was it, what was it that they suggested in those words "this" or "that" which I have just written? I pray you in your mercy to keep such things from the soul of your servant. How filthy, how shameful were these things they were suggesting! And I was blushing for shame, because I could still hear the dim voices of those vanities, and still I hung back in hesitation. And again she [the virtue, Continence] seemed to be speaking: "Stop your ears against those unclean members of yours, so that they may be mortified. They tell you of delights, but not of such delights as the law of the Lord your God tells." So went the controversy in my heart—about self, and self against self.

And now from my hidden depths my searching thought had dragged up and set before the sight of my heart the whole mass of my misery. Then a huge storm rose up within me bringing with it a huge downpour of tears. I flung myself down on the ground somehow under a fig tree and gave free rein to my tears; they streamed and flooded from my eyes, an acceptable sacrifice to Thee. And I kept saying to you, not perhaps in these words, but with this sense: "And Thou, O Lord, how long? How long, Lord: Wilt Thou be angry forever? Remember not our former iniquities." For I felt that it was these which were holding me fast. And in my misery I would exclaim: "How long, how long this 'tomorrow and tomorrow'? Why not now? Why not finish this very hour with my uncleanness?"

[Augustine heard the voice of a girl saying pick up the Bible and read.] I checked the force of my tears and rose to my feet, being quite certain that I must interpret this as a divine command to me to open the book and read the first passage which I should come upon. For I had heard this about Anthony: he had happened to come in when the Gospel was being read, as though the words read were spoken directly to himself, had received the admonition: Go, sell all that thou hast, and give to the poor, and thou shalt have treasure in heaven, and come and follow me. And by such an oracle he had been immediately converted to you. I snatched up the book, opened it, and read in silence the passage upon which my eyes first fell: Not in rioting and drunkenness, not in chambering and wantonness, not in strife and envying; but put ye on the Lord Jesus Christ, and make not provision for the flesh in concupiscence. [Romans 13:13,14] I had no wish to read further; there was no need to. For just as I had reached the end of this sentence it was as though my heart was filled with a light of confidence and all the shadows of my doubt were swept away. For you converted me to you in such a way that I no longer sought a wife nor any other worldly hope. I was now standing on that rule of faith, just as you had shown me to her [his mother] in a vision so many years before.[98]

This was the defining moment in Augustine's Christian life, and his experience is very important for understanding the theology he bequeathed to the Catholic Church. It also helps us understand the shift that was taking place in the meaning of Christianity.

Augustine certainly believed that Jesus took away the guilt of his sin. In Book IX of his *Confessions*, he describes his mother's faith in wonderful, Christ-centered terms. As the day of her death drew near, Monica had no concern over how or where she would be buried. She had only one desire, that she be

remembered at Your altar, where she had served You with never a day's absence. From that altar, as she knew, the holy Victim is made available to us, He through whom the record of debt that stood against us was annulled. He has triumphed over an enemy, who does keep a tally of our faults and looks for anything to lay to our charge, but finds no case against Him. In Him we win our victory. Who will reimburse Him for that innocent blood? Who will pay back to Him the price He paid to purchase us, as though to snatch us back from Him?[99]

But if one evaluates Augustine on the basis of his writings, it would be hard to prove that sin, guilt, and the grace of God's forgiveness in Christ was in the forefront of his mind.[100]

---

[98]Augustine, *The Confessions of Saint Augustine*, trans. Rex Warner (New York: New American Library, 1963), pp. 179-183 (*The Confessions*, Book VIII, 11,12).

[99]Augustine, *The Confessions of Saint Augustine,* trans. Maria Boulding (Hyde Park, New York: New City Press, 2012), p. 235 (*The* Confessions, Book IX, 36, capitalization of pronouns referring to Christ added).

[100]When asked if Augustine understood the scriptural meaning of God's grace, seminary professor and church historian E. C. Frederick said that in his formal writings, he didn't think Augustine did. But Augustine revealed a better understanding of grace in his letters. This would make sense, because when a person is counseling or comforting others, God's forgiveness naturally comes to the fore, as it did when Augustine was describing his mother's comfort when she was dying.

The passage of Scripture that led to Augustine's conversion was a passage in which Paul urges Christians to live in service to God and put off their sins (Romans 13:13,14). Christians put off their sins as they put on the Lord Jesus Christ. But in this passage, Paul says nothing about what it means to put on Jesus Christ.

It was a law passage that gave Augustine the grace he needed to break his bondage to sin. Augustine taught that we are saved by grace alone. But he defined grace in line with his conversion experience: as a "sanative" or healing power from God, which enabled him to live a God-pleasing life. Forgiveness was always there, but "becoming more God-pleasing" was the dominant theme.

Alister McGrath describes this in terms of justification. He writes,

> Justification is about "being made just"—and Augustine's understanding of *iustitia* is so broad that this could be defined as "being made to live as God intends man to live in every aspect of his existence," including his relationship with God, with his fellow men, and the relationship of his higher and lower self.[101]

When one's religious climate is shaped by the yearning to overcome sin, the message of forgiveness recedes into the background and the search for infused grace comes to the fore. Infused grace might come through a powerful experience, as in Augustine's case, or it may come in association with the Christian Church. Over time, the Catholic Church came to see itself as a dispenser of this kind of grace through its sacramental system. For example, the sacraments of marriage and ordination dispensed grace to fulfill the requirements of those institutions. The sacrament of last rites dispensed grace to a dying person to remain firm in the faith until the end. When sanative grace replaces grace as God's forgiveness in Christ, the subject shifts to one's improvement in life and the question always becomes, "What must I *do* to receive this grace."

All this developed slowly over the centuries after Augustine's death. But considering how important Augustine was, his lack of keeping Christ at the forefront of his theology made it easier for Catholic theology to develop as it did.

A quick look at three of Augustine's books will illustrate some of these points.

---

[101]McGrath, *Iustitia Dei,* Vol. 1, p. 36. The battle between his higher and lower self is Augustine's way of talking about his struggle with sin in terms of "the neo-Platonic anthropological model favored by Augustine" (McGrath, p. 36).

The Confessions

When Augustine was 43, he began writing his confessions. He had been a baptized Catholic for ten years and a priest for six. The bishop of the African town of Hippo was soon to retire and wanted Augustine to be his replacement. There were some questions about Augustine's promotion to the bishopric. It may be that members of the church at Hippo and others in the surrounding territory questioned the procedure and possibly the sincerity of Augustine's conversion. Augustine wrote *The Confessions* to give people insights into his journey through life and his victory of faith. It is a compelling story that resonates with many who struggle to overcome sin.

We have already focused on Augustine's conversion, which comes near the end of his life's history. Now we'll focus on the very first paragraph of *The Confessions*, which sets the pace for the journey he was about to describe.

In the first paragraph of *The Confessions* Augustine admits that humans are mortal and sinful and that God gives evidence that he resists the proud. In spite of this, Augustine writes, human beings find joy in praising God. In the next part of the sentence, he gives the reason why. This is the basic reason for everything that happened, leading up to his conversion. He writes, "You have made us for yourself, and our heart is restless until it finds rest in you."[102]

This passage is quoted by Christians of all denominations, including Lutherans. What does Augustine mean by that? One could argue that Augustine was restless because of his sins, the pain of his conscience, and his anticipation of the final judgment.

But one could also argue that Augustine was thinking more in terms of Plato's thought than the teaching of Paul. While Paul says that human beings were "dead in the trespasses and sins in which [they] once walked" (Ephesians 2:1), Plato taught that human beings share a memory of the Source from whom they came and yearn to be reunited with him. True happiness, they believe, is found through "participation in the one God by clinging to him in love," which Augustine believed was a goal "common to both Christians and Platonists and, thus, which establishes common ground between them."[103]

---

[102] Augustine, *The Confessions*, p. 39. My translation of the Latin, ". . . *quia fecisti nos ad te et inquietum est cor nostrum, donec requiescat in te.*" https://faculty.georgetown.edu/jod/latinconf/1.html, accessed January 2023.

[103] William Babcock, "Introduction," in Augustine, The City of God, Vol. 1 (Hyde Park, NY: New City Press, 2012), pp. xx-xxi.

But Scripture does not credit people with a pious yearning to be reunited to God and find peace with him. We like to think that we are searching for God, but Paul says that "no one understands; no one seeks for God" (Roman 3:11). Paul says that by nature our minds are "set on the flesh," "hostile to God," and unable and unwilling to submit to God's law (Romans 8:7).

There is a search going on. But it's not a search our hearts are engaged in. It is God searching for us. People might be looking to God for answers, but they are invariably looking for answers to human questions, questions they themselves are asking. Yet God alone has the right to determine the questions people should be asking him. He bids us ask the question, "How can I find rest from the accusing voice of my conscience." His answer is, "Through Christ, who sacrificed himself for you and created peace between us." Paul found rest in Christ's sacrifice for him, which enabled him to cease trying to find peace in the Law. And this rest was his reason for serving God and giving up his sins.

If restlessness is defined by being guilty of sin and liable for punishment, that is one thing. But if restlessness is defined by being trapped in sins one cannot give up, that is another. As we see from his confessions, Augustine was restless in the latter sense.

The City of God

The City of God is a work completed by Augustine later in his life, written over the years A.D. 412 to A.D. 426. In A.D. 410, Germans from northern Europe sacked the city of Rome and were in the process of conquering the Roman Empire. Many were blaming Christianity for Rome's downfall, claiming that the Roman gods were punishing the empire for turning its back on them and worshiping the Christian God. In *The City of God* Augustine contrasts the City of Men, made up of people who have not come to faith, with the City of God, made up of people whom God has drawn to himself and who will live with him into eternity.

William Babcock begins his introduction to the most recent translation of *The City of God* with these words:

> "Two loves," Augustine writes, "have made two cities. Love of self, even to the point of contempt for God, made the earthly city; and love for God, even to the point of contempt for self, made the heavenly city." (XIV,28). For all its vast scale and intricate complexity, *The City of God* is a story of love. It is, however, a love story played out in cosmic setting,

across an immense historical range, and within complicated patterns of social order.[104]

The work is divided into 22 "books" or long chapters. In the first 10 books, Augustine does apologetics at its best. He defends his hope in the true God by exposing and completely destroying the Roman and Greek system of gods. He describes their evil and arbitrary nature, how their system is based on baseless legends, and its aimless search to identify to which god one should turn to for help in this or that situation. The remaining books trace the progress of the City of God throughout history, starting with Adam and Eve.

As noted above, *The City of God* is a story of love—of God's love for us and of our love for him. But we must ask, what is the primary way God reveals his love to us? Is it through the gracious forgiveness he won for us by the sacrifice of his Son? Or is it through the gracious power he gives that enables us to rise above wills held captive by sin?

Augustine defines both cities in terms of the latter meaning of grace: "What gives birth to citizens of the earthly city, however, is a nature vitiated by sin, and what gives birth to citizens of the heavenly city is grace liberating that nature from sin."[105]

Augustine has great insight into the differences between the two cities. But, in the opinion of this author, he does not give Christ the place he deserves as the reason why God loves us and why the two cities exist. When sinners treasure forgiveness as their greatest gift, the entire Scripture opens up as the story of how God fulfilled his promise to restore us to himself in Christ. But when grace becomes the power to overcome one's sinful nature, Christ has a way of fading into the background.

Books 11-22 of *The City of God*, which trace the course of the Church through history, contain references to Christ and they mention certain aspects of his work. But Augustine moves from creation to the final judgment without giving much attention to the life and death of Jesus Christ as related in the four Gospels. He doesn't include a section on why Jesus was on the cross or the importance of his resurrection. Rather, he moves from one relatively minor question to the next—questions often of a philosophical nature. Perhaps they were important questions in his day, especially among scholars, but they are

---

[104]Babcock, "Introduction," in Augustine, *The City of God,* Vol. 1, p. ix.

[105]Augustine, *The City of God,* Vol. 2 (Hyde Park, NY: New City Press, 2012), p. 141. (Book XV).

hardly central to the Christian faith and existence of the City of God, which is forgiveness in the face of the guilt of our sin.

Instructing Beginners in Faith

In his mature Christian years, Augustine wrote a book to a deacon in the North African city of Carthage by the name of Deogratias, advising him on how to give basic instructions to people interested in becoming Christian. They had heard the basics of Christianity and were interested in learning more about it. Before a person was accepted for formal instruction in the faith—in what we might call an adult Bible information class—he or she went through a set of lectures designed to help them decide if they wanted to start formal instructions.[106]

How does the Gospel fare in this work? Sadly, not so well. It is always risky to judge a book based on what the author chose not to include in it. But this was a book to help a person inquiring about the Christian faith. Somewhere, you would think, Augustine would include a description and explanation of Jesus' life and work. His advice should have been, "Above all, don't miss this!"

Augustine understood the terror people feel in the presence of God. He can safely say, he remarks, that no one "comes wishing to become a Christian who has not in some way or other been struck by fear of God."[107] The antidote to such fear is the knowledge that God loves people. But Augustine doesn't link God's love with the sacrifice of the Lamb, at least not as consistently as we would like. Augustine describes justification in terms of regeneration rather than forgiveness. We find our hope, Augustine writes, "only in him who through his work of justification makes both them and you the kind of people that you are."[108]

The book is filled with practical advice. At one point Augustine helps Deogratias deal with inquirers who show up at a bad time, when Deogratias has a busy schedule or is so distraught over a congregational problem that he is "unable to deliver his address calmly and congenially." Here keeping Christ at the center, Augustine advises: "If this is the case, our love toward those for whom Christ died—those whom he wanted to ransom, at the price of his blood, from the

---

[106] Augustine, *Instructing Beginners in Faith,* ed. Boniface Ramsey and trans. Raymond Canning (Hyde Park, NY: New City Press, 2006). pp. x-xv. For more on this process of becoming a member of the Church, see the introduction by Raymond Canning.

[107] Augustine, *Instructing Beginners in Faith,* p. 21.

[108] Augustine, *Instructing Beginners in Faith,* p. 108.

death of the errors of this world" would give him the strength he needed to help this new believer.[109]

Augustine composed a short explanation that Deogratias could use if he didn't have much time. Forced to condense his thoughts, Augustine got right to the basics: Just as sin entered the world through one man, "in the same way too . . . through one man, who is also God, the Son of God, Jesus Christ, all the sins of the past would be wiped away and all who believe in him would enter into life."[110]

Nevertheless, he advises Deogratias that if his student is "exceptionally dull" or is not opening up to what Deogratias is telling him, he should be content to teach him the basics: "Thus, while all the other points can be mentioned briefly in passing, it is those that are most essential—namely, the unity of the Catholic Church, temptations, the Christian way of life—that we must instill in him, evoking fear in view of the judgment to come."[111] But Christ is not mentioned in the list of essentials, and this is a book devoted to helping an inquirer learn about Christianity.

Here and there, Augustine makes good statements about Jesus' true work as the world's Savior from sin, but they are incidental. And they do not reflect the way St. Paul puts the cross of Christ at the center of his instruction.

After Augustine

Considering Augustine's importance in the life of the Catholic Church, it is reasonable to assess the development of the Catholic Church against the backdrop of his life and writings. A number of trends had been developing in the Catholic Church during the previous 350 years. Augustine solidified some of those trends and added to them. The Roman Catholic, or Western Church, came to define God's grace in Augustinian terms. It defined grace as an infusion of power rather than by St. Paul's definition of grace as God's forgiveness. Our contention is that the modern apologetic movement has grown in a religious climate more like the one created by Augustine than the one created by Paul.

What follows are teachings and trends that developed in the Catholic Church after Augustine.

---

[109] Augustine, *Instructing Beginners in Faith,* p. 52.

[110] Augustine, *Instructing Beginners in Faith,* p. 114.

[111] Augustine, *Instructing Beginners in Faith,* p. 48.

A higher view of human spirituality

Based on his yearning for morality, Augustine taught the integrity of the human will. That is, Augustine taught that mankind's desire to do good and to praise God has not been compromised by sin; it is merely held captive by sin. Alister McGrath explains this distinction: "The free will is not lost, nor is it non-existent; it is merely incapacitated, and may be healed by grace. In justification, the 'free will held captive' becomes the 'free will set free' by the action of healing grace."[112] This also came out of Augustine's experience. He yearned for the power to live an upright life, and this yearning was proof that his will was free. But the fact he could not do what he yearned to do indicated that something was holding him back—something that only God's grace could correct.

Augustine taught that mankind did not lose the image of God when Adam and Eve fell into sin. He equated the image of God with the power of reason and understanding. After the fall, the image of God was merely corrupted and mankind was no longer able to participate in God. Yet the image of God was not lost, and its presence makes human beings capable of union with God. Augustine writes,

> But the mind must first be considered as it is in itself before it becomes a partaker of God, and His image must be found in it. For, as we have said, although worn out and defaced by losing participation of God, yet the image still remains. For it is His image in this very point, that it is capable of Him; which so great good is only made possible by its being His image.[113]

Augustine's phrase "partaker of God" reflects his understanding of grace. Human beings have lost "participation in God." But because they still possess God's image, human beings are still "capable of Him;" that is, they are still capable of being receptacles of the "great good" God wants them to have.

This has application to modern apologetics. Paul says that Christians "have put off the old self with its practices and have put on the new self, which is

---

[112]McGrath, *Iustitia Dei*, Vol. 1, pp. 26-27, 30. McGrath uses the Latin terms, which are translated in the quotation above. *Liberum arbitrium captivatum* is translated, "free will held captive"; *liberum arbitrium liberatum* is translated "free will set free"; *justificare* is translated "to justify." McGrath adds the point he made previously: "Augustine understands the verb 'to justify' to mean 'to make righteous,' an understanding of the term which he appears to have held throughout his working life," pp. 30-31.

[113]Augustine, "St Augustine: On the Holy Trinity; Doctrinal Treatises; Moral Treatises" in *Post-Nicene Fathers,* ed. P. Schaff (Grand Rapids: Eerdmans), 3:189.

being renewed in knowledge after the image of its creator" (Colossians 3:9-10). Through the renewing message of Christ, Christians begin to put on the image of God, which was lost after the fall. The renewing message of Christ, not the abilities of the image of God retained after the fall, is the starting point when talking with an unbeliever.

The foundation was laid for the idea that people are searching for God.

Augustine's *Confessions* is a prayer of praise to God for everything God had done for him. But as we noted previously, in the first paragraph of the book he made a statement about human nature that sets the pace for the book and for how he analyzed his life. He wrote,

> Man wants to praise you, man who is only a small portion of what you have created and who goes about carrying with him his own mortality, the evidence of his own sin and evidence that you resist the proud. Yet still man, this small portion of creation, wants to praise you. You stimulate him to take pleasure in praising you, *because you have made us for yourself, and our hearts are restless until they can find peace in you.*[114]

Who would disagree with that? God *has* made us for himself, and our lives are filled with guilt over sin and the specter of his punishment.

But that's not what Augustine is saying. Augustine knew from his conscience that sex outside of marriage is wrong and that the pursuit of fame is a sinful, worldly activity. But for a long time—until his conversion experience—he couldn't rid himself of these sins.

Augustine was restless. But what made him restless was his lack of ability to stop sinning. Augustine's restlessness was more a matter of stymied morality rather than a matter of unresolved guilt. Before people know God's love in Christ, they do not yearn for God or to serve him. Paul wrote, "For the mind that is set on the flesh is hostile to God, for it does not submit to God's law; indeed, it cannot. Those who are in the flesh cannot please God" (Romans 8:7,8). Human beings may feel guilt. They might see the damage sin causes in their lives and yearn for the power to change. But they are not restless for God himself.

Avery Dulles helps us see the implications of Augustine's view of human restlessness for the study of apologetics, especially the area of apologetics that urges

---

[114]Augustine, *Confessions,* p. 17 (Book 1.1, "Thou resisteth" changed to "you resist." Emphasis added.).

people to adopt the Christian worldview: "As compared with their Protestant counterparts, Catholics characteristically put greater emphasis on the inner dynamism of the human spirit toward union with the God who, as Augustine said in his *Confessions*, has made us for Himself. *If our hearts cannot be at rest except in Him, the search for God must be part of the human condition.*"[115]

Here's the point of application to apologetics: If "the search for God" is "part of the human condition," then apologists have a natural point of contact with an unbeliever and the argument for Christianity can proceed on logical grounds. But if not, some other point of contact must be found.

The foundation was laid for experientialism.

Augustine's conversion experience is one of the most well-known stories in Church history. It is held up as a model for all Christians to follow. There are many forms of conversion experiences and they come in varying degrees of intensity.

But there are some problems with Augustine's type of conversion experience. People assume that such conversion experiences are found in Scripture, and it is understandable for people to assume they are. But they must be read into Scripture. Scripture describes many people who were converted to Christianity. But Scripture never records anyone who had a conversion experience like Augustine's, and Paul never urges people to have one. Rather, Paul always points to Christ and his forgiving work and urges people to *believe* in Christ's sacrifice for them. This is always Paul's motive for godly living.

Many of the Jewish people in Jesus' day rejected him. But others did not. John wrote, "But to all who did receive him, who believed in his name, he gave the right to become children of God" (John 1:12). To *receive* Christ is to *believe* in him—that he is God's Son sent to deliver us. It does not mean to ask him to dwell in us and seek an experience which convinces us that he is present in us. Our certainty lies in what Christ did for us long ago, which we believe is true. It does not lie in our being united with him in the present.

A conversion experience becomes a substitute source of power and assurance. Its power is credited to the indwelling of Christ, but it is not necessarily linked to the work of Christ. Recall that Augustine's conversion happened while he was reading a passage where Paul was describing what God wanted him to do.

---

[115]Dulles, *A History of Apologetics,* p. 366 (emphasis added).

From Augustine's day forward, power and certainty were found either in mystic experiences, or for most in the experience of the mass or by partaking of the sacraments of the Church.

Augustine gave philosophy a foothold in the Church

Augustine's former mentor, the philosopher Plato, engaged in rigorous debates to discover the best way for people to live. All the ancient philosophers did the same. Although Augustine rejected Plato's pagan ideas, he was sympathetic with Plato's goal. Augustine substituted the teachings of Christ for the conclusions of Plato's reason. Gould and Davis write: "Augustine believed that Christianity and philosophy were significant conversation partners. Augustine appropriated much of Plato and Neoplatonism into service in explicating and defending Christian theology."[116]

Augustine's philosophical beginnings also shaped how he defended the Christian faith. Beilby explains, "Augustine seeks to locate his approach to defending the faith in a thoroughly developed philosophical framework," and "Augustine's articulation of the importance of reason and the reasonability of faith set the tone for apologetic work in the Middle Ages."[117]

In the centuries immediately following Augustine, how to use philosophy (human arguments) to define and defend the Christian faith was not as actively pursued. But in the 11th century, and especially when universities became the center of learning in Europe, interest in philosophy resurfaced. With Thomas Aquinas (1225–1274), "the introduction of the major writings of Aristotle into scholastic thought changed this. The ancillary role of philosophy was replaced by a philosophy which stood in its own rights."[118]

A new direction for the teaching of predestination

We can include Augustine's definition of predestination into the list of his teachings that shifted the nature of his gospel.

Scripture teaches that God wants all people to be saved. It also teaches that by nature all people choose to reject Christ. But it teaches that God has chosen some to hear and believe that Christ saved them from their sins. And by his

---

[116]Gould and Davis, *Four Views on Christianity and Philosophy*, p. 16.

[117]Beilby, *Thinking About Christian Apologetics*, pp. 45-46.

[118]Bernard Ramm, *Varieties of Christian Apologetics* (Grand Rapids: Baker, 1973), p. 95.

grace, through the message of Christ crucified for the sins of the world, he would give them faith and eternal life.

For Augustine, though, predestination was no longer God's gracious choice to bring certain people to faith in Christ. People were predestined, but the result of predestination was not faith in Christ's work. Rather, it was the reception of power that Augustine had received. In that context, God set up a series of life events that would move one of his elect to the point of receiving and experiencing victory over sin.

Predestination was discussed like this: God could have prepared a world containing any set of circumstances, ranging from a world in which all were saved to a world in which no one was saved. But in his infinite knowledge and wisdom, he chose to create and direct the events of this world so that those he had predestined to come to faith would come to faith.[119]

In the case of the lost, why didn't God set up a series of events that would lead to their conversion? That is the mystery. The opportunities he gave them to receive his grace, however, was real, and their natural refusal to accept it made them guilty.

This way of thinking contributed to how little Augustine emphasized Christ in some of his major writings. He simply did not emphasize freedom in Christ through the forgiveness of sin won for all, as Scripture does. Of course, Augustine believed those facts and found his final comfort there, like he did at the death of his mother. But it was not the center of his teaching and writing as it was for Jesus, Paul, and the other New Testament writers. Augustine focused on "the submission of the individual's whole being to God," as Alister McGrath puts it.[120]

Looking ahead, we will conclude that how a church views these topics—the human nature, the human will, the image of God, and the nature of predestination—will shape how it spreads and defends the Gospel and its hope. It shaped Roman Catholicism as it moved forward into the Middle Ages (A.D. 500–1500). And it shapes how modern apologists approach their ministry. In chapter 8, we will demonstrate that modern apologists share many of Augustine's beliefs.

---

[119]See Eugene Portalie, *A Guide to the Thought of Saint Augustine* (Chicago: Henry Regnery Company, 1960), p. 201.

[120]McGrath, *Iustitia Dei*, Vol. 1, p. 35.

The foundation was laid for making Christianity logical.

Interestingly, something happened after Augustine's death that happened after the Reformation. The leader of the Swiss Reformation, John Calvin, taught predestination in a way similar to Augustine, as a bare decree of God that went two ways: God chose some to be saved and he chose others not to be saved. Calvin's followers were divided. Some agreed with Calvin, but many chose to believe that salvation came to those who *chose* to believe the Gospel.

Something similar happened in the early Church after Augustine died. The Church debated Augustine's position on predestination and rejected it. They moved Catholic teaching in a direction that gave human beings the natural ability to accept or reject Christianity. People could choose to become more filled with God's grace in association with the Catholic church, or they could avoid the Church and the grace it had to offer.

Avery Dulles describes life in the Catholic Church:

> The Evangelists, particularly John, teach that a sincere acceptance of the Christian message requires that one experience the inner attraction of grace and be willing to live up to the moral demands of the Gospel. To those who are called and are willing to sacrifice all else for the following of Christ, the Gospel gives a joy and peace that are not of this world.[121]

This view of Christianity and the Gospel makes sense to human reason. It appeals to the restless human yearning for morality and offers power to satisfy that yearning. The experience it produces comes from being attracted by the Church's grace and by keeping the Law (described as the "moral demands of the Gospel").

This is a shifted view of Christianity resulting from the shift in the way grace is understood—away from God's favor in Christ to the power to become moral. Lutheran theologian Francis Pieper writes, "Substituting grace in the sense of *gratia infusa*, or a good quality in man, for the *gratuitus favor Dei*, or combining the two, is the fundamental error of all who within Christendom depart from the pure Christian doctrine."[122]

---

[121]Dulles, *A History of Apologetics*, p. 25.

[122]Francis Pieper, *Christian Dogmatics, Vol. II (St. Louis: Concordia, 1951), p. 11. Gratia infusa* refers to grace as the power to overcome sinful actions. *Gratuitus favor Dei* refers to the gracious favor of God in Christ and forgiveness.

This is what Augustine started. Although he knew that Jesus' death had won the forgiveness of sins, what he yearned for was freedom from temptation and the sins he was finding impossible to overcome.

All Christians yearn to be more God-like. We ask for God's forgiveness and a greater desire to serve him. But forgiveness is at the heart of everything. When we are forgiven, we know the way to God. And the only way there is to grow in the ability to serve God is to reflect on what he has made us to be, forgiven sons and daughters. What's more, whenever the law says, "You shall," our sinful nature springs to life and does the opposite. But when Christ removes the demands of the law, our sinful nature has nothing to react to, and we become truly free to serve God and do what his law says. Only the freedom from sin and guilt, given us through Christ's cross, unites us with Christ and frees us to serve him "in the new way of the Spirit" (Romans 7:6).

People are always tempted to follow the principle that when they give up sin they have taken the first step to be at peace with God. Lutheran theologians call this the *opinio legis*, the idea (*opinio*) that a person can find access to God by keeping the law (*legis*).

The *opinio legis* is deeply entrenched in the human heart. It was hard at work in Paul's day. Many Jews insisted that if Gentiles (non-Jews) wanted to become followers of God, they had to submit to certain Old Testament laws, particularly the law of circumcision. Some of Paul's new Gentile converts were heavily influenced by this.

Paul was surprised at how quickly the members of his churches in Galatia had forgotten the Gospel he had taught them. Paul wrote, "Now that you have come to know God, or rather to be known by God, how can you turn back again to the weak and worthless *elementary principles of the world*, whose slaves you want to be once more?" (Galatians 4:9).

The basic principles of the world are not just wrong ideas in general. Rather, they are wrong ideas about how to earn God's favor, namely, by using the Law rather than by relying on the cross of Christ. Paul makes this point to the Colossians: "See to it that no one takes you captive through hollow and deceptive philosophy, which depends on human tradition and the basic principles of this world rather than on Christ" (Colossians 2:8 NIV 84). Paul contrasted the basic principles of the world with Christ's work for us, "Since you died with Christ to the basic principles of this world, why, as though you still belonged to it, do you submit to its rules: 'Do not handle! Do not taste! Do not touch!'" (Colossians 2:20,21 NIV84).

Augustine cannot be blamed for the work-righteous system of religion that in later years developed in the Roman Catholic Church. Yet he shifted the meaning of justification from God's declaration of forgiveness to God's infusion of power for godly living. This, in turn, turned the Church's eyes away from repentance, faith, forgiveness, and freedom in the kingdom of God. And it opened the door to Church members catering to their natural *opinio legis,* that is, to the legalistic basic principles of how the world tries to gain God's favor.

In Part 2 of this book, we looked at the faith we are called on to affirm and defend. We saw that the entire Bible revolves around sin, repentance, God's Savior from sin, and forgiveness. But Augustine led people to ask, "What must *I do* to be justified and receive God''s grace? He also accompanied this with a set of unscriptural ideas that made it possible for people to do this—the availability of infused grace, the idea that human beings retain the image of God, and the human God-pleasing yearning for morality.

Faith in forgiveness through the cross of Christ is humanly foolish. But the desire to receive God's favor through the Law makes sense because it is in line with mankind's natural way of thinking. Christianity thus becomes rational, and it can be described and defended by human logic.

Those, especially in the Lutheran Church, who argue for the logical nature of Christianity must continually remind themselves of this. There may be rational arguments and evidence for various Christian truths. For example, it *is* beneficial to keep the Law, evidence *does* point to the miraculous nature of Scripture, or Jesus *was* a real, historical person. But one cannot claim that Christianity per se is rational. That claim opens the door to redefining Christianity and mixing the Law into the Gospel. And it invariably includes a heightened view of mankind's spiritual ability and a redefinition of Christ's ministry.

Anecdotes on reason and apologetics from Catholic history

How important was the use of philosophy and rational discussion (dialectics) in the early Catholic church? In the second half of the middle ages (the years starting around A. D. 1000) there were three general schools of thought. Some argued for an unrestricted use of philosophy and rational discussion. Others were skeptical and even hostile toward philosophy and had in mind the ancient

Church father Tertullian's question: "What has Jerusalem to do with Athens, the Church with the Academy."[123]

Some believers used human reason and philosophy "to discern the rational grounds for their own commitment to Christ and to the Church."[124] Others, like some modern apologists, believed that rational arguments could help spread the Gospel. James Beilby writes that "Alan of Lille [d. 1202], for example, sought to rely solely on rational arguments for the truth of various Christian doctrines because he was convinced that Muslims could not be persuaded by arguments from Scripture."[125]

Once philosophy was allowed into the Church, Scripture had a hard time keeping its place as the Church's sole source of faith and teaching. The following anecdotes will give us a feel for that.

Anselm of Canterbury (1033–1109) and the monks of Bec

Some think that apologetics has value to lead a person to faith but that once that person comes to faith, apologetics is no longer necessary. The following anecdote, however, demonstrates that doubt is not unique to unbelievers. Believers also have doubts.

Anselm, who would later become the archbishop of Canterbury, joined a monastery in the French town of Bec at age 27. The abbot of Bec, Lanfranc, embraced the moderate position on the use of philosophy. The monastery had opened a school, not just for monks but for the children of the nobility. The school became the foremost seat of learning in Europe and famous for solid scriptural teaching and for not allowing philosophy to overstep its bounds.

During his years at Bec, Anselm taught and wrote. He was not dealing with skeptics and atheists, however. He was teaching and writing for monks, dedicated and ambitious Christians who wanted to understand logically and philosophically what they believed.

Anselm agreed with Lanfranc about the proper role of philosophy. But Anselm had a more expansive view of the role that philosophical reasoning could play in understanding religious truth. Thomas Williams explains that Anselm taught what he called "the reason of faith," meaning "the intrinsically rational

---

[123]Tertullian, "Prescription Against Heretics," chapter 7.
Dulles, A History of Apologetics, p.91.
[125]Beilby, *Thinking About Christian Apologetics,* p. 47.

character of Christian doctrines, in virtue of which they form a coherent and rationally defensible system."[126] Avery Dulles says that for Anselm "faith is objectively rational." This is because God "is supreme truth and hence eminently intelligible; and all that God does is conformed to reason."[127]

The monks came to Anselm with a request. Anselm describes the nature of their request:

> Some of the brethren, that is to say, some of the monks of Bec, have often eagerly entreated me to write down some of the things I have told them in our frequent discussions, about how one ought to meditate on the divine essence, and about certain other things related to such a meditation, as a sort of pattern for meditating on these things. Having more regard for their own wishes than to the ease of the task or my ability to perform it, they prescribed the following form for me in writing this meditation: Absolutely nothing in it would be established by the authority of Scripture, rather, whatever the conclusion of each individual investigation might assert, the necessity of reason would concisely prove, and the clarity of truth would manifestly show that it is the case, by means of plain, unsophisticated arguments, and straightforward disputation.[128]

The monks were not questioning their faith. They merely wanted Anselm to help them think it through logically without resorting to the authority of the Scriptures or the Church. But their request, of course, shows they thought it could be done. Anselm obliged and wrote the *Monologion*, in which he explained the faith *sola ratione* (by reason alone)."[129] Most significant, in the *Monologion* Anselm gave a number of logical proofs for the existence of God, which he reduced to one—the validity of which is still debated among philosophers today. It's called Anselm's Ontological Argument.[130]

---

[126]Thomas Williams, *Reason & Faith: Philosophy in the Middle Ages,* Lecture 7, in The Great Courses (Chantilly, VA: The Teaching Company, 2007).

[127]Dulles, *A History of Apologetics,* p. 100.

[128]Williams, *Reason & Faith: Philosophy in the Middle Ages,* Lecture 7, in The Great Courses, quoting from the preface to the *Monologion.*

[129]Dulles, *A History of Apologetics,* p. 101. From Anselm, Monologion, 1.1, Deane, 38.

[130]1. It is a conceptual truth that God is a being than which none greater can be imagined. *2.* God exists as an idea in the mind. 3. A being that exists as an idea in the mind and in reality is, other things being equal, greater than a being that exists only as an idea in the mind. 4. Thus, if God exists only as an idea in the mind, then we can imagine something that is greater than God. 5. But we cannot imagine something that is greater than God. 6. Therefore, God exists.

The benefit of demonstrating the rationality of Christian teaching, Anselm says, is to help his readers so that "as far as possible they may always be ready to convince anyone who demands of them a reason of that hope which is in us."[131] Anselm believed that "the common ground between [unbelievers] and believers is not faith but reason."[132] Unbelievers have no alternative but to discuss the Christian faith on the basis of their reason. Therefore, when Christians understand the rationality of what they believe, they can speak with unbelievers on their own terms.[133] Dulles writes, "In raising so clearly the question of the intrinsic demonstrability of Christian faith, Anselm made an epochal contribution to the history of apologetics."[134]

This account introduces one aspect of apologetics Lutherans sometimes don't speak about much. Most often apologetics is discussed in the context of explaining Christianity to skeptics. But in this case the question came from believers—from monks in a monastery. When Lanfranc, who by then was the archbishop of Canterbury, read the *Monologion*, he asked, "Where's the Scripture?" But Anselm and the monks of Bec already knew what Scripture said. What they were looking for were logical reasons for why they believed it.

This opens up the question of the relationship between apologetics and Christian belief. If a believer comes to you and asks why they should believe a certain teaching *of Scripture*, what role should arguments from reason—from apologetics—play in the answer?

Peter Abelard (1079–1142) vs. Bernard of Clairvaux (1090–1153)

Sometime after the incident at Bec, a controversy started between a scholar, Peter Abelard, and a monastic, Bernard of Clairvaux. Abelard was the most brilliant scholar of the first half of the 12th century. Bernard was the most well-known and powerful man in the church—at times likely more powerful than the pope himself. Soon after his death, Bernard was elevated to sainthood.

Up to the 12th century, most teaching and study took place in monasteries. But as more people from outside the monastery began seeking an education, teachers began to accommodate. Some monasteries opened their doors to local people. Some teachers began opening private schools.

---

[131]Dulles, *A History of Apologetics,* p. 102.

[132]Dulles, *A History of Apologetics,* p. 102.

[133]Dulles, *A History of Apologetics,* p. 102. See Cur Deus Homo 1.2, Deane, 182.

[134]Dulles, *A History of Apologetics,* p. 104.

In time, what we call universities began to form. The universities were always under the oversight of the Catholic Church, of course. But they were also places where teachers could teach what they wished, more than they could in the monasteries. This is the context in which Peter Abelard taught.

Abelard was a philosopher. He subjected every idea to the scrutiny of human reason. This included the teachings of the Catholic Church. In one of his most famous books, *Sic et Non*, (*Yes and No*), Peter listed teachings of the Catholic Church and showed the wide variety of ways those teachings had been taught. He didn't offer his opinion on which way was best. His purpose was to open the door for human reason to decide.

Bernard, on the other hand, championed adherence to Church doctrine. He was a mystic. His goal was to contemplate the love of God, draw nearer to him, and experience union with him already in this life. Jon Sweeney describes Bernard's view of faith and reason:

> If you have any interest in knowing what's true, Bernard says again and again, you must first have faith. It is by faith that God purifies your heart. Unless you first abandon yourself to God, you will never know God.[135]

Peter, who championed reason, reversed Bernard's position on faith leading to understanding. He said that nothing can be believed if it is not first understood. Sweeny writes that Peter feels

> he is simply stating a fact. His challenge of reason, although less grounded in the Bible and tradition, was, he thought, essential for religious people who were beginning to interact with science, logic, art, and people of other religious traditions with competing worldviews. . . . Not only does one need to believe in order to understand, but nothing can really be believed unless it is also understood.[136]

The problem was not so much *what* Abelard taught but *how* he arrived at the truth. Sweeney writes, "It was the style, not the substance, that condemned Peter."[137]

---

[135]Jon M. Sweeney, *The Saint vs. The Scholar: The Fight Between Faith and Reason* (Cincinnati, OH: Franciscan Media, 2017), p. 118.

[136]Sweeney, *The Saint vs. The Scholar,* p. 119.

[137]Sweeney, *The Saint vs. The Scholar,* p. 120.

The story of Bernard and Abelard is one of the most drama-filled and intriguing stories in Church history.[138] It ends with Bernard calling a council in A.D. 1141 at which Abelard and his writings were condemned. Avery Dulles describes the event like this:

> The contest between Abelard and Bernard has remained vivid in Western memory, for it symbolizes the tension between two Christian attitudes that recur in every generation—an apologetically inclined mentality, which seeks to find as broad a common ground as possible with the non-Christian, and a strictly dogmatic stance, which would safeguard the integrity of the faith even at the price of placing severe limits on the free exercise of reason.[139]

At work were the two basic forces that were causing a shift in the meaning of Christianity. Bernard sought to protect the human desire for union with God, and such a desire could be carried out only in the context of the Catholic Church and its historic teachings. Abelard sought to protect the human desire to make sense out of what one believed, which could only be carried out by the free use of human reason.

But did either of these goals bring people to know their sin and God's forgiveness in Christ?

Thomas Aquinas (1225–1274)

Within a hundred years of Abelard's censure for using reason and philosophy as he did, reason and philosophy became a completely legitimate tool for discovering truth in the Catholic Church. During those hundred years, the writings of the ancient philosopher Aristotle were being rediscovered by the Western world and translated into Latin.

Aristotle's brilliant and rigorous analysis of the world provided a framework around which Christian teaching could be taught and even defined. Looking ahead, in the 1800s the Catholic Church found itself with a problem. A movement in Europe called the Enlightenment claimed that reason *alone* is the road to the truth. Of course, if that is true, truth becomes a matter of opinion, which,

---

[138]See the Wikipedia article on "Peter Abelard." At the end of the article, the "onstage and onscreen" section lists recent plays and movies that have featured Abelard's story, including a stage play as recent as 2019.

[139]Dulles, *A History of Apologetics,* p. 109.

in turn, leads to the idea that there is no absolute truth. In the late 1800s, this idea was finding its way into the Catholic Church.

To reverse this trend, in 1879 Pope Leo XIII issued an encyclical "On Christian Philosophy." However, instead of simply jettisoning the power of human reason and starting with a fresh look at Scripture, Leo wanted the Church to use reason in the best way possible.

He urged Catholic scholars to engage in an aggressive study of Thomas Aquinas. To Leo, no one had combined reason and Christian teaching better than Aquinas. Leo considered Aquinas' synthesis of Christian teaching and the ideas of the ancient philosopher Aristotle to be Rome's best line of defense against Enlightenment relativism. As a result of this encyclical, new editions of Aquinas' works were published, and Catholic scholars have been analyzing his thought ever since.

We return to Aquinas. Aquinas believed that if philosophy is done well, its conclusions will match what God has revealed in Scripture and through the Catholic Church. Of course, some teachings like the Trinity or Jesus' incarnation can be known only through revelation and cannot be understood by human reason. But in regard to the traditional categories of knowledge that human philosophy concerns itself with—for example, the existence of God and what we can learn about him from nature—clear and unbiased logical discussion will arrive at truths that match what God has revealed to us.

Ralph McInerny describes how Aquinas approached the use of reason:

> Thomas studied [Aristotle] closely and learned an enormous amount of truth. The basic characteristic of Thomas is that there can be no real conflict between what is known and what is believed, between faith and reason, between philosophy and theology. If philosophers think they know something that is in conflict with faith, Thomas would proceed . . . in the conviction that something must have gone wrong in the philosophical discourse that led to a conclusion which contradicts the faith, [and upon closer examination], the reasonableness of belief is made clear.[140]

---

[140]Ralph McInerny, *A First Glance at St. Thomas Aquinas* (South Bend, IN: University of Notre Dame Press, 1990), p. 62.

Philosophy, if done well, can become a source of truth and along with Scripture can become one of "the two main sources of Christian theology."[141]

A sample of Aquinas' apologetics

Thomas wrote a book titled *On the Truth of the Catholic Faith Against the Errors of the Unbelievers.*[142] It is thought that he was asked to help Christian missionaries in Spain defend the faith against the Muslims who had conquered the southern part of that country. What is of interest is how Thomas recommends approaching unbelievers. His conviction that faith and reason are not in conflict establishes the point of contact between Christians and unbelievers.

In this book he separates truths that can be discovered by reason and truths that can be learned only through God's revelation. In the first category (truths that can be discovered by reason) Aquinas includes a human being's natural search for "true happiness," which in Christian terms he calls "the ultimate perfection." He writes, "Moreover, no instrument can achieve its ultimate perfection by the power of its own form, but only by the power of the principal agent, *although by its own power it can provide a certain disposition to the ultimate perfection.*[143]

Aquinas is saying that people know God exists and that he is far above us. They also realize that one form (a human being) cannot be in the presence of another form (God) unless that person is infused with qualities that must be received from the other form, qualities they don't possess naturally. This is a simple, logical conclusion, which a person can arrive at through rational thought.

Furthermore, Aquinas says that by nature people have "a certain disposition" to unite with "the ultimate perfection." That is, deep down inside people desire to be in the presence of God and to share in him. However, without the qualities of the form (God) whom they seek, such a thing is an impossibility. The various forms of infused grace that empower a person to become more God-like are available only in the Catholic Church. This, of course, points out one's total dependence on the sacraments found only in the Catholic Church.

[141] Allen, *Philosophy for Understanding Theology,* p. 1.

[142] *Summa Contra Gentiles.*

[143] Aquinas, *Summa Contra Gentiles,* Book Three, Chapter 147.6, trans. Vernon J. Bourke. https://isidore.co/aquinas/ContraGentiles3b.htm#147. Accessed Jan 2023 (emphasis added).

In that same paragraph Aquinas continues the argument: God's grace must reside in people if they are to become more like him. This is because the "ultimate perfection" cannot simply be *given* to a person; he or she must personally take part in the process of being transformed—"in order that man may be brought to his ultimate end *by his own operations*."[144]

And since a person is personally involved in using God's grace to effect their transformation, salvation becomes a matter of doing and merit. Aquinas puts it like this: "A form must be superadded to him from which his operations may get a certain efficacy *in meriting* his ultimate end."[145]

To summarize: For people to live eternally in God's presence, they themselves must become like more like God—something which they have a deep-seated yearning to do. They can do this only through God's grace—his undeserved transformative power—available only in the Catholic Church. Salvation then becomes something people achieve through God's power within them *and* something they merit. This makes sense and unbelievers, they say, should agree with that.

While saying Mass on December 6, 1273, Aquinas had a mystical experience, a vision of some sort, which put an end to his scholarly work. When his secretary urged him to continue work on the *Summa*, he replied, "I cannot, because all that I have written now seems like straw."[146] Aquinas followed Peter Abelard on the path of reason, but all his scholarly labor seems to have been trumped by an experience of God, which Bernard of Clairvaux spent his life waiting for.

The historic shift from the "foolishness of God" to a reasonable religion

The message of Scripture is quite simple. God warns in no uncertain terms that everyone faces the horror of his coming judgment when their sin will be brought to light and punished. The good news is that people can face the coming judgment in confidence and peace. And that will be easy to do because the world's sins have already been punished and the debt people owed to God has already been forgiven.

---

[144] Aquinas, *Summa Contra Gentiles,* Book Three, Chapter 147.6 (emphasis added).

[145] Aquinas, *Summa Contra Gentiles,* Book Three, Chapter 150.6 (emphasis added).

[146] Anthony Kenny, *Aquinas* (Oxford: Oxford University Press, 1980), p. 26.

God calls on people to be reconciled to him, to call him their Father and consider themselves to be his children. That's also easy because God, through the work of his Son, is already reconciled to the people of the world. If a barrier still exists, it exists between human beings toward God, for people know that their sin deserves God's punishment. "Face that fact," God tells us. "But then live in the fact that I'm already reconciled to you through the life and death of my Son."

God wants his people to love and serve him. That is also easy. God tells his people: "Through faith in what my Son did for you, you died and rose with him. You are rid of your sins. You are no longer a slave to sin but a slave to the righteousness I have given you. And because you died with Christ, you are dead to the Law—all of it. It plays no role in your winning my favor or in getting you to Heaven. What's more, you can love others as I love you. You can serve me and your neighbor in a new way." Paul calls this the "way of the Spirit" who has brought you to Christ, and not in "the old way of the written code," driven by fear and guilt (Romans 7:6).

The simple message of forgiveness, reconciliation, and the new life that come through God's forgiveness and peace gives us eternal hope, "the ultimate perfection," to use Aquinas' phrase.

All this is quite easy. But if we learn one thing from Church history, it's how hard it is to maintain this simple definition of the Gospel, how easily the Gospel is abandoned or its meaning altered, how easily faith becomes a product of human reason, and how quickly salvation becomes something to be earned. Grace to live in service to God comes only by deepening one's understanding of how God served us in Christ. And ironically, the teaching that tells us to forsake the claims of our own piety causes our piety to grow.

But the early Church neglected justification by faith. Daniel Clendenin comments on the lack of the New Testament Gospel in the Eastern Orthodox Church: "In the history of Orthodox theology . . . it is startling to observe the near total absence of any mention of the idea of justification by faith. . . . In fact, the most important text of Orthodox theology, John of Damascus' *Orthodox Faith*, never even mentions the idea."[147]

Alister McGrath says the same about the Western Church: "It has always been a puzzling fact that Paul meant so relatively little for the thinking of the church

---

[147]Daniel Clendenin, *Eastern Orthodox Christianity: A Western Perspective* (Grand Rapids: Baker, 1994), p. 123.

during the first 350 years of its history. To be sure, he is honored and quoted, but—in the theological perspective of the West—it seems that Paul's great insight into justification by faith was forgotten.[148]

Christianity became a way to satisfy the natural desire that all people have, namely, to live in the best way possible. This had been the goal of ancient philosophy. Christianity became a *super philosophy*. It had the same goal as secular philosophy but believed it could do what secular philosophy was unable to do.

At the point when Christianity was considered to be the only true philosophy, it became philosophy, and to a large extent human reason and logic were used to define and defend it. The ancient Greek philosophy of Plato, and later the philosophy of Aristotle, provided tools to analyze and discuss Christian teaching.

Christianity never lost its basic purpose to give people peace with God and the hope of eternal life with him. But grace defined as an infusion of power to put off sin tended to replace, or at least to overshadow, Scripture's message of God's gracious favor in Christ. Having a supply of infused grace, which was available in the Catholic church, gave people the peace and hope they were looking for. But when people are taught to yearn for infused grace, they can only ask: "What must I *do* to get it?" On the other hand, when people come to believe that their sins are forgiven, they can only say, "Praise be to God for this wonderful gift."

Experiential religion also grew in prominence. People turned to experience— either their own or that of Christians of the past—to verify that their faith is true. Church sacraments, spiritual exercises, methods to keep oneself on the path of faith, and ways to yield oneself to Christ—these largely defined the Christian life.

When Lutherans discuss problems in the Roman Catholic Church leading up to the Reformation, they most often focus on the work righteous nature of Catholic teachings. But this was only the outcome of the shift of focus that transpired in the early Church. Francis Pieper's statement quoted previously in the section on Augustine bears repeating: "Substituting grace in the sense of *gratia infusa*, or a good quality in man, for the *gratuitus favor Dei*, or combining the two, is the fundamental error of all who within Christendom depart from the pure Christian doctrine."[149]

---

[148]McGrath, *Iustitia Dei*, Vol. 1, p. 19.

[149]Pieper, *Christian Dogmatics*, Vol. II, p. 11.

Summary

Soon after the apostles died, the Christian Church began to lose the Gospel. The goal of helping people become righteous through an infusion of God's power replaced God's goal of letting people know that they are righteous through faith in Christ.

In time, the Christian Church became engulfed in teachings and practices that promoted human works rather than faith in Christ. Augustine was a major contributor to this shift of the Gospel's meaning.

When the Church adopted the world's idea that freedom comes through keeping the Law, the doctrines of Christianity became more logical. Christians turned to human philosophy as an aid to understand and explain Christianity. The search for power to become God-pleasing shaped the development of the Church's doctrine, especially the Church's sacramental system. The mystical experience became a tool many used to become close to God.

Chapter 7

Making Christianity Reasonable—After the Reformation

Martin Luther (1483–1546)

When a Christian is primarily concerned with the power *to do* something, Christianity becomes just that, a matter of *doing*. When growth in morality rather than God's forgiveness becomes one's reason for becoming a Christian, uncertainty and doubt are close at hand. Is my faith and life growing fast enough? Am I worthy of God's blessing? Have I sufficiently paved the way for my prayers to reach God? Can I really be sure of spending eternity with him? When Christ's work of *justification* is defined as "to make a person righteous," concern over spiritual growth or the lack of it replaces confidence in the perfect forgiveness we have in Christ. Christ's role as Judge replaces his role as Savior. In that context, a system of merits evolved in the Catholic Church. Penance, visiting the remnants and shrines of the saints, works of piety, the monastic life, purgatory after death—all were designed to make up for sin and to give hope.

This describes the Christian world in Martin Luther's day. The message of forgiveness was taught, but it was greatly overshadowed by the need to become worthy of God's love. Luther tried to find peace in this system. But he realized he could not.

When Luther came to faith, he was not in a struggle to conquer this or that sin. He was struggling with guilt before God. So he became a monk. What better place than a monastery to devote oneself to finding peace with God? Then he became a priest, but even the power to administer the sacraments did not calm his guilty conscience. Then he was chosen to become a doctor of the church. Although he grew more and more learned, he still could not learn how to be at peace with God.

With God's help, however, he found the answer. He tells us what he found and where he found it:

My situation was that, although an impeccable monk, I stood before God as a sinner troubled in conscience, and I had no confidence that my merit would assuage him. Therefore I did not love a just and angry God, but rather hated and murmured against him. Yet I clung to the dear Paul and had a great yearning to know what he meant.

Night and day I pondered until I saw the connection between the justice [or righteousness] of God and the statement that "the just shall live by his faith." Then I grasped that the justice of God is that righteousness by which through grace and sheer mercy God justifies us through faith. Thereupon I felt myself to be reborn and to have gone through open doors into paradise. The whole of Scripture took on a new meaning, and whereas before the "justice of God" had filled me with hate, now it became to me inexpressibly sweet in greater love. This passage of Paul became to me a gate to heaven.[150]

Luther had to realign his thinking

Luther knew the works of Thomas Aquinas, who was most responsible for giving the Catholic church its formal theology and who relied heavily on the philosophy of Aristotle to define Catholic doctrine. Aquinas left Luther cold, and Luther would have nothing to do with him. He considered Thomas' theology to be "nothing more than pagan Aristotelianism with a Christian veneer."[151]

But Augustine was another matter, and Luther did not give up on him so quickly. Luther was a monk in the Augustinian order. He took that name seriously. While in the monastery, he devoured the works of Augustine.

Luther had been taught that he himself was responsible for doing what was necessary to find peace with God. But from Augustine, he learned the opposite. Good works could be done only *by the grace of God*. This teaching of Augustine kept Luther from sheer despair.

But as important as this was for Luther, Augustine's teaching of "by grace alone" was only a part of Luther's struggle. Luther also had to wrestle with what Augustine meant by grace. Augustine thought that God gave him the grace he needed to overcome the sins that plagued him, but Augustine's focus was still on overcoming sin.

---

[150]Roland Bainton, *Here I Stand* (Nashville: Abingdon, 1950), p. 66.

[151]Becker, *The Foolishness of God*, p. 25.

Luther's struggle was different. It was more basic. It got to the heart of the issue. Luther's focus was on God himself. How could a sinner be at peace with God? Even more basic: How did God expect a sinner to find peace with him?

Recall that Augustine had received his understanding of grace when he read a moral exhortation (Romans 13:13,14), which also shaped his understanding of justification. Augustine understood Romans 1:17 like this: If a member of the city of God were asked to name the supreme good and the supreme evil, he or she would call eternal life the supreme good and eternal death the supreme evil. The Christian would continue and explain how the supreme good is achieved:

> *To attain the one and avoid the other we must live rightly.* That is why Scripture says, *The just person lives by faith* (Romans 1:17). For we do not yet see our good, and as a consequence, we must seek it by believing. Nor is it in our power to live rightly by our own efforts unless we are helped in believing and praying by the one who gave us the very faith by which we believe that we must have his help.[152]

By contrast, Luther received grace through a careful reading of that same passage, Romans 1:17, "For in the Gospel a righteousness from God is revealed by faith, for faith, just as it is written, 'The righteous will live by faith.'" Gradually, Luther realized that he and Augustine had less in common than he originally thought. Even if God might give him the power to do good works, peace with God would still be related to what he *did*. And that's what troubled him.

Luther expressed the difference between himself and Augustine in a "table talk" in 1531:

> It was Augustine's view that the law, [when] fulfilled by the powers of reason, does not justify, even as works of the moral law do not justify the heathen, but that if the Spirit assists, the works of the law do justify. The question is not whether the works of the law justify, but whether the law, kept with the Spirit's help, justifies. I reply by saying, No. Even if in the power of the Holy Spirit a man were to keep the law completely, he ought nevertheless to pray for divine mercy, for God has ordained that man should be saved not by the law but by Christ. Works never give us a peaceful heart. Christ would never have been sad in spirit unless he

---

[152] Augustine, *The City of God,* Vol. 2, p. 354 (Book 22.5). Emphasis added

had been pressed hard by the Law, to which he subjected himself for our sake.[153]

Between posting the 95 Theses in 1517 and his confession of faith at the Diet of Worms in 1521, Luther grew in his understanding that God's grace first and foremost was the forgiveness of sins. He learned that justification was God's act of *declaring*, opposed to *making*, a person to be righteous in Christ.

The Catholic Church never lost sight of Christ. But it did lose sight of why God sent him. Luther restored the good news that Christ's righteous life was God's gift to us and that his unjust suffering was the suffering we justly deserve. When we compare Luther with Jesus and the apostle Paul, we see that they all emphasized the guilt of sin and the coming judgment. And they all centered their message on God's gracious forgiveness. They all closely linked Christian service to God with the fact that "the Son of Man came not to be served but to serve, and to give his life as a ransom for many" (Matthew 20:28). While Augustine found his answer to sin through the experience of an infusion of power, Luther found his answer on "daily contrition and repentance," which led him to treasure the Gospel and enabled him to do God's will with a willing spirit.

Luther's conversion was his discovery of what God had done for him 1,500 years before he was born. Luther described the history of that event in the first hymn he wrote for congregational singing:

Fast bound in Satan's chains I lay;
Death brooded darkly o'er me.
Sin was my torment night and day;
In sin my mother bore me.
Yet deep and deeper still I fell;
Life had become a living hell,
So firmly sin possessed me.

My own good works availed me naught,
No merit they attaining;
My will against God's judgment fought,
No hope for me remaining.
My fears increased till sheer despair
Left naught but death to be my share
And hell to be my sentence.

---

[153]Martin Luther, *Luther's Works*, ed. and trans. Theodore G. Tappert, American Edition, Vol. 54 (Philadelphia: Fortress Press, 1967), p. 10.

He spoke to his beloved Son:
"'Tis time to have compassion.
Then go, bright Jewel of my crown,
and bring mankind salvation.
From sin and sorrow set them free;
Slay bitter death for them that they
May live with you forever."

"The foe shall shed my precious blood,
Me of my life bereaving.
All this I suffer for your good;
Be steadfast and believing.
Life shall from death the victory win;
My innocence shall bear your sin,
And you are blest forever."[154]

Luther and Scripture

The message of Christ crucified is "a stumbling block to Jews and folly to Gentiles" (1 Corinthians 1:23). This message does not come as an answer to human yearnings; people don't look for salvation through something as humble as a person dying on a cross. It cannot be explained philosophically. What philosopher would try to convince a fellow philosopher that salvation by crucifixion is a viable way to a true and happy life? It cannot be proved and defended by human logic. One might find ample proof that a person mentioned in Scripture lived or that some event related by Scripture actually happened, but there is nothing to prove that Jesus' death erased the guilt of the world's sins. Luther thanked God for revealing that to him in the pages of Scripture.

Luther found peace in the Bible. The Bible revealed that God had forgiven him 1,500 years before he was born. For faith and life he needed nothing more than what Scripture told him: The guilt of *your* sin has been removed, the path to God is clear of the debris of *your* sin, and God has reconciled himself to *you*. Luther found complete assurance in what God's Word told him: "Jesus loves me; this I know. For *the Bible* tells me so.

Throughout the ages Christians have taught that God's Word has power. Modern apologists confess the same. But the shift in the meaning of the Gospel,

---

[154]*Christian Worship: A Lutheran Hymnal* (Milwaukee, Northwestern Publishing House, 1993), 377: 2,3,5,8.

which we have been plotting in this section, compromises that confession. Using logic to support faith, crediting humans with a natural yearning for God and morality, finding assurance in conversion experiences—all these remove a Christian's sole dependence on the power of the Word.

God's grace comes through Scripture. In Scripture people read that God sent his Son to suffer the punishment they deserve for their sins. They learn from Scripture that God is at peace with the world. They hear in Scripture the eternal seriousness of their sins and the urge to repent and live in the peace of Christ.

As such, Scripture is a means, or channel, through which God's grace comes to us. The Gospel message will always remain a stumbling block and foolishness, said Luther. But that's OK. "We must take care not to deface the Gospel, to defend it so well that it collapses. Let us not be anxious: the Gospel needs not our help; it is sufficiently strong of itself. God alone commends it, whose it is."[155]

In future chapters we will hear about the power of the Word and Luther's complete reliance on it.

Philip Melanchthon (1497–1560)

The Lutheran Reformation teaches that God will maintain the preaching of the Gospel. But it also teaches that the desire to shift the meaning of the Gospel is hardwired into all people. The problem is not a denominational issue but a personal one. We treasure the teachings of the Lutheran Church because they are drawn from Scripture and teach us to center our faith on sin and grace, on guilt and forgiveness. But we see many in the Lutheran Church who have shifted the meaning of Christianity in some of the ways noted previously.

Philip Melanchthon was Luther's close friend and the invaluable co-leader of the Reformation. He articulated its teachings in clear and compelling language. But under the surface, there was a problem in Melanchthon's spiritual understanding, which after Luther's death would cause problems in the Lutheran Church.

Leading up to the Reformation, many in the Roman Catholic Church adopted *religious humanism*. Religious humanists considered the goal of Christianity to help a person lead a moral life. They were *humanists* because human beings, they believed, have a natural desire for holiness. But they were *religious* because they knew that human nature is weak and that sinful people cannot

---

[155]Beilby, *Thinking About Christian Apologetics*, p. 56.

live a moral life by their own strength. They need God's help—an infusion of grace—to achieve the holiness they desire.

When Philip Melanchthon came to Wittenberg, he was a religious humanist. Under Luther's influence, he came to embrace the Gospel. And he also accepted as scriptural what Luther said in his 1525 *Bondage of the Will* about mankind's complete bondage to sin. The humanist would claim that knowing God implies a desire to serve him and knowing the law implies a desire to keep it. Luther and Melanchthon countered by saying that knowing these things has the opposite effect. Mankind rebels against the law he sees in his heart and suppresses the knowledge of God who is the source of that law.

Nevertheless, there was always an undercurrent of humanism in Melanchthon. In 1525 he wrote, "I am conscious of the fact that I have never theologized for any other reason than to improve my morals."[156]

Early in the Reformation, Melanchthon and Luther focused on the law as God's tool to help people realize their sins and guide them in service to the Lord and their neighbor. Over time, however, Melanchthon more and more emphasized the natural law as it is reflected in philosophy and government. In the process, the roles of church and government were merged. Paul Peters described Melanchthon's change: "Both the ecclesiastical order as well as the secular order were to serve as a disciplinary force of mankind. Melanchthon's influence is focused on the moral influence of the commonwealth. He is not any more concerned about the invisible, purely inner religious life of the Church."[157]

Boa and Bowman make an observation in regard to Melanchthon's view of apologetics: "Philip Melanchthon, in particular, was in his later years more appreciative of classical apologetics than Martin Luther had been, and presented arguments in the Thomistic fashion in the later editions of his Loci communes."[158]

Melanchthon also lumped together two things that must always remain separate: the bondage of the will in coming to faith and serving God with a willing spirit and the freedom of the will in external, natural matters—matters that relate to keeping order and peace in the world. Melanchthon credited the

---

[156]Fred Bente, "Historical Introductions to the Symbolical Books of the Evangelical Lutheran Church" in *Concordia Triglotta* (St. Louis: Concordia, 1921), p. 105.

[157]Paul Peters, "Melanchthon the Humanist," *Wisconsin Lutheran Quarterly*, Vol. 44 (October 1947), pp. 291-296.

[158]Boa and Bowman Jr., *Faith Has Its Reasons*, p. 51.

human will with more power than it has. He affirmed the *human* desire for holiness before God and gave it a role in conversion. This is called *synergism*, the teaching that God and people work together to effect conversion. After Luther's death, Melanchthon's ideas surfaced in the *Synergistic controversy* in the Lutheran Church, which caused the Lutheran Church untold problems.

John Bunyan (1628–1688)

John Bunyan, the author of *Pilgrim's Progress*, shows you don't have to be a Lutheran to understand the Gospel as Luther understood it.

Bunyan had been baptized as a baby but had fallen away from God. He married when he was 20 and afterward began to struggle spiritually. In *Grace Abounding to the Chief of Sinners* he describes his struggle.

In that book, Bunyan did not dwell on a desire to put off sin. His chief concern was the guilt of his sin. He wanted to find peace with God. He prayed that God would not forsake him eternally and studied the Bible for some assurance of God's mercy.

> Thus I went on for many weeks, sometimes comforted, and sometimes tormented; and especially at some times my torment would be very sore. . . .

> But one day, as I was passing into the field, and that too with some dashes on my conscience, fearing lest yet all was not right, suddenly this sentence fell upon my soul, "Thy righteousness is in heaven;" and methought withal, I saw with the eyes of my soul, Jesus Christ at God's right hand; there, I say, as my righteousness; so that wherever I was, or whatever I was doing, God could not say to me, "He wants my righteousness," for that was just before him. I also saw, moreover, that it was not my good frame of heart that made my righteousness better, nor yet my bad frame that made my righteousness worse; for my righteousness was Jesus Christ himself, "the same yesterday, today and forever."

> Now did my chains fall off my legs indeed; I was loosed from my afflictions and irons; my temptations also fled away; so that from that time those dreadful Scriptures of God [i.e., concerning Esau's rejection] left off to trouble me: now went I also home rejoicing, for the grace and love of God; so when I came home I looked to see if I could find that sentence, "Thy righteousness is in heaven," but could not find such a

saying; wherefore my heart began to sink again, only that was brought to my remembrance, "He is made unto us of God, wisdom, righteousness, sanctification, and redemption." By this word I say the other sentence is true.

For by this Scripture I saw that the man Christ Jesus, as he is distinct from us, as touching his bodily presence, so he is our righteousness and sanctification before God. Here therefore I lived, for some time, very sweetly at peace with God through Christ. Oh! Methought, Christ! Christ! There was nothing but Christ that was before my eyes. . . . Now Christ was all; all my righteousness, all my sanctification, and all my redemption.[159]

These words show a Christian like Luther, who found his assurance of God's forgiveness and gift of righteousness in the words of Scripture.

August Hermann Francke (1663–1727)

However, not all yearnings for piety are the same. Christians have a *divine* yearning for piety. They confess that Jesus died for their sins. They know the Holy Spirit is living in them and that their citizenship is in Heaven. They want to put off the deeds of the sinful nature and aim for perfection in how they live. They yearn for a deeper understanding of God's promises in Christ. They know that victory over sin comes from a growing appreciation of the height and breadth and depth of God's forgiving love for them. And so they want to let the Holy Spirit have his way in their lives and please the Lord more and more in how they live.

And they pray for the grace to serve God better. The grace they are looking for—spiritual gifts, positions of service in the church, greater wisdom and understanding, greater holiness in life, greater courage to give a reason for our hope—is always associated with the grace of God's favor in Christ. These graces help extend God's kingdom and serve the body of Christ. Within that context—a context the Bible writers never lost sight of—the yearning for grace is a *divine* yearning, worked in our hearts by God.

But there is a natural—a *human*—yearning for what is called grace. It does not flow from the Gospel as much as from the bare desire to keep the Law, or to be

---

[159]Hugh T. Kerr and John M. Mulder, *Conversions* (Grand Rapids: Eerdmans, 1983), from *Grace Abounding to the Chief of Sinners* in *The Complete Works of John Bunyan* (Philadelphia, 1874), pp. 54-56, 59.

a moral person, or to overcome sin. The Lutheran church leader, August Hermann Francke had such yearnings.

In 1685 August Francke graduated from the German Lutheran university at Leipzig. He was a brilliant young student, ready to serve as a pastor or professor. He had studied the teachings of Scripture about Jesus' life and death for the sins of the world, God's love and favor in Christ, and the blessings of membership in God's kingdom. But for years he struggled in vain to overcome sins of vanity and pride over his academic prowess and the honors he received. For this reason he was in doubt that he was a true, justified Christian.

The immediate occasion for his "conversion" was an invitation to preach a sermon. His long-drawn-out struggle for holiness came to a head as the Sunday when he was to preach approached. He was plagued by the thought: "I do not find the faith in myself that I am to demand of my hearers."[160]

The following lengthy excerpt from his autobiography describes what happened. When Francke was about 24 years old, he began to drive himself

> to gain a deeper understanding of my miserable condition and to truly see myself so that my soul might be freed. I cannot point to anything specific that prompted me to do this other than that I did not find the faith in myself that I was to demand in the sermon. The fact that my theological studies, however, led only to knowledge that I was absorbing with my intellect, made me realize that I could not possibly betray people. I could not allow myself to accept a position in the church and preach to people about things I was not convinced of in my heart.
>
> My circle of friends were people of the world and I continued to be attracted by sin. I fell into my long-time habits, but in spite of everything, God on high moved my heart to humble itself before him, to ask him for grace, and repeatedly to fall on my knees, asking that he would change the course of my life and turn me into an upright child of God.
>
> The fact that I still did not possess true faith troubled me more and more. I wanted to find encouragement in my text and use it to chase away my sadness, but it wasn't enough. Up to now I used arguments that made sense to my reason, but I had little experience in the new way of the Spirit. I thought I would now help myself in this new way,

---

[160]Peter Erb, ed. *Pietists, Selected Writings* (New York, Paulist Press, 1883), p. 102 (paraphrased).

but the more I tried to help myself, the deeper I fell into restless doubt. I thought I would support myself with the Holy Scriptures, but then I thought, "who knows if the Scriptures really are God's Word." After all, the Turks have their Koran and the Jews their Talmud. Who knows who is right? These thoughts became more and more powerful so that finally there was nothing I had learned throughout my whole life—particularly in the eight years I had studied theology and learned of God's will and essence—that I still believed to be true.

I saw my entire life. Everything I had ever done, said, or thought, was nothing but sin and an abomination to God. I paced back and forth in my agitation; then I fell on my knees before the one I did not know. Yet I prayed that if there really was a God, that he might have pity on me. I did this often.

When I was with other people, I hid my inner misery as much as I could. Once when I had finished eating, I wanted to go with a friend to the superintendent who lived in the area, and my friend consented. We had hardly sat down when the superintendent began to discuss with us how a person can know whether he has faith or not. As I sat there I began to wonder whether it was by accident that I should be listening to this kind of discourse, which was so important to me, considering that no one in the whole world knew the least about my condition. I listened to him with rapt attention, but my heart would not be still. I was all the more convinced that I had no real faith, for I saw in myself the exact opposite of the signs of faith as Scripture describes them.

I again got down on my knees and called out to that God whom I did not know or believe in, to save me from my wretched condition—if there truly was a God. At that point the Lord heard me, the living God, from his holy throne, as I was down on my knees. So great was his fatherly love that he did not remove from me my doubt and turbulence of heart in a gradual way—with which I would have been satisfied—rather, he did it instantly so that I would all the more be convinced and my confused reason would be reined in lest it turn on God's power and faithfulness. For this reason he answered my prayer as he did. As one turns over his hand, so all my doubt was taken away; I was assured in my heart of the grace of God in Christ Jesus, I knew God not only as God, but as my father. All sadness and restlessness of heart was at once taken away and immediately I was showered with a stream of joy, so that with complete courage I praised the Lord who had given me such grace.

I stood up with a completely different mind than the one I had when I kneeled down. For I kneeled with great sorrow and doubt, but I arose with unspeakable joy and certainty. It was as if I had lived my life in a deep sleep and everything I had done was a dream, and now for the first time I was awake. It was as if I had been dead, but behold, I am alive.

That night I couldn't stay in bed, but I jumped up and praised the Lord my God. You angels in heaven, I cried out, join me in praising the name of the Lord, who has shown to me such compassion. My reason stood at a distance, for the victory had been ripped from reason's hands, for the power of God had made it submit to faith.

For a while, however, I thought that all this might be something natural. Couldn't a person experience such great joy in a natural way? But I was completely convinced to the contrary. The whole world, with all its joys and glories, could not instill a sweetness like this in the human heart. I knew by faith that after this taste of the grace and goodness of God, the world with its attractions to worldly delights would have little influence on me anymore. The streams of living water were sweet to me now and I would have no trouble forgetting the stinking swamp of the world.

This, therefore, is the time I consider myself to have been truly converted. For from this point on my Christianity had a place to stand, and since that time it has been easy for me to deny ungodly ways and earthly delights and to carry on a chaste, righteous, and godly life in this world. And whereas I had previously made a god out of learning, I now saw that faith like a mustard seed was more valuable than a hundred sacks of learning, and that everything I had learned at the feet of Gamaliel was nothing but dregs compared to the surpassing knowledge of Jesus Christ, our Lord.[161]

Who cannot identify with Francke? Sins continue to plague all Christians. But Francke and all believers have a choice. Should we patiently listen to Scripture reveal and remind us of what God has done for us in Christ, asking God to fill us with Christ's forgiveness and love and thereby free us from the power of our sins? Or should we search for an experience like Francke had?

---

[161] For more of the account in translation, see Robert Koester, *The Spirit of Pietism* (Milwaukee: Northwestern, 2013), pp. 168-183.

As we see from Francke's autobiography, it was his experience that confirmed the existence of God, the reality of his faith, and the truth of Scripture. Francke certainly treasured the Word of God but his certainty lay in his experience. That became Francke's apologetic.

John Calvin (1509–1564)

John Calvin was a younger contemporary of Martin Luther. He was a French scholar in the Catholic Church. He joined the Reformation in his late teens or early 20s. He was forced to leave France and took up residence in Geneva, Switzerland. He gradually assumed leadership of the Swiss Reformation, which had begun in the early 1520s under Ulrich Zwingli (1484–1531). John Calvin established the Swiss Reformation's doctrinal position, which came to be called *Calvinism.*

The German and Swiss reformers broke away from the Catholic Church, rejecting its work-righteousness. They embraced the Gospel of God's free forgiveness and confessed that we are saved by grace through faith alone. They agreed on many points of teaching, but they parted company on other points.

Calvin established the Reformed church, an arm of the Reformation distinct from Lutheranism. The Reformed church had its own way of approaching the Christian religion. An understanding of John Calvin is important because he is the fountainhead of most of today's protestant churches, which is the primary home of the modern apologetic movement.[162]

Calvin never gave apologetic arguments a role in spreading the Gospel. But his theology includes a cluster of teachings that fostered the use of reason and helped create the kind of religious environment where apologetic arguments could play an important role. The cluster of teachings we will look at are similar to the cluster of teachings we looked at in our study of Augustine. In this section on Calvin and the next, where we will look at Jacob Arminius' modification of Calvinism, we'll examine that claim.[163]

---

[162]Calvin is the direct fountainhead of modern Reformed churches that identify closely with Calvin, and he is the indirect fountainhead of modern churches that identify more closely with Jacob Arminius. We noted that strict Calvinists tend to avoid using apologetic arguments while Arminians are open to their use. In a general way, however, understanding Calvin is very important for understanding modern apologetics. Jacob Arminius rejected and changed some of Calvin's teachings, but he was still a follower of Calvin and retained the basic Reformed outlook on Christianity.

[163]In the analysis of Calvin's theology that follows, I will be primarily drawing from four articles in *The Cambridge Companion* to John Calvin, edited by Donald K. McKim. All

Calvin's sense of the divine

Scripture teaches what has become known as "total depravity." Sin so completely dominates the natural human heart and mind that people can do nothing spiritually good. At birth we are spiritually dead, hostile to God, and unable to serve him in love.

Martin Luther reflects this teaching in his Small Catechism: "I believe that I cannot by my own thinking or choosing believe in Jesus Christ, my Lord, or come to him. But the Holy Ghost has called me by the Gospel, enlightened me with his gifts, sanctified and kept me in the truth faith."[164]

Calvin also taught total depravity and devoted several sections of *The Institutes of the Christian Religion* to a complete description of the depth of human sin. Calvin confessed that everyone would search for the Creator whose wisdom and love is reflected in his creation, "did not the depravity of the human mind lead it away from the proper course of investigation" (I.2.2).[165]

But there's a snag in Calvin's doctrine of total depravity. Calvin taught that people have what he called the *sensus divinitatis*, that is, a knowledge of the true God deeply implanted within them. Calvin wrote,

> That there exists in the human mind and indeed by natural instinct, some sense of the Deity, we hold to be beyond dispute, since God himself, to prevent any man from pretending ignorance, has endued all men with some idea of his Godhead, the memory of which he constantly renews and occasionally enlarges, that all to a man being aware that there is a God, and that he is their Maker, may be condemned by their own conscience when they neither worship him nor consecrate their lives to his service. (I.3.1)

---

the authors have Calvinist roots, are world-class Reformation scholars, and are experts on John Calvin. The four articles are "Calvin's Theology" by I. John Hesselink, "Calvin's Ethics" by Guenther H. Haas, "Calvin on Piety" by Joel R. Beeke, and "The Place of Calvin in Christian Theology" by B. A. Gerrish.

[164]Martin Luther, *"The Creed,"* in David P. Kuske, *Luther's Catechism* (Milwaukee: Northwestern Publishing House, 1982), p. 5.

[165]Calvin published many sermons and commentaries on the Bible. But his most well-known work is T*he Institutes of the Christian Religion*. Quotations from *The Institutes* are taken from John Calvin, *The Institutes of the Christian Religion,* 1559 Edition, trans. Henry Beveridge. Kindle file. *The Institutes* is divided into books, chapters, and sections. In this book all references to *The Institutes* will be in text. For example, the reference (I.2.2) refers to book 1, chapter 2, section 2.

According to Calvin, people have this natural instinct "from the womb" (I.3.3), "thoroughly fixed, as it were, in our very bones" (I.3.3). It's like a seed planted in all people, from which "the religious propensity springs" (I.3.2). It is "a memory" that God constantly renews and occasionally enlarges" (1.3.1). Even those who suppress this sense find it resurfacing at various times in their lives, in times of difficulty, for example. Although "nature herself allows no individual to forget, though many, with all their might, strive to do so" (I.3.1).

This teaching is Calvin's logical conclusion from the fact that "there never has been, from the very first, any quarter of the globe, any city, any household even, without religion, this amounts to a tacit confession, that a sense of Deity is inscribed on every heart" (I.3.1).

We remember that in Romans 1:19 Paul wrote, "For his invisible attributes, namely, his eternal power and divine nature, have been clearly perceived, ever since the creation of the world, in the things that have been made. So they are without excuse." Here we see a difference between Paul and Calvin. Paul was not teaching that people have a *sensus divinitatis* inscribed within them from birth. Rather, he was saying that when people look outside of themselves at the world around them, they must logically conclude that a creator–God exists and that he is eternal, powerful, and divine.

The problem with Calvin's *sensus divinitatis* is that it mitigates the depth of human sin. Although Calvin says that people stifle their knowledge "partly by ignorance, partly by evil intent" (I. 1. Introduction), the teaching that all people have a *sensus divinitatis* can easily lead to the idea that people retain within themselves something of the image of God and a certain degree of spiritual ability.

Calvin himself opened the door to this idea. He wrote, "But though experience testifies that a seed of religion is divinely sown in all, scarcely one in a hundred is found who cherished it in his heart, and not one in whom it grows to maturity" (I.4.1). Although no one allows the knowledge of God "to grow to maturity," Calvin says that here and there a person can be found who "cherishes it." Calvin, in fact, uses the ancient philosopher Plato as an example of the latter. He wrote, "This did not escape the observation even of philosophers. For it is the very thing which Plato meant when he taught, as he often does, that the chief good of the soul consists in resemblance to God; i.e., when, by means of knowing him, she [the soul] is wholly transformed into him" (I.3.3).

Both Paul and Calvin taught that people suppress what they know about God. But Paul used that fact to point out human guilt and our absolute need for God's gift of righteousness. Calvin, on the other hand, taught that although people suppress the sense of the divine, this sense is a positive quality within human beings that can make a positive contribution.

Calvin's emphasis on piety

Calvin's major theological work was *The Institutes of the Christian Religion*. But Calvin did not consider this to be a summary of *Christian teaching*, but rather a summary of *what leads to piety*. I. John Hesselink in his article "Calvin's Theology" says that Calvin "calls his book not a *summa theologiae* but a *summa pietatis*. The secret of his mental energy lies in his piety; its product is his theology, which is his piety described at length."[166]

If one were to ask Luther why Christian teaching is useful, he would answer, "Because there I learn how I can be saved from sin, death, and the devil." Hesselink indicates that Calvin might answer that question differently. He writes, "We shall see that a constant concern of Calvin's theology was always the promotion of piety or godliness and the '*usefulness*' of true doctrine."[167]

In the second book of *The Institutes*, Calvin describes a Christian's goal. Once the Holy Spirit breaks through a person's resistance and leads a person to the truth and goodness that can only be found in God, he or she

> must learn to expect and ask all things from him, and thankfully ascribe to him whatever we receive. For this sense of the divine perfections is the proper master to teach us piety, out of which religion springs. By piety I mean that union of reverence and love to God which the knowledge of his benefits inspires. For, until men feel that they owe everything to God, that they are cherished by his paternal care, and that he is the author of all their blessings, so that naught is to be looked for away from him, they will never submit to him in voluntary obedience; nay, unless they place their entire happiness in him, they will never yield up their whole selves to him in truth and sincerity. (I.ii.1)

---

[166]I. John Hesselink, "Calvin's Theology," in *The Cambridge Companion to John Calvin*, ed. Donald K. McKim (Cambridge: Cambridge University Press, 2004), p. 77, quoting John T. McNeill from the forward to the McNeil-Battles edition of *The Institutes*, p. 8.

[167]Hesselink, "Calvin's Theology," in *The Cambridge Companion to John Calvin*, p. 76 (emphasis added).

In his *Commentary on Romans*, Calvin wrote, "The state of the case is really this,— that the faithful are never reconciled to God without the gift of regeneration; nay, we are for this end justified,—that we may afterwards serve God in holiness of life."[168]

B. A. Gerrish explains the place of justification in the theology of Calvin in contrast to Luther:

> For Luther, "grace" was nothing but the favor or good will of God in freely justifying the sinner. Not that Luther was uninterested in "sanctification": as he put it in his treatise *Against Latomus* (1521), appealing to Romans 5:15, besides the *grace* that forgives the sinner there is the *gift* that little by little heals the sin.

> Calvin, by contrast, taught a "double grace" that both justifies and sanctifies (*The Institutes* III.11.1; cf. III.3.1), and his thinking was marked by a concern to balance these two gifts of participation in Christ. In a sense, he even gave the pre-eminence to sanctification, or the cultivation of purity of life, since he could say that the Lord freely justifies his own *in order that* he may restore them to true righteousness by sanctification (*The Institutes* III.3.19). . . . To be sure, Calvin could call justification "the sum of all piety" (*The Institutes* III.15.7), but it was more characteristic of him to describe justification as the main *hinge* on which religion turns, or the *foundation* on which to build piety toward God (*The Institutes* III.11.1; cf. III.15.1).[169]

Gerrish—who is not a Lutheran—offers this striking contrast between Luther's piety and that of Calvin:

> Luther's great boon to the church was his profile of the Christian as one who lives in the liberating joy of unconditional forgiveness. . . . The Calvinist profile of the Christian portrays a dutiful son, pledged to willing obedience, although it is not filial obedience but fatherly indul-

---

[168]John Calvin, *Commentary on Romans,* Romans 6:2: "Who have died to sin, etc." https://www.studylight.org/commentaries/eng/cal/romans-6.html accessed April, 2023.

[169]B. A. Gerrish, "The Place of Calvin in Christian Theology," in *The Cambridge Companion to John Calvin,* ed. Donald K. McKim (Cambridge: Cambridge University Press, 2004), p. 297 (emphasis original).

gence alone that secures the relationship (*The Institutes* III.11.6,16,22; III.19.5)."[170]

Calvin wanted to balance justification and sanctification. Guenther Haas, however, gives a significant example of one area of Christian teaching where Calvin came down decidedly on the side of sanctification. Traditionally, the Law is said to have three purposes: to point out sin, to keep order in society, and to reveal how God wants Christians to live. For Luther, the most important use was the first use, "the accusing and killing function." This use was most important because it served to make people realize their need for a Savior. Calvin, however, claimed that showing Christians how to live was the "proper purpose for which the law was originally intended."[171] For Calvin the third use was most important because it served "as a positive instrument to enable believers to understand and embody the will of God in their lives."[172] In other words, Luther saw the Law primarily as God's tool to show people their sin and need for a Savior while Calvin saw the Law primarily as God's tool to show Christians how to live. Gerrish observes that Luther and Calvin would often discuss the Law in similar ways, but "it is a question of where the accent falls."[173]

Guenther Haas writes, "The goal of the Christian life, for Calvin, is the restoration of the image of God which sin has distorted and defaced."[174] Haas explains that Calvin gives the Law a major role in this process. First, it is the best source of instruction on the nature of God's will. Second,

> because believers still struggle with sin, the law has the power to exhort them to holiness, especially when they become weary, complacent, or apathetic. [Quoting Calvin:] "The law is to the flesh like a whip to an idle and balky ass, to arouse it to work." It remains "a constant sting" that arouses believers to obedience, strengthens them to press on, and draws them back from sin.[175]

---

[170]Gerrish, "The Place of Calvin in Christian Theology," in *The Cambridge Companion to John Calvin*, p. 297.

[171]Haas, "Calvin's Ethics," in The *Cambridge Companion to John Calvin*, p. 100. Also see Gerrish, "The Place of Calvin in Christian Theology," pp. 297-298, where he compares Melanchthon to Calvin on this point.

[172]Guenther H. Haas, "Calvin's Ethics," in *The Cambridge Companion to John Calvin*, ed. Donald K. McKim (Cambridge: Cambridge University Press, 2004), p. 100.

[173]Gerrish, "The Place of Calvin in Christian Theology," in *the Cambridge Companion to John Calvin*, p. 298.

[174]Haas, "Calvin's Ethics," in *The Cambridge Companion to John Calvin*, p. 95.

[175]Haas, "Calvin's Ethics," in *The Cambridge Companion to John Calvin*, p. 101, quoting *The Institutes* II.7.12; II.8.1,51.

But Scripture teaches that a person's sinful nature is outright hostile to God's Law, and the Law cannot whip it into service, at least not the willing service God is pleased with. And Christians are new creations, brought into being by the Gospel. And only the Gospel "draws us back from sin" and into willing service.

Calvin mixes the Law and the Gospel. Hesselink contrasts Luther and Calvin on this point:

> Luther, in his conflict with the Roman Catholic Church, emphasized the distinction between Law and Gospel. For him, human effort, good works, and the curse and wrath of God are represented in the Law. . . . The Gospel, on the contrary, is sheer grace, a freely offered gift, to be accepted by trust and faith. Calvin, no less than Luther, stressed that faith is grounded exclusively in God's gracious promises in the Gospel. But Calvin was equally emphatic in his insistence that the Word of God that frees us by his promises at the same time makes a total claim upon us through his commands.[176]

The idea that God's Word frees us but also forces us to get serious about God's Law has a Law-centered ring to it. It appeals to the natural *opinio legis*, the natural human desire to make God's Law the focus of one's Christianity.

Calvin's gospel: Union with Christ

Calvin taught that a person is justified by faith alone. Like Luther, Calvin taught that justification is not the process of *making* a person righteous but of God *declaring* that person righteous in Christ. We quote one example among many:

> Our acquittal is in this, that the guilt which made us liable to punishment was transferred to the head of the Son of God. We must specially remember this substitution in order that we may not be all our lives in trepidation and anxiety, as if the just vengeance which the Son of God transferred to himself were still impending over us" (II.16.5).

For Calvin, justification was nothing other than the forgiveness of sins.

Nevertheless, Calvin's teaching on justification did not follow the pattern of Scripture. Once again, we note how Scripture presents the teaching of justification: Jesus paid for the guilt of all people's sins, which is the same as saying

---

[176]Hesselink, "Calvin's Theology," in *The Cambridge Companion to John Calvin*, p. 82.

that God forgave all people's sins, which is the same as saying that God justified all people. We do nothing to have the guilt of our sins removed, or to earn the right to God's forgiveness, or to be declared justified before God. Christ alone procured this blessing for every man, woman, and child on earth. The *benefit* of what Christ did for all people is ours simply *by believing it to be true.*

This is *not* how Calvin would teach justification by faith. The problem does not lie with a misunderstanding of justification. Rather, it lies with his understanding of the way faith acquires justification.

In Scripture, justification flows directly from faith. A Christian simply believes what Christ has already done. Calvin, however, puts something between faith and justification, namely, union with God through the Spirit, thus separating the two.

At the outset of the third book of *The Institutes*—where Calvin describes how people receive the blessings of the Gospel—he writes,

> The first thing to be attended to is that so long as we are without Christ and separated from him, nothing which he suffered and did for the salvation of the human race is of the least benefit to us. To communicate to us the blessings which he received from the Father, he must become ours and dwell in us. . . . All which he possesses being nothing to us until we become one with him. (III.1.1)

Justification is by faith, Calvin says, but before a person can be justified by faith, Christ must come to dwell in that person's heart. Until that union is achieved, everything Christ did for the world "is of the least benefit to us" and is "nothing to us."

Immediately the question arises: How can I be united with Christ so that I can be justified by faith? With Calvin, we are once again being forced to ask what we must do. This is an important issue and seems to be part of an ongoing discussion among Reformed theologians.

Reformed teacher Michael Horton interprets Calvin to say that justification is the basis of our union with Christ.[177] He quotes Calvin from his commentary

---

[177] The material in this and the next two paragraphs is from Lee Gatiss, "The Inexhaustible Fountain of All Good Things: Union with Christ in Calvin on Ephesians," Section 2.1, "Benefits Together," Themelios, Vol 34. No 2 https://www.thegospelcoalition.org/themelios/article/the-inexhaustible-fountain-of-all-good-things-union-with-christ-in-calvin-o/, accessed April 2023.

on Ephesians 3:17: "Most people regard partaking of Christ and believing in Christ as the same thing. But our partaking of Christ is rather the effect of believing." Here Horton finds support for his claim in Calvin's statement, "Forensic justification through faith alone is the fountain of union with Christ in all of its renewing aspects." In other words, when we believe in Christ's work, which justifies us, we are then united with Christ and receive all his blessings.

However, another Reformed theologian, Lee Gatiss, says that Horton misinterprets Calvin. He is surprised, he says, when he finds Reformed theologians like Michael Horton "arguing for that more Lutheran conception as if it were Calvin's." He argues that the word *justification* does not occur in the words Horton quotes, either in the surrounding context or in Ephesians 3:17 itself. He says that on close examination, Calvin is teaching the same thing he teaches in other places, namely, that *faith* leads to union with Christ, not to *justification*, and once a person is united with Christ, then the person receives the grace of justification.[178]

Gatiss then presents the key argument: How can "one of the benefits of union with Christ" be the "basis for the union itself." That is, how can faith in justification be the basis of "the union in and through which it [justification] is received"?[179] Gatiss' way of answering this fits with Calvin's statement quoted above, namely, that nothing Christ has done for us is of any value "until we become one with him." And when a person is united with Christ, that person receives all the blessings Christ has to give. Membership in God's family, wisdom, understanding, joy, confidence—they all become ours, *as well as* grace to be justified (forgiven) and grace to be sanctified (to grow in piety). On this point, it is hard to claim that Calvin taught what Horton says he taught: that justification by faith leads to union with Christ. Rather, Calvin taught that union with Christ leads to our justification.

Joel Beeke in his article "Calvin on Piety," emphasizes this point. Calvin's

> sermons, commentaries, and theological works are so permeated with the union-with-Christ doctrine that it becomes the focus for Christian faith and practice. Calvin says as much when he writes, the "joining together of Head and members, that indwelling of Christ in our hearts—in short, that mystical union—are accorded by us the highest degree of

---

[178]Lee Gatiss, "The Inexhaustible Fountain."
[179]Lee Gatiss, "The Inexhaustible Fountain."

importance, so that Christ, having been made ours, makes us sharers with him in the gifts with which he has been endowed.[180]

This then is Calvin's gospel: Through faith we are united with Christ. Once we are united with Christ, we possess all his blessings, including grace to be justified apart from anything we do, and grace to grow in holiness through the power and influence of the Holy Spirit living within us.

Making union with Christ the heart of Christianity, however, leads to problems. There is a difference between preaching about what God *wants us to have* and what God *has already given us.* Something that has already been done comes by faith in the fact that it has been done. Something that *will* be done raises nagging questions: How will Christ do it for me? When will he do it? What must happen before he does it? Those questions must be answered before a Christian can be certain of his or her faith, certain that Christ is in them, and certain that they have been justified.

Second, it can desensitize Christians to the relationship between justification and sanctification. Calvin wrote, "Although we may distinguish them [justification and sanctification], Christ contains both of them inseparably in himself. Do you wish, then, to attain righteousness in Christ? You must first possess Christ; but you cannot possess him without being made partaker in his sanctification, because he cannot be divided into pieces" (III.16.1). Calvin did teach, in fact, the correct relation between the two—that we serve the Lord because he has freed us from the guilt of our sins. But when union with Christ becomes the goal, through which we received the gifts of justification and sanctification, the relationship between the two can't help but break down.

In Scripture, the meaning of the Gospel and the meaning of faith in the Gospel are very specific: Christ died for the sins of the world, and peace with God comes through that faith. In Scripture, the meaning of Christian piety is also specific. When a person believes the Gospel, they die to sin and rise to live with Christ. They become slaves of the righteousness Christ has given them. They are no longer slaves to sin. They are set free from the law and can now serve God "in the new way of the Spirit and not in the old way of the written code" (Romans 7:6). The Spirit, who leads Christians to know Christ's forgiveness, uses that as his springboard to instill in them "love, joy, peace, patience, kindness, goodness, faithfulness, gentleness, self-control" (Galatians 5:22,23). And

---

[180]Joel Beeke, "Calvin on Piety," in *The Cambridge Companion to John Calvin,* ed. Donald K. McKim (Cambridge: Cambridge University Press, 2004), pp. 127-128, quoting *The Institutes* III.11.9.

as we learn from other places in Scripture, all those qualities flow from the fact that Christ has justified us and the Spirit has led us to believe it.

Calvin's faith, however, was faith in a more general group of promised blessings. It was faith in God's goodness, holiness, and power over all things. It was faith in God's desire to restore to mankind the blessings they lost when they fell into sin. It was faith in Christ as the one through whom we can receive those blessings.

To be sure, when a person comes to faith as Calvin describes it, God's forgiveness in Christ *can* become the main focus, as it does in the hearts of many Evangelical/Reformed believers whose faith and lives center on the cross of Christ. And simply belonging to a Lutheran church does not guarantee the correct focus. But Calvin's general definition of faith makes it easy for a Christian to center his or her life on one or the other of God's promised blessings.

Calvin tried to be reasonable

The goal of modern apologetics is to show a skeptic that Christianity is a reasonable religion. Calvin helped to create a culture in which such a claim can be made. The emphasis on piety and the more general nature of faith make it easier for a modern apologist to argue for Christianity, while understanding the nature of faith as the acceptance of God's forgiveness in Christ makes it more difficult.

Calvin certainly accepted many truths of Scripture that reason cannot fathom, the Trinity and the incarnation of Christ, for example. Nevertheless, Calvin gave reason a greater role than Scripture allows. We'll focus on one of Calvin's most controversial teachings, *double predestination.*

Calvin's teaching on predestination was not based on any clear passages of Scripture. Rather, it was forged by Calvin's logic. In Calvin's system—where union with Christ must take place before a person is justified—there is need to explain how a completely sinful human being who lacks any spiritual power can be united with Christ. Calvin's explanation is that God works directly on a person's heart and mind with his irresistible power to bring that person to faith. Since this is so—the focus being God's irresistible power and not God's invitation to believe in his Son—God obviously must want some to be saved and others to be condemned.

This was Calvin's teaching of double predestination. He wrote,

> By predestination we mean the eternal decree of God, by which he determined with himself whatever he wished to happen with regard to every man. All are not created on equal terms, but some are preordained to eternal life, others to eternal damnation; and, accordingly, as each has been created for one or other of these ends, we say that he has been predestinated to life or to death. (III.21.5)

Calvin knew exactly what he was saying. He commented in *The Institutes*, "The decree is dreadful indeed, I confess" (III.23.7).

The following two Scripture passages create a logical problem:

> "In him we have obtained an inheritance, having been predestined according to the purpose of him who works all things according to the counsel of his will" (Ephesians 1:11).

> "God our Savior desires all people to be saved and to come to the knowledge of the truth. For there is one God, and there is one mediator between God and men, the man Christ Jesus, who gave himself as a ransom for all" (1 Timothy 2:3-6).

Calvin had a choice and he chose to remain faithful to the first passage and logically taught double predestination. But in the process, he denied that "God wants all people to be saved." One of Calvin's followers, Jacob Arminius (whom we will look at next), wanted to remain faithful to the second passage, so he taught that God wants all people to be saved but denied Scripture's teaching of predestination. In the process, he logically gave human beings partial credit for choosing to accept the Gospel, and in the process he logically denied Scripture's teaching that salvation comes to God's elect by his grace alone.

The only way to confess both passages is to take a very illogical position and simply accept what both passages teach: God predestined some to come to faith and God wants all people to come to faith.

Martin Luther is often lumped together with John Calvin in regard to his teaching on predestination. Luther did teach predestination. However, he refused Calvin's logical conclusion, that is, that God predestined some to salvation and others to damnation. Luther respected and taught both of the passage quoted above. And he blames his critics for not

> making any distinction between God preached and God hidden, that is, between the Word of God and God himself. God does many things that

he does not disclose to us in his word; he also wills many things which he does not disclose himself as willing in his word. Thus he does not will the death of a sinner according to his word; but he wills it according to that inscrutable will of his. It is our business, however, to pay attention to the word and leave that inscrutable will alone, for we must be guided by the word and not by that inscrutable will. After all, who can direct himself by a will completely inscrutable and unknowable? It is enough to know simply that there is a certain inscrutable will in God, and as to what, why, and how far it wills, that is something we have no right whatever to inquire into, hanker after, care about, or meddle with, but only to fear and adore.[181]

Calvin saw a mystery in the teaching of predestination. His mystery was why God elected this particular person to come to faith and that particular person to be damned. Calvin's mystery, however, came only after he had traveled a good way down the path of logic and arrived at his teaching of double predestination. For Luther, however, the mystery was that according to Scripture, God wants two opposite things to happen. This is not logical. But once it became clear that this is what Scripture taught, Luther simply shut down his human reason and refused to let his logic go any further.

Thus Luther created a climate in which the Word, not human reason or logic, had the final say. Calvin helped create an idea that has always existed in the Reformed church—that neither God nor his Word can be illogical.

But the desire to be logical came at a price. Double predestination required other teachings to support it. Calvin taught "irresistible grace." If certain people are elected to salvation, there is nothing those people can do to resist God's will to bring them to faith.

Double predestination also led to the teaching of "limited atonement"—that Christ died only for those whom God predestined to salvation. There is some question as to whether Calvin himself taught limited atonement. But later Calvinists concluded that God would *not* have sent his Son to die for those he had not predestined to be saved.[182]

---

[181]Martin Luther, *Luther's Works*, ed. and trans. Philip S. Watson, American Edition, Vol. 33 (Philadelphia: Fortress Press, 1972), p. 140.

[182]Roger Nicole, "John Calvin's View of Limited Atonement," *Westminster Theological Journal*, Vol. 47, No. 3 (Fall 1985), https://www.apuritansmind.com/arminianism/john-calvins-view-of-limited-atonement/, accessed April. 2023. Whether or not Calvin believed in universal atonement—that Christ died for all people—is debated. Limited atonement seems to follow logically from his teaching on double predestination,

To summarize so far, Calvin emphasized piety. He taught that people had an inborn sense of God's existence. He defined faith in a more general way, which encompassed all the blessings God wants to give those who believe. And he was willing to use human reason to avoid contradictions in Scripture. These teaching opened the door to a subtle form of experientialism.

Calvin and the experience of faith

Many of Calvin's followers were troubled by two logical questions. First, how can I be sure I'm among the predestined? Second, how can I know my faith is genuine?

For those whose faith lies in what Christ has already done for them, the answers are easy: Because we believe in Christ, we know we are among the elect. Because we believe in Christ, our faith is genuine. We identify with the Christians in Rome, *all* of whom Paul described as "those whom he predestined" (Romans 8:30). We put our hope of salvation in the forgiveness already gained for us by Christ.

But when a Christian thinks of predestination as God's eternal decision to unite people to Christ, it becomes more difficult to be sure of one's predestination. That is to say, predestination loses its Scriptural anchor—its objective anchor— namely, Christ and the forgiveness he already won. And it turns one's mind to a bare decree God made in eternity past.

As mentioned previously, Scripture teaches that all of God's elect will come to faith and will persevere in faith. Scripture also warns every Christian against falling away from faith and returning to a life of sin and unbelief. These two teachings are contrary, humanly speaking. Yet we believe them both because that's what Scripture teaches. But when Scripture points us to what Christ did for the world, he becomes the reason why we have God's blessings as believers. And he is the reason why a person who has fallen from faith can return to membership in God's family.

Calvin's understanding of predestination completely muddied those waters. His understanding of predestination focused people on themselves. In a world where not everyone has been united with Christ, people were led to wonder: If

---

for why would Christ die for those whom God chose to go to Hell? Nicole concludes, "Our conclusion, on balance, is that definite atonement fits better than universal grace into the total pattern of Calvin's teaching." The teaching of limited atonement became an official Reformed teaching at the Synod of Dort in 1617–1618, after Calvin's death.

God is all-powerful, he should successfully bring everyone to faith. And if God is all-loving, he *would* give his grace to all people. Since this has not happened, Christians ask, "Can I be sure God wants me to be united with Christ? Can I be sure I will never fall from faith?"

Calvin's logic forced Christians to ask even more sinister questions. Calvin's followers wondered about those who confessed their faith, joined a Christian church, and then fell away. Calvin would respond, "That's what God predestined would happen." But some would object, "If these people truly believed, they must have been one of the elect. And if that's the case, God would not have allowed them to fall away." To this Calvin would answer, "Their faith was not genuine." Some would respond, "But these people confessed their faith, just like I did. We worshiped side by side, we sang the same hymns, and we offered to God the same prayers. We helped the poor together, we visited the sick, and we even suffered for our faith." Calvin would respond, "Nevertheless, your friend did not have genuine faith."

This is not a hypothetical conversation. In Book III, Chapter 2 of *The Institutes,* Calvin addresses these concerns. Calvin begins his discussion by outlining his argument:

> I am aware it seems unaccountable to some how faith is attributed to the reprobate, seeing that it is declared by Paul to be one of the fruits of election; and yet the difficulty is easily solved: for though none are enlightened into faith, and truly feel the efficacy of the Gospel, with the exception of those who are fore-ordained to salvation, yet experience shows that the reprobate are sometimes affected in a way so similar to the elect, that even in their own judgment there is no difference between them. (III.2.11)

Calvin is saying that if a person comes to faith and experiences the blessings of the Gospel, it is because that person has been predestined to salvation. However, some of those predestined to damnation seem to display a faith similar to those predestined to salvation. The elect are tempted to interpret this as true faith. But they are mistaken, for only the elect have true faith.

Calvin devotes two long sections of *The Institutes* to explain this problem. He acknowledges that Jesus and the writer of Hebrews ascribe what seems to be true faith to some who fall away. The writer of Hebrews refers to people who fall away as those "who have once been enlightened, who have tasted the heavenly gift, and have shared in the Holy Spirit, and have tasted the goodness of the word of God and the powers of the age to come" (Hebrews 6:4,5). And in the parable of the sower and the seed, Jesus speaks about those who when they "hear the word, receive it with joy" but then "fall away." Jesus speaks about others "who hear" and start to grow, whose fruit "does not mature" (Luke 8:13,14) (III.2.11,12).

Calvin explains that such people do not "truly perceive the power of spiritual grace and the sure light of faith." The Lord has given them "such a sense of his goodness as can be felt without the Spirit of adoption" so that the Lord can better "convict them, and leave them without excuse." He says that "the elect alone have that full assurance which is extolled by Paul, and by which they are enabled to cry, Abba, Father," and God "effectually seals in them the grace of his adoption, that it may be sure and steadfast." He argues that in this process "there is nothing to prevent an inferior operation of the Spirit from taking its course in the reprobate" (III.2.11,12).[183]

Calvin continues to describe the difference between the faith of a true believer and that of a reprobate:

> We may add, that the reprobate never have any other than a confused sense of grace, laying hold of the shadow rather than the substance, because the Spirit properly seals the forgiveness of sins in the elect only, applying it by special faith to their use. Still it is correctly said, that the reprobate believe God to be propitious to them, inasmuch as they accept the gift of reconciliation, though confusedly and without due discernment; not that they are partakers of the same faith or regeneration with the children of God; but because, under a covering of hypocrisy, they seem to have a principle of faith in common with them. Nor do I even deny that God illumines their minds to this extent, that they recognize his grace; but that conviction he distinguishes from the peculiar testimony which he gives to his elect in this respect, that the reprobate never attain to the full result or to fruition. (III.2.11,12)

> When he shows himself propitious to them, it is not as if he had truly rescued them from death, and taken them under his protection. He only gives them a manifestation of his present mercy. In the elect alone he implants the living root of faith, so that they persevere even to the end. Thus we dispose of the objection, that if God truly displays his grace, it must endure for ever. There is nothing inconsistent in this with the fact

---

[183]"Reprobate" is Calvin's term for those whom God has elected to damnation.

of his enlightening some with a present sense of grace, which afterwards proves evanescent. Although faith is a knowledge of the divine favor towards us, and a full persuasion of its truth, it is not strange that the sense of the divine love, which though akin to faith differs much from it, vanishes in those who are temporarily impressed. The will of God is, I confess, immutable, and his truth is always consistent with itself; but I deny that the reprobate ever advance so far as to penetrate to that secret revelation which Scripture reserves for the elect only. (III.2.11,12)

Thus their knowledge stopping short leaves them only mid-way; not so much confirming and tranquilizing the mind as harassing it with doubt and disquietude. Very different is that feeling of full assurance which the Scriptures uniformly attribute to faith—an assurance which leaves no doubt that the goodness of God is clearly offered to us. This assurance we cannot have without truly perceiving its sweetness, and experiencing it in ourselves. (III.2.11,12)

In order for a Christian to be sure of their election and that their faith is certain, Calvin says, they must be convinced that they have the "special faith" of the true believer, the "peculiar testimony which he gives to his elect," "the living root of faith," "that secret revelation which Scripture reserves for the elect only." Believers will always lack assurance of true faith unless they are "perceiving its sweetness, and experiencing it in ourselves" (III.2.11,12).

Joel Beeke writes,

Calvin's piety is evident in people who recognize through *experiential faith* that they have been accepted in Christ and engrafted into his body by the grace of God. In this "mystical union," the Lord claims them as his own in life and in death. They become God's people and members of Christ by the power of the Holy Spirit.[184]

Calvin and the Word

Certainty derived from an experience is often seen as a characteristic of Arminianism. But we see that its roots are found in Calvinist theology. The Calvinistic experience of union with Christ, although perhaps not as dramatic, is no different than Augustine's or August Francke's conversion experiences. It is

---

[184]Beeke, "Calvin on Piety," in *The Cambridge Companion to John Calvin*, p. 125 (emphasis added).

the point at which Christ comes to live in a person and empowers that person to be justified by faith and to live a God-pleasing life.

Guenther Haas writes,

> The radical transformation of the human heart that enables sinners to understand and embrace God's moral order for their lives is the result of union with Christ. This doctrine lies at the heart of Calvin's teaching on salvation and the Christian life. . . . He dwells in them so that they are progressively able to live the life that is pleasing to God. Thus, Christians have communion with Christ in both the grace of justification and sanctification.[185]

Calvin left his followers to search for evidence that they were truly converted and united with Christ and that evidence is found in Christian living—sanctification. It is inevitable that Calvinists emphasize the latter grace, the grace of sanctification.

Francis Pieper writes in his *Christian Dogmatics,*

> At the outset Calvinists often give a perfectly correct definition of saving grace, namely, God's gracious disposition in Christ or the forgiveness of sins; but by their denial of universal grace, and the resultant denial of the appropriation of grace through the Word of the Gospel and the Sacraments, they are carried into the Roman current of "infused grace" as the basis for the remission of sins.[186]

Calvin's emphasis on piety, his teaching of union with Christ, the logic of double predestination, and certainty of faith based on an analysis of one's faith experience all shifted the meaning of the Gospel as it had been shifted in the previous 1,500 years of Church history. Rather than, "How can I find a gracious God?" the question was, "How can I be united with God; how can I find the power I need to live a moral life?"

Hesselink notes some distinctive features of Calvin's theology.[187] One distinctive feature concerns the relation of the Word and the Spirit. He writes,

---

[185]Haas, "Calvin's Ethics," in *The Cambridge Companion to John Calvin,* p. 94.

[186]Pieper, *Christian Dogmatics,* Vol. III, p. 121.

[187]Hesselink is drawing on material from German theologian Walter Kreck's essay, titled "Die Eigenart der Theologie Calvins" (The Distinctiveness of Calvin's Theology).

Calvin differs from Luther who emphasized the objective external Word in his conflict with the spiritual radicals. The result was the danger of uniting Word and Spirit so completely as to run the risk of identifying them. Calvin, in contrast to Luther, maintains that the Word and Spirit are intimately related but that they must also remain distinct and not to be identified. The Spirit can, and sometimes does, work without the Word.[188]

I think it would be difficult to prove that Luther so united the Word and the Spirit that he ran the risk of identifying them. Yet he did link them more closely than Calvin. In Calvinism there is little or no concept of what Lutherans call "the means of grace."

God's Word is our link to God, for it is through the Word that the Spirit tells us about Christ. On the other hand, Calvin's gospel was more general. It was a series of blessings given us by God. As such, it did not come through a message but through the Spirit himself who comes directly from God to the elect. One might say that the Spirit himself is the means of God's grace.

Through the Spirit, the Christian begins to receive God's blessings. He or she gradually grows in piety, accepts Scripture as God's Word, and knows he or she is forgiven. Conversion in Calvin becomes a bare work of the Spirit, not necessarily the Spirit working through the message of Christ. Calvin valued God's Word highly. But to him, the union of the believer with God must precede a Christian's appreciation of the Word. Calvin writes,

> The testimony of the Spirit is more excellent than all reason. For as God alone is a fit witness of himself in his Word, so also the Word will not find acceptance in men's hearts before it is sealed by the inward testimony of the Spirit. The same Spirit therefore, who spoke through the mouth of the prophets must penetrate into our hearts to persuade us that they faithfully proclaimed what had been divinely commanded. (I.7.4)

Since the grace of God is the message of his favor in Christ rather than a group of general blessings, Luther took some statements of Scripture more literally than Calvin did. For example, baptism actually saves us because it washes away our sins and gives us a good conscience toward God. We find God's forgiveness in the Lord's Supper because Christ's body and blood are really there, and it is

---

[188]Hesselink, "Calvin's Theology," in *The Cambridge Companion to John Calvin*, p. 80.

through Christ's body and blood that God established his New Covenant with us.

The second distinctive feature that Hesselink notes is about the importance of the mystical union of Christ with Christians. Scripture certainly teaches the union that exists between Christ and his people, and so does Martin Luther. But Hesselink contrasts Luther and Calvin like this: "To contrast Luther and Calvin on this point, it could be said that Luther lays more emphasis on Christ *for us*, Calvin on Christ *in us*."[189] Here again we see the shift of emphasis, from forgiveness to piety.

Calvin on apologetics

This distinction between Calvin and Luther has implications for how a Christian uses apologetic arguments. Evangelical/Reformed Christians emphasize the act of receiving Christ into one's life, or being "born again." Conversion, therefore, becomes more of a process leading to a person's reception of the Spirit rather than the simple act of believing what Scripture says about God's forgiveness in Christ. Modern apologetic arguments become part of the process leading to the decision to receive Christ, or the Spirit, into one's life. But modern apologetics cannot easily be made to fit with the point of time when the Spirit leads a person to realize the guilt of their sin and believe in Christ's forgiveness. This will come up again in more detail later in this book.

For Calvin, apologetic arguments are ineffective unless the Holy Spirit convinces a person of their truth. Avery Dulles explains:

> Arguments such as these, Calvin maintains, are available in case anyone should wish to establish the validity of the Scriptures on rational grounds; but Calvin admits that the arguments do not give full conviction unless confirmed by the inner testimony of the Spirit. On the other hand, he who has the Spirit's own witness does not need to rely on any rational arguments.[190]

Calvin said he could easily refute the skeptic using the evidence for the truth of Scripture. Nevertheless, that would be fruitless. Bernard Ramm explains: "These evidences are no match for human depravity. If we use them as battering rams against unbelief they simply bounce back! The wall remains firm.

---

[189]Hesselink, "Calvin's Theology," in *The Cambridge Companion to John Calvin*, p. 81 (emphasis added).

[190]Dulles, *A History of Apologetics*, p. 150.

Therefore, Calvin does not appeal to them as the means whereby human unbelief is crashed through."[191]

Calvin will not find assurance in apologetic arguments, but neither does he find assurance first and foremost in Scripture. A person must first have the Spirit. Calvin writes, "Scripture will ultimately suffice for a saving knowledge of God only when its certainty is founded upon the inward persuasion of the Holy Spirit." (1.8.13).[192] Thus Calvin depends on the direct intervention of the Holy Spirit to supply proof that Scripture and Christianity are true. In a sense, that is his apologetic.

Luther on the other hand, reflecting the teaching of Scripture, would say that the Word has power and that the Spirit comes to us through the Word of God and the Gospel message. This makes the Word self-authenticating, needing no apologetic argument for its truth.

Summary of Calvin

Let's quickly sum up Calvin's influence on Christianity and on the use of apologetics.

Calvin gave more emphasis to piety than to forgiveness. The emphasis on piety or morality is the starting point of lifestyle and worldview apologetics. This can be contrasted with an emphasis on the guilt of sin and God's solution in Christ.

Calvin's gospel was that people could have a union with Christ, through which God bestows all his blessings, especially justification and sanctification.

Calvin taught that God was never illogical. For example, Calvin succumbed to logic when wrestling with Scripture's teaching of predestination. Thus he helped establish a climate of reason, which is conducive to the use of apologetics.

Calvin taught that human beings are corrupt but maintain a sense of the divine, which gives them the ability to recognize the truth when they see it. Evidentialists and even presuppositionalists believe that this sense establishes a common ground between them and unbelievers.

Calvin taught that only those who are united with Christ can verify that the Word is true. While Calvin had a negative view of apologetics, this opened the

---

[191]Ramm, *Varieties of Christian Apologetics,* p. 175.
[192]See *The Institutes* I.1.7,8 for more on Calvin's view of apologetics.

door for teaching that God's Word is not self-authenticating, but must be verified by an outside source.

Jacob Arminius (1560–1609)

Not long after Calvin died, a Dutch Calvinist theologian, Jacob Arminius, rose to prominence in the Reformed Church. In many ways he remained a Calvinist, and although he started a new strain of Calvinism, it was built on the Calvinism we have examined in the previous pages. Arminius changed the shape of Calvinism by rejecting Calvin's teaching of double predestination. Arminius believed that God wants all people to be saved. This belief, shared by many, started a controversy among the followers of Calvin. Arminius died in the middle of the controversy, but his position created a division among Calvinists.

Both he and Calvin were faced with the question of why some come to faith and why others don't. Calvin found his answer in double predestination. Arminius focused on the many passages of Scripture that say God wants all people to be saved, and he found his answer in the teaching of *prevenient grace.*

In a nutshell, the teaching of prevenient grace says that when Adam and Eve fell into sin, they completely lost the image of God, became totally sinful, and were completely unable to come to faith. However, on account of Christ's work, God gave them and their descendants prevenient grace. This grace did not lead them to faith. Rather, it "came before" faith (which is what *prevenient* means) and gave them the spiritual ability to choose to believe.

In his book *Prevenient Grace,* W. Brian Shelton explains,

> The distinction between Calvin and Arminius on this point [total depravity] is not really the quantity of sin that every person inherits from Adam, but whether human beings remain in a state of absolute depravity before God. Calvin believed . . . that humankind is left in a state of total depravity. On the other hand, Arminius believed that God's grace subsequentially extends to all humankind, so that we now live in a state of repaired depravity.[193]

Arminius' idea of prevenient grace takes the ball out of God's court and puts it into the court of the unbeliever who hears the Gospel. The unbeliever is ultimately accountable for deciding to accept Christianity (or, to use Calvin's

---

[193]W. Brian Shelton, *Prevenient Grace: God's Provision for Fallen Humanity* (Anderson, IN: Francis Asbury Press, 2014), p. 105.

teaching of union with the Spirit, to accept the Spirit—or Christ—into one's heart). One's conversion often comes at the end of a process in which a person becomes more and more receptive to Christianity and finally invites Christ into their lives. We will return to the role of a conversion experience in modern apologetics in a future chapter.

John Wesley (1703–1791)

Ted Campbell in his book *The Religion of the Heart* traces the various Pietist type movements that surfaced throughout Europe after the Reformation. In his description of Methodism, Campbell writes, "Throughout their works, John and Charles Wesley stressed the centrality of religious experience and the way of salvation punctuated by such experiences."[194]

John Wesley yearned to be rid of his sins. He described the ten years before his true conversion as a time when he was in "abject bondage to sin."[195] At that time he was a believer but had still not received the grace he was looking for. He confessed that his service to sin was "unwilling, but still I served it."

Wesley described his bondage: "I was still 'under the law,' not 'under grace.'" Here he is quoting Paul: "For sin will have no dominion over you, since you are not under law but under grace" (Romans 6:14). There is a big difference, however, between what Paul was saying in that passage and how Wesley interpreted it. Wesley was looking for a special type of grace that would raise him above his daily struggle against his sinful nature. Paul, on the other hand, was saying that believers are under God's gracious favor in Christ, who has freed them from the curse and demands of the law. Now they can serve God willingly because they are no longer driven by the Law. This parallels what he wrote in Romans 6:11,12: "You also must consider yourselves dead to sin and alive to God in Christ Jesus. Let not sin *therefore* reign in your mortal body, to make you obey its passions."

Wesley was looking for an infusion of power, not for a greater understanding of the freedom from the law which he had in Christ. He had observed that power at work in others and he wanted it for himself. We see that in the portion of his autobiography leading up to his conversion experience.

---

[194]Ted Campbell, *The Religion of the Heart* (Columbia, SC: University of South Carolina Press, 1991), page 121.

[195]The autobiographical material that follows is taken from *Wesley's Journal,* Volume 1. This volume contains Wesley's journal from October 14, 1735 to November 29, 1745. The references below are from May 1738, paragraphs 10–14.

A friend named Peter Boehler had explained "salvation by grace" to him. To Boehler, grace meant grace as received by Augustine or August Francke. But Wesley doubted that such grace was real. He wrote, "Nor could I therefore allow it be true, till I found some living witnesses of it." Boehler replied that he could show him witnesses—the very next day, if Wesley wanted. Wesley wrote,

> The next day, he came again with three others, all of whom testified, of their own personal experience, that a true living faith in Christ is inseparable from a sense of pardon for all past, and freedom from all present sins. They added with one mouth, that this faith was the gift, the free gift of God; and that he would surely bestow it upon every soul who earnestly and perseveringly sought it.

Wesley resolved to seek the grace they had spoken about. In that context he recorded his well-known conversion,

> I continued thus to seek it (though with strange indifference, dullness, and coldness, and unusually frequent relapses into sin) till Wednesday, May 24. I think it was about five this morning that I opened my Testament on those words: "There are given unto us exceeding great and precious promises, even that ye should be partakers of the divine nature."

> In the evening I went very unwillingly to a society in Aldersgate Street, where one was reading Luther's Preface to the Epistle to the Romans. About a quarter before nine, while he was describing the change which God works in the heart through faith in Christ, I felt my heart strangely warmed. I felt I did trust in Christ, Christ alone for salvation, and an assurance was given me that he had taken away *my* sins, even *mine*, and saved *me* from the law of sin and death.[196]

In this quotation, we see a mixture of two things that gave Wesley his assurance of salvation in Christ. The first was the knowledge found in Scripture, that Christ took away the guilt of every sin he had committed and that he had saved him from the law, which arouses sin and ends in death. The second was the experience of finding his heart strangely warmed, which backed up the words of Scripture.

Ted Campbell writes, "John and Charles Wesley had been preaching a more or less Evangelical doctrine of justification, even before they themselves

---

[196]End of quotations from John Wesley's journal.

experienced the assurance of pardon."[197] That is, they were *already* preaching the message that led Luther to faith in the first place and subsequently changed his life. But the change in life Wesley yearned for had not happened. The message from Luther he heard at Aldersgate did not supply the change he was looking for. Stanley Ayling wrote that from the time of his meeting with Boehler, Wesley "looked with anxious expectation toward his own instantaneous conversion."[198] And because such a conversion did not occur as he desired, he often doubted that he was a Christian. Ayling writes, "That there is any clear boundary between Wesley's life before [the meeting at Aldersgate] and his life after that point is a proposition which accords neither with the apparent facts nor even with a good deal of Wesley's own subsequent testimony."[199]

He came to teach that after coming to faith, Christians should seek an experience of the Holy Spirit. He called this "entire sanctification" or "perfectionism." This experience did not make a person perfect, but it provided the power to live one's Christian life on a higher moral plane than faith in Christ's forgiveness was able to provide. In this we see a parallel between Wesley and the German pietist August Francke. In fact, Wesley was attracted to German Pietism and made a trip to Germany to visit a group of Moravian pietists. He was deeply influenced by their piety and worked to incorporate their spirit into his own life. Peter Boehler, mentioned previously, was a Moravian pietist.

Methodism spread to America and had a profound effect on American religion. Methodists were active in the First Great Awakening in the 1730s and 1740s. Methodist preachers followed the westward expansion in the U.S. in the 19th century and conducted countless revival meetings in towns established on the frontier. At the end of the 19th century, the Methodist church in the United States started to liberalize and lost its original fervor. The concern of many over this trend led to the Holiness Movement, and the Holiness Movement became the springboard of the Pentecostal Movement.

All believers treasure God's forgiveness

A bewildering variety of denominations and nondenominational groups have spun off from the original Calvinistic Reformed churches. But these groups, even the ones who follow the teachings of Jacob Arminius, all retain the broad

---

[197]Campbell, *The Religion of the Heart*, page 120.

[198]Stanley Ayling, *John Wesley* (New York: William Collins Publishers, Inc., 1979), p. 92.

[199]Ayling, *John Wesley*, p. 93.

contours of Calvin's teachings. They can all be called Reformed. Out of these movements grew the many denominations, particularly the Arminian church bodies, that take part in the modern apologetic movement.

What we have been describing is not merely faith versus reason. Rather, it is a shifted form of Christianity, which is reasonable, versus the Scripture's message of sin and grace, which is not. In the next chapter, we'll see that the shift we have been describing underlies modern apologetic thinking.

Before we continue, however, we must remind ourselves that wherever God's Word is read and proclaimed, people are hearing that they are forgiven in Christ and are living in the hope of this truth. They are looking beyond the brief time they will spend in this world—looking ahead to their eternity with God. Regardless of what blessings God gives, withholds, or takes away in this life, believers in Christ know that perfection awaits them in the presence of God's glory—all because of the cross.

This is not a matter of confessional Lutherans versus non-Lutherans. Many Lutherans have succumbed to the Gospel in its shifted form. And many who belong to a church where the shifted Gospel has become formalized in its theology nevertheless share the hope given in Scripture.

We have examined the problems that surfaced in already in the early Church. We should also listen to the hope shared by Christians in every time and place.

The hymn "O Sacred Head, Now Wounded" is attributed to Bernard of Clairvaux, the 12th century Catholic abbot and mystic we met earlier in the previous chapter. In the 17th century, Lutheran hymn writer Paul Gerhardt prepared a lengthier version for Lutheran churches. Here are some of the words he used that were written by Bernard:

> My burden in your passion,
> Lord, you have borne for me,
> For it was my transgression,
> my shame, on Calvary.
> I cast me down before you;
> wrath is my rightful lot.
> Have mercy, I implore you;
> Redeemer, spurn me not!
>
> What language shall I borrow
> to thank you dearest Friend,

For this, your dying sorrow,
your pity without end?
Oh, make me yours forever,
and keep me strong and true;
Lord, let me never, never
outlive my love for you.

Lord, be my consolation,
my shield when I must die;
Remind me of your passion
when my last hour draws nigh.
My eyes will then behold you,
upon your cross will dwell;
My heart will then enfold you—
who dies in faith dies well![200]

John Donne, English poet, scholar, and clergyman, expressed his hope in "A Hymn to God the Father." In lofty yet beautiful words he expressed his thanks to God.

Wilt thou forgive that sin where I began,
which was my sin, though it were done before?
Wilt thou forgive that sin, through which I ran,
and do run still, though still I do deplore?
When thou hast done, thou hast not done,
for I have more.

Wilt thou forgive that sin which I have won
others to sin, and made my sin their door?
Wilt thou forgive that sin which I did shun
a year or two, but wallow'd in a score?
When thou hast done, thou hast not done,
For I have more.

I have a sin of fear, that when I have spun
my last thread, I shall perish on the shore;
But swear by thyself, that at my death thy Son
shall shine as he shines now, and heretofore;
And, having done that, thou hast done;

---

[200]*Christian Worship* (Milwaukee: Northwestern Publishing House, 2021), 105: 2-4.

I fear no more.[201]

Stuart Townend, who attends an independent church in Brighton, England, has written hymns that express the Gospel in clear and winsome terms and have given them a place in confessional Lutheran churches. The hymn "How Deep the Father's Love for Us" is a good example.

How deep the Father's love for us
How vast beyond all measure
That He should give His only Son
To make a wretch His treasure.
How great the pain of searing loss;
The Father turns His face away
As wounds which mar the Chosen One
Bring many sons to glory.

Behold the man upon a cross
My sin upon His shoulders.
Ashamed, I hear my mocking voice
Call out among the scoffers.
It was my sin that held Him there
Until it was accomplished.
His dying breath has brought me life
I know that it is finished.

I will not boast in anything
No gifts, no power, no wisdom,
But I will boast in Jesus Christ.
His death and resurrection.
Why should I gain from His reward?
I cannot give an answer.
But this I know with all my heart:
His wounds have paid my ransom.[202]

The issues covered so far in this book, although discussed in the context of the modern apologetic movement, could be discussed in many other contexts. That's because they are at the heart of proclaiming and holding on to the faith delivered to all the saints.

---

[201]John Donne, "A Hymn to God the Father," https://www.poetryfoundation.org/poems/44115/a-hymn-to-god-the-father, accessed May, 2023.
[202]*Christian Worship*, 523:1-3.

Summary

A Catholic monk, Martin Luther, realized that the meaning of the Gospel had changed. After a great struggle in trying to become righteous as God demanded, Luther realized that peace with God was his because of Jesus' work, which he could have simply through faith.

After the Reformation, the same problems that surfaced in the early Church began to surface in Lutheranism and in other Reformation churches. This shift affected the Lutheran church through people like Philip Melanchthon and August Francke. It shaped the foundation of the Swiss Reformation under John Calvin.

Calvin's theology is the foundation of most Protestant churches in America. It has taken on various forms under the influence of men like Jacob Arminius and John Wesley. Although the message of forgiveness through faith is taught in most Wesleyan churches, the emphasis is often on piety and receiving the power to live an upright life.

Chapter 8

Modern Apologetics Depends On a Reasonable Gospel

Introduction

Earlier in this book, we offered a quotation from Boa and Bowman that bears repeating. They pointed out that in the apologetic world, "there is significant debate concerning the theological foundation of apologetics. To some extent apologetic methods are related to the way one understands and interprets Christian theology."[203] Boa and Bowman are referring to differences within the Evangelical/Reformed world. But if differences exist among apologists whose doctrines come from a single source, John Calvin, you have to wonder about the differences in apologetics between Calvinistic churches and Lutheran churches.

Martin Luther uncovered the Gospel of Jesus Christ after it lay buried for centuries under the teachings of a Church infected with the "gospel" of infused grace. Scripture teaches the good news that Christ died for the world's sins. Therefore, all people can know and believe that Christ died for *their* sins. Scripture teaches that in Christ there is peace between God and the world. Therefore all people are at peace with God.

These blessings became ours when the Son of God died on a Roman cross and they were proven to be ours when Jesus rose from the dead. This is the Gospel we are defending. A believer's life of piety and service to God have a vital place in the Christian faith. But what we are defending is where it all starts—with the good news that sin was paid for at the cross and that God is at peace with the world.

Every apologist must answer questions like these: Do my apologetic arguments lead directly to a defense of this Gospel? Do my apologetic arguments defend the world's forgiveness won through Christ's death on a cross? Do my

---

[203]Boa and Bowman Jr., *Faith Has Its Reasons*, p. 40.

apologetic arguments defend the truth that God, in Christ, is at peace with the world? And can an apologetic argument defend the fact that forgiveness and peace is mine through faith alone?

In the last two chapters, we isolated several important new doctrines that redefined, or "shifted," Christianity and the Gospel. In these chapters we also saw that although Calvin and Arminius taught justification by faith, they did not completely shake themselves of ideas that led to the shift.

In this chapter, we'll see that the same ideas are held by churches that have given rise to the modern apologetics movement.

The goal of modern apologetics: to prove that Christianity is reasonable

Proving that Christianity is reasonable: to unbelievers

The modern apologetic goal is to assemble as many reasons as possible to prove that Christianity is reasonable and to use those reasons to convince people to become Christians.

In the introduction to *Five Views on Apologetics*, Steven Cowan says that apologetics "is an intellectual discipline that is usually said to serve at least two purposes: (1) to bolster the faith of Christian believers, and (2) to aid in the task of evangelism." It works to refute "objections to the Christian faith," and to offer "positive reasons for the Christian faith."[204]

Boa and Bowman list four things apologetics offers.

> *Proof:* Apologetics involves marshaling philosophical arguments as well as scientific and historical evidence for the Christian faith. *Defense:* It clears away any intellectual difficulties that nonbelievers claim stand in the way of their coming to faith. More generally, the purpose of apologetics as defense is not so much to show that Christianity is true as to show that it is credible. *Refutation:* This function focuses on answering, not specific objections to Christianity, but the arguments non-Christians give in support of their own beliefs. *Persuasion:* It persuades them to apply its truth to their life. Persuade people to commit their lives and

---

[204]Cowan, *Five Views on Apologetics,* p. 8.

eternal futures into the trust of the Son of God who died for them. We might also speak of this function as evangelism or *witness*.[205]

But they add, "Not everyone agrees that apologetics involves all four of these functions."[206]

The general goal of modern apologetics is to demonstrate that a person can become a Christian without sacrificing reason and logic. According to Boa and Bowman, the arguments used by classical and evidentialist apologists "are thought to prepare the mind for faith."[207] According to John W. Montgomery, the evidence brings nonbelievers to a point of decision in which they have good grounds for "experientially trying" Christianity. He writes, "Absolute proof of the truth of Christ's claims is available only in personal relationship with Him; but contemporary man has every right to expect us to offer solid reasons for making such a total commitment."[208]

In *Thinking About Christian Apologetics*, James Beilby writes, "The task of apologetics, therefore, is to acknowledge the multiplicity of reasons that might motivate a person's distrust toward the Gospel of Jesus Christ and offer them sound arguments for the reasonability of a stance of basic trust."[209]

Clark Pinnock says that apologists do not need to coerce people to accept the Christian faith "but to make it possible for them to do so intelligently."[210] He hopes that classical apologetics will be more and more used "as a reasonable modern response to reasonable modern people who want a reason why they should believe."[211]

Apologist Alister McGrath describes how he understands the relation between apologetics and evangelism. He says that conversion is ultimately the task of evangelism. Apologetics, on the other hand, is about preparing the way for such a conversion: "It's about clearing away rubble and debris in the path of evangelism."[212] It does this by showing that Christianity is "rationally

---

[205]Boa and Bowman Jr., *Faith Has Its Reasons*, pp. 5 –6 (abridged; emphasis original).

[206]Boa and Bowman Jr., *Faith Has Its Reasons*, p. 7.

[207]Boa and Bowman Jr., *Faith Has Its Reasons*, p. 236.

[208]Montgomery, *Faith Founded on Fact*, p. 40.

[209]Beilby, *Thinking About Christian Apologetics*, p. 173.

[210]Sproul, Gerstner, and Lindsley, *Classical Apologetics*, p. 126, quoting Clark Pinnock, *Set Forth Your Case: Studies in Christian Apologetics* (Nutly, NJ: Craig, 1968), p.41.

[211]Sproul, Gerstner, and Lindsley, *Classical Apologetics*, p. 16.

[212]McGrath, *Mere Apologetics*, p. 78.

compelling."[213] He writes, "Apologetics can be thought of as getting a serious conversation under way by getting our audience interested and intrigued by the deep questions we are exploring. Apologetics begins the conversation; evangelism brings it to its conclusion."[214]

Lee Strobel talks about the place apologetics played in his own decision to become a Christian. In *The Case for Christ,* he writes, "Yes, I have to take a step of faith as we do in every decision we make in life. But here's the crucial distinction: I was no longer trying to swim upstream against the strong current of evidence; instead, I was choosing to go in the same direction that the torrent of facts was flowing. That was reasonable, that was rational, that was logical."[215] He describes his feeling when he finally came to faith, "I know that some people feel a rush of emotions at such a moment; as for me, however, there was something else that was equally exhilarating: There was a rush of reason."[216]

William Lane Craig sees an even broader goal for apologetics:

> If the Gospel is to be heard as an intellectually viable option for thinking men and women today, then it is vital that we as Christians try to shape American culture in such a way that Christian belief cannot be dismissed as mere superstition. This is where Christian apologetics comes in. If Christians could be trained to provide solid evidence for what they believe and good answers to unbelievers' questions and objections, then the perception of Christians would slowly change. . . . I'm saying that arguments and evidence will help to create a culture in which Christian belief is a reasonable thing. They create an environment in which people will be open to the Gospel.[217]

In another place Craig writes, "Apologetics is therefore vital in fostering a cultural milieu in which the Gospel can be heard as a viable option for thinking people. . . . It will be apologetics which, by making the Gospel a credible option for seeking people, gives them, as it were, the intellectual permission to believe."[218]

---

[213]McGrath, *Mere Apologetics,* p. 19.

[214]McGrath, *Mere Apologetics*, p. 123.

[215]Lee Strobel, *The Case for Christ: A Journalist's Personal Investigation of the Evidence for Jesus* (Grand Rapids: Zondervan, 2016), p. 290.

[216]Strobel, *The Case for Christ,* p. 291.

[217]Craig, *On Guard,* p. 18.

[218]Morley, *Mapping Apologetics,* p. 221, quoting William Lane Craig, *Reasonable Faith,* p. 19.

Proving that Christianity is reasonable: to believers

Modern apologists argue that if apologetics plays a role in calming the skeptic in the hearts of unbelievers, it is also an important tool for calming the skeptic in the hearts of Christians.

In *A History of Apologetics* Catholic theologian Avery Dulles says that in addition to developing apologetic arguments for groups outside the church, apologists "came to recognize that every Christian harbors within himself a secret infidel. . . . Every Christian must somehow come to terms with the current objections to religious faith and weigh the legitimacy and rationality of his own commitment."[219]

John Frame puts it this way, "For the believer, apologetics gives *reassurance* to faith as it displays the rationality of Scripture itself."[220] He writes, "Believers themselves sometimes doubt, and at that point apologetics becomes useful for them even apart from its role in dialogue with unbelievers."[221]

Classical apologist William Lane Craig says, "Since almost all intelligent adult Christians are bombarded throughout their education and adult life with multifarious defeaters for Christianity, it seems that for a great many, if not *most*, people, *rational argument and evidence will be indispensable to the sustenance of their faith.*"[222]

Gary Habermas notes how much Christians should appreciate the evidence for Christ's resurrection that comes from outside Scripture: "Is there enough evidence for a rational person to be justified in concluding that Jesus' resurrection was a real event in history? Christians should be delighted to find that the evidence for Jesus' resurrection is extremely compelling."[223]

Modern apologists speak of a Christian's need to grow beyond a childhood faith. Joshua Chatraw, in *Apologetics at the Cross*, confesses: "All my life I had been desperately taught the 'whats' of Christianity, that is, the content of Christianity. Now I was desperately searching for what Timothy Keller calls

---

[219]Dulles,*A History of Apologetics,* pp. xx, xxiii.

[220]Frame,*Apologetics to the Glory of God,* p. 26 (emphasis added).

[221]Frame,*Apologetics to the Glory of God,* p. 2.

[222]William Lane Craig, "Classical Apologetics," in *Five Views on Apologetics*, ed. Stephen Cowan, p. 33 (emphasis added).

[223]Habermas and Licona, *The Case for the Resurrection of Jesus,* p 28.

the 'whys' of Christianity, the answer to the question, 'Why should I believe this?'"[224]

Tim Keller advises that Christians wrestle with the arguments of the skeptics as if they were their own: "It is no longer sufficient to hold beliefs just because you inherited them. Only if you struggle long and hard with objections to your faith will you be able to provide grounds for your beliefs to skeptics, *including yourself,* that are plausible rather than ridiculous or offensive."[225]

Some say that apologetics only leads to the point where the Holy Spirit takes over and convinces a person of the truth of the cross. At that point, it would seem, apologetics is no longer necessary. But such a position overlooks the ongoing struggle every Christian is engaged in: the struggle to answer the new and sometimes more serious doubts Satan continuously lays on their path.

A reasonable Gospel makes Christianity reasonable

Apologetics is not about whether a Christian ought to use logic and reason. Without logic and reason, we couldn't understand what God tells us in his Word. We could never figure out what God wants us to believe and how we should live as his sons and daughters. Nor could we rule out misinterpretations of Scripture.

Modern apologists, however, use logic to show that it's reasonable to become and remain a Christian. They claim that all the teachings of Scripture are reasonable, including the Gospel message. John Frame, a Calvinist apologist, speaks about two aspects of conversion:

> The question, "Where does faith come from?" may be taken in two senses. (1) It may be asking the *cause* of faith. In that sense, the answer is that God causes faith by his own free grace. This is the regenerating work of the Holy Spirit. (2) Or it may be asking the *rational basis* of faith. In that sense, the answer is that faith is based on reality, on truth. It is in accord with all the facts of God's universe and all the laws of thought that God has ordained. The Holy Spirit does not cause us to believe lies. He is the God of truth, and so he makes us believe what is

---

[224]Joshua D. Chatraw and Mark D. Allen, *Apologetics at the Cross: An Introduction for Christian Witness* (Grand Rapids: Zondervan, 2018), p. 19.

[225]Keller, *The Reason for God,* p. xxiii (emphasis added).

true, what is in accord with all evidence and logic. The faith he gives us agrees with God's own perfect rationality.[226]

Frame also writes: "The Spirit does not work 'magically,' but through reasons. Therefore, the Spirit's work is not to persuade us of something for which there are no rational grounds, but rather to persuade us by illumining the rational grounds which obligate us to believe. Spirit-created faith is not 'blind.'"[227]

But can the Gospel *as preached by Paul* ever be acceptable to human reason? And who says that for the Holy Spirit to work, his message must be acceptable to human reason? When we studied the meaning of the Gospel in part 2, we heard Paul say that unbelievers consider the Gospel *unreasonable*. The Gospel is "folly to those who are perishing . . . . a stumbling block to Jews and folly to Gentiles" 1 Corinthians 1:18,23). Paul says that it is God's will to save those who believe by using "the folly of what we preach" (1 Corinthians 1:21).

As we have seen, Scripture puts the emphasis on the heart of the Gospel, namely, the forgiveness of sins. To be sure, the Gospel is good news that God also gives Christians a wide range of blessings. But God's forgiveness in Christ and the work of his Son, who reconciled him to us, is the reason why God gives us all the blessings we have. Paul writes, "He who did not spare his own Son but gave him up for us all, how will he not also with him graciously give us all things?" (Romans 8:32). In fact, only in the context of living under the cross does God's way of dealing with us make our lives understandable—whether he bestows a blessing that makes life easier or a blessing that makes life more difficult.

References to Jesus' forgiveness can be found in modern books on apologetics. But as I read apologetic literature, I found only a few who worked to define the meaning of the gospel.[228] The books I read spoke of "the Gospel" and the

---

[226]John Frame, "Presuppositional Apologetics," in *Five Views on Apologetics*, ed. Stephen Cowan, pp. 209-210.

[227]Morley, *Mapping Apologetics*, p. 107.

[228]For example, Gary Habermas writes, "Through Jesus one can have sins forgiven and receive eternal life. This good news or gospel is the primary message that Christians should want to share" (Habermas, and Licona, *The Case for the Resurrection of Jesus*, p. 25). Gregory Koukl in his book *Tactics* advocates the "Columbo" approach to apologetics. He tries to get people to say what they know and then show the logical need for the Gospel. This works particularly well to talk about sin, and it leads directly to the forgiveness people have in Christ. His questions bring "commonsense intuitions to the surface so I could use them to make a point." He gives a couple good examples on pages 98-108, the second being his conversation with a lawyer whose sense of right and wrong, justice, and accountability for committing a crime easily led to the message

Christian "worldview," but they seldom defined the Gospel as God's grace in Christ alone, and the Christian worldview was often little more than a moral outlook on life with God at the center.

The Gospel in Evangelical/Reformed Christianity as defined by John Calvin, Jacob Arminius, and John Wesley certainly includes the message of God's forgiveness. But they define the Gospel in a more general way than Lutherans do—as good news that if we are united with Christ, submit ourselves to God, and follow his will, all of his blessings can be ours.

In modern apologetic literature, the Law is often mixed with the true Gospel as it has been through much of Church history. When that happens, the Gospel becomes more in tune with how human beings think salvation ought to be achieved. In the process, it becomes a matter of doing. It becomes associated with the way human beings naturally think. And it becomes more reasonable and subject to human proofs and argumentation.

The possession of God's image makes Christianity reasonable

In general, modern apologists build on a foundation that contributed to the shift of the gospel. It has an overly optimistic view of people's innate spiritual abilities.

Mankind was created in the image of God. That much is clear. But what exactly is the image of God? And to what extent was the image of God affected by the fall into sin? What does it mean that Christians are renewed in the image of God?

Answers to these questions range far and wide, and we will look carefully at what Scripture says about the image of God later in the chapter on apologetics and God's grace. But for now, we will simply point out that modern apologists, especially those whom we are calling worldview apologists, believe that people retain the image of God. They believe that by virtue of their having the image of God they have some amount of spiritual life remaining in them. Also, the

---

that God punished his Son for the sins people commit (Gregory Koukl, *Tactics* [Grand Rapids: Zondervan, 2019] p. 106). John Frame summarized the Gospel: "Scripture tells us of our creation in God's image, our fall (through Adam) into sin, and God's free gift of his only Son to die an atoning death for our sin and to raise us up with him in newness of life." And he gets to the heart of the Christian faith: "So biblical religion alone, of all the religions and philosophies of the world, provides an authoritative answer to the question that we most need to ask of God: How can my sins be forgiven?" (Frame, *Apologetics to the Glory of God*, p. 122).

image of God gives all people a natural affinity to God and a sense of how God wants them to live. Because they retain the image of God, the apologist and the unbeliever are on common ground and the unbeliever will find the apologist's message reasonable.

The teaching that people retain the image of God is present in John Calvin's writings. Recall that Calvin taught "total depravity," that is, that human beings are totally sinful. However, he also taught that people retain the image of God. John Frame explains the position of strict Calvinist Cornelius Van Til on the image of God: "Van Til argues that part of that image is knowledge of God, which, though repressed (Rom.1), still exists at some level of his thinking. That is the point of contact to which the apologist appeals."[229]

Frame explains his own position: "It is to that clear self-revelation of God to the unbeliever, known but suppressed, that the apologist appeals."[230] When an apologist urges unbelievers to come to faith in the Christian religion, the apologist is simply asking them to accept what they know is true by virtue of the image of God in them. Frame writes, "If faith is in accord with God's own thought, then it will also be in accord with human reasoning at its best, which images God's."[231]

Most modern apologists, especially evidentialists, would agree with Frame. But evidentialists (who usually reject Calvin's teaching of total depravity) give the image of God even more credit than strict Calvinists do. They believe that the image of God gives people far more natural ability to process truth and arrive at the proper conclusions than Calvin or Van Til ever did.

---

[229]Frame, *Apologetics to the Glory of God,* p. 83.

[230]John M. Frame, *Cornelius Van Til: An Analysis of His Thought* (Phillipsburg, NJ: P&R Publishing, 1995), p. 116.

[231]Frame, "Presuppositional Apologetics," in *Five Views on Apologetics*, ed. Stephen Cowan, p. 210. These quotations help us understand the "presuppositional" position on apologetics versus the "evidentialist" position. Most evidentialists are Arminians and have an optimistic view of mankind's natural spiritual ability to conclude that Christianity is truth. They credit this to mankind's being created in the image of God. In other words, most Arminian apologists simply present evidences for the truth of Scripture and its message, confident that their unbelieving listeners will be able to understand it and draw the "obvious" conclusions about the Christian religion. On the other hand, Calvinist presuppositionalist theologians believe the point of contact in an unbeliever lies much deeper, almost completely suppressed by the effects of sin. A presuppositionalist simply presents the truth, hoping that God will lead the truth to resonate with the truth the unbeliever possesses because of the image of God. But the evidentialist believes he can argue with the unbeliever and seek a verdict for Christianity based on the evidence. Nevertheless, all Evangelical/Reformed apologists believe they can reach unbelievers because all people possess the image of God.

All members of Evangelical/Reformed churches believe with John Calvin that people retain the image of God and have a certain natural ability to understand the truth. This, in turn, makes Christianity reasonable.

The presence of natural yearnings makes Christianity reasonable

When Christians hear the word *apologetics* today, many think about historical proofs from history for the reliability of Scripture and the verification of it message. But modern apologetics is more than that. Many apologists work less with historical evidence and more with showing that only Christianity can satisfy people's natural human yearnings. These natural yearnings provide apologists with a hook to show that it's reasonable to believe in Christianity.

The belief that people retain the image of God leads directly to the teaching that people have natural human yearnings originating from the image of God within them. These yearnings are considered noble and should be affirmed.[232]

Alister McGrath writes, "As Augustine, Pascal, and Lewis appreciated, recognizing we are made in the image of God provides a powerful theological foundation for Christian apologetics. It means we are able to use the deep human longing for truth, beauty, and goodness to help people orient themselves toward their ultimate origin and goal—the living and loving God."[233]

Augustine taught that the human heart was restless until it found its rest in God. This restlessness, at least in Augustine's case, resulted in a yearning to live according to God's will. Subsequent Roman Catholic theology taught that people retain the image of God. It taught that people have free will and want to love and serve God but need the help of the sacraments offered in the Catholic Church to find the power they need to do that.

Catholic theologians have long based an apologetic on human needs and yearnings. Avery Dulles quotes a number of 19th-century theologians on this topic. John Henry Neumann wrote, "There is only one Religion in the world which tends to fulfill the aspirations, needs, and foreshadowings of natural faith and devotion," for Christianity alone has a "definite message addressed to all mankind." Isaac Hecker, a 19th century Catholic priest and church leader,

---

[232] Avery Dulles credits Schleiermacher with this approach. Dulles writes, "Schleiermacher was perhaps the first to construct a thoroughgoing 'inner apologetic' that proceeds through the progressive unfolding of the innate longing for communion with God." (*A History of Apologetics*, p. 213).

[233] McGrath, *Mere Apologetics,* p. 104.

wrote, "The innate yearning of the human heart for authority and for union with something greater than itself is uniquely satisfied by the Catholic Church with her authoritative teaching and her sacramental system." Gilbert Chesterton, English convert to Catholicism and apologist, wrote, "We are born in a state of confusion, and when we arrive at faith we realize that Christianity is more natural to us than we to ourselves."[234]

These yearnings can take various forms. In a culture where God's will, the final judgment, and Heaven and Hell are clearly in view, people yearn for an infusion of power to be worthy of God and worthy to go to Heaven. In a more mystical context, people yearn for a more intimate experience of God's presence.

In an increasingly secular world, recent generations have grown up on self-help books, or on promises that money, power, and possessions lead to happiness. But deep down inside they sense that there is more to life. They yearn for purpose and fulfillment. These yearnings, it is claimed, can be traced back to the voice of God's image within them. And regarding such people, John Frame writes, "A person with a wish to be fulfilled is often on the road to belief."[235]

The following quotations will present a general picture of what apologists are thinking when they use human yearnings to spread the Gospel. The quotations will be organized around some key apologists. Please don't assume that the apologists agree on every point.

C. S. Lewis was a modern pioneer on using yearnings in apologetics. James Beilby writes that Lewis developed "a powerful argument for Christian belief from the universal sense of longing humans feel."[236] Beilby says,

> One commentator has suggested that "there probably is no more dominant theme in all of Lewis's writings than this theme of longing." Drawing on Pascal, Lewis held that humans have a "god-shaped hole" in their hearts. . . . Similarly, he argued, "If we are really the products of a materialistic universe, why is it we don't feel at home in it?"[237]

James Carnell was the second president of Fuller Theological Seminary (1954–1959) and an apologist early in the modern movement. Brian Morley writes,

---

[234]Dulles, *A History of Apologetics,* pp. 248, 253, 293.

[235]Frame, *Apologetics to the Glory of God,* p. 37.

[236]Beilby, *Thinking About Christian Apologetics,* p. 77.

[237]Beilby, *Thinking About Christian Apologetics,* pp. 77-78, quoting Will Vaus, *Mere Theology: A Guide to the Thought of C. S. Lewis* (Downer's Grove, Ill.: InterVarsity Press, 1998), pp. 21, 23.

"Carnell's characteristic point of contact is the felt needs of the nonbeliever. If believers do not show nonbelievers how Christianity meets their needs, they will conclude that the Gospel is irrelevant."[238] Carnell explains that the apologist is helping the unbeliever find true wisdom, which he defines:

> Wisdom is a matter of choosing the right value, just as rationality is a matter of choosing what is consistent. . . . Thus the apologist works on more than one level, showing that Christianity is both rational and desirable, and that the alternatives are neither—that the choice is between Christianity and despair.[239]

John Warwick Montgomery, who began his career early in the movement and is still an active apologist today, says that "the Christian revelation satisfies the deepest general and particular longings of the human heart." Among those longings he lists (1) a sound value system, (2) an integrated personality, (3) genuine friendship, (4) the assurance that life has a purpose, and (5) ultimate fulfillment.[240] He then goes on to show how Christianity satisfies those longings.

British scientist, theologian, and apologist Alister McGrath speaks about the human desire for God. He calls it a "homing instinct for God." He explains,

> Although this takes various forms, it is most commonly framed in terms of a deep human awareness of a longing for something that is not possessed but whose attraction is felt. Christian apologists argue that this deep sense of yearning for something transcendent is ultimately grounded in the fact that we are created to fellowship with God, and will not be fulfilled until we do so.[241]

McGrath notes that this "homing instinct for God" is one of the elements of human existence that can serve as touch points for apologists as they make a case for Christianity. McGrath calls them "clues" that can get unbelievers to think about reality. They can be used "to help others begin to realize how Christianity has the power to make sense of what we think, see, and experience—and to

---

[238]Morley, *Mapping Apologetics,* p. 162, quoting Edward John Carnell, *The Kingdom of Love and the Pride of Life* (Grand Rapids: Eerdmans, 1960), p. 6.

[239]Morley, *Mapping Apologetics,* p. 164, quoting Edward John Carnell, *A Philosophy of the Christian Religion* (Grand Rapids: Eerdmans, 1952), pp. 44-45.

[240]Montgomery, *Tractatus Logico-Theologicus,* p. 190.

[241]McGrath, *Mere Apologetics,* p. 109.

encourage them to discover Christianity's deeper power to transform human life."[242]

Timothy Keller, who pastored the fast-growing Redeemer Church in New York City, explains the goal of his ministry: "You cannot, therefore, deal with your hideousness and self-absorption through the moral law, by trying to be a good person through an act of will. You need a complete transformation of the very motives of your heart."[243] That is why Jesus was born: "The Son of God was born into the world to begin a new humanity, a new community of people who could lose their self-centeredness, begin a God-centered life, and, as a result, slowly but surely have all other relationships put right as well. . . . If you respond to him, all your relationships will begin to heal." [244]

Keller talks about forgiveness, but it is usually in view of what it means for life: "I discovered, however, that the gospel contained the resources to build a unique identity. In Christ I could know I was accepted by grace not only despite my flaws, but because I was willing to admit them."[245]

In a particularly eye-opening statement, Chatraw and Allen not only define natural human yearnings, but they create an antithesis between using human yearnings and using the message of sin—at least as it is preached in the churches they are familiar with: "This use of the law to reveal sin is biblical, and in some contexts, it still can prove quite effective in initial conversations. However, for many today, being presented with a divinely instituted law that 'they must be accountable to, or else' will not fit within their current framework."[246]

Gregory Koukl is a refreshing contrast to this emphasis. In his book *Tactics*, he also refers to the longings people have without God. But he does the opposite of what Chatraw and Allen recommend. He is concerned with sin and guilt.

In one place, Koukl describes a young lady, Holly Ordway. Holly was an atheist. At one point she began to realize how empty she was: "However satisfied I declared myself intellectually, . . . atheism . . . was a terrible place to live." She called that time in her life "the winter of her soul."[247] When she began to study Christianity, for the first time she realized that Christianity, not atheism,

[242]McGrath, *Mere Apologetics*, p. 95.
[243]Keller, *The Reason for God*, p. 184.
[244]Keller, *The Reason for God,* pp. 230, 231.
[245]Keller, *The Reason for God,* p. 287.
[246]Chatraw and Allen, *Apologetics at the Cross,* p. 248.
[247]Koukl, *Tactics*, p. 238.

described the world as she experienced it. But then, as Koukl explains, Holly went further. He writes, "The disturbing part for her was this: the brokenness that was real was also moral and personal. . . . She was guilty, and she knew it."[248]

Koukl talks about the similar experience of a French philosopher, Guillaume Bignon. Bignon was studying the New Testament but couldn't get past the question, Why did Jesus have to die? Koukl tells what Bignon related to him: "Then something unexpected happened. 'God reactivated my conscience,' he told me. 'That was not a pleasant experience. I was physically crippled by guilt, not knowing what to do about it.' Suddenly it dawned on him. 'That's why Jesus had to die. Because of *me*. Because of *my* guilt.'"[249]

Koukl describes his debate with Deepak Chopra, prominent in the New Age Movement. Koukl felt outgunned. But instead of pitting himself against Chopra, he decided to pit Chopra against Christ. He says, "This move is especially important when dealing with the most offensive detail of our message—which is also *the* central claim of the gospel—that Jesus is the Savior of the world, the only one capable of rescuing us from judgment and restoring us to a relationship with the Father."[250]

Those examples from Koukl are not the norm in modern apologetic literature. They illustrate what in this book we are calling sin and grace apologetics. There is no doubt that sinful self-love ends badly and causes people to lose purpose and fulfillment. And using other people for one's own goals certainly affects life adversely. But that is not proclaiming the guilt of sin and the cross of Christ, which is why the Christian Church exists.

Christianity is reasonable when mixed with philosophy

It is claimed that a Christian's use of philosophy was affirmed already in the early church: "Standing on [Mars Hill in Athens], Paul began the 'great conversation' that continues to this day between the philosophers and Jesus and his followers. Very early in the history of the Christian church, Christianity and philosophy became partners."[251]

---

[248]Koukl, *Tactics*, p. 239.

[249]Koukl, *Tactics*, p. 239 (emphasis original).

[250]Koukl, *Tactics*, p. 242 (emphasis original).

[251]Paul Gould and Richard Davis, eds., *Four Views on Christianity and Philosophy,* pp. 15,16.

Some early church leaders accepted philosophy wholeheartedly. Others, like the early church father Tertullian, believed that philosophy has no place in Christianity. Gould and Davis picture the relationship like this: "Most Christians found a middle way between these extremes [completely accepting or rejecting philosophy], bringing philosophy and Christianity into conversation in order to understand truth and live the good life."[252]

Philosophy is a big word for a relatively simple activity: human beings using human reason to understand the physical world and reality in general. Philosophers categorize and define all areas of knowledge.

Many aspects of philosophy are good. Norman Geisler credits philosophy with providing the essential tools "of clear, consistent, and correct thinking."[253] This is what Martin Luther was referring to when he stood firm in his teachings at the 1521 Diet of Worms. He stated that he would not take back his writings unless shown by Scripture *and by reason* that the conclusions he drew from Scripture were faulty.

However, modern apologists see a greater role for philosophy. Norman Geisler put it this way: "Apologetics involves the construction of good arguments or the supplying of good evidence in justification of the basic truth of Christianity," a task which "falls squarely on the shoulders of philosophy."[254]

Gould and Davis, in their introduction to *Four Views on Christianity and Philosophy*, speak of "a natural affinity between philosophical reflection and religious instinct" and credit this affinity for "a positive relationship" between the two.[255] We note that this affinity became greater the more Christianity shifted from a focus on God's forgiveness and the blessings Christians have in Christ to people's natural human yearnings to live a pious and blessed life. This shift provided more opportunity for philosophy to supplement the truth found in Scripture.

Philosophy helps modern apologists in various ways. It helps apologists understand the culture in which people live. Philosophical thought helps uncover the emptiness of the secular worldview and the blessings of the Christian

---

[252]Paul Gould and Richard Davis, eds., *Four Views on Christianity and Philosophy,* p. 16.

[253]Boa and Bowman Jr., *Faith Has its Reasons,* p. 79, quoting Norman Geisler and Paul Feinberg, *Introduction to Philosophy: A Christian Perspective* (Grand Rapids: Baker, 1980), p. 76.

[254]Boa and Bowman Jr., *Faith Has Its Reasons,* p. 79, quoting Geisler and Feinberg, *Introduction to Philosophy,* p. 78.

[255]Gould and Davis, eds., *Four Views on Christianity and Philosophy,* p. 11.

worldview. It helps show that Christianity is the only religion with a worldview that works.

The philosophy of religions helps apologists evaluate non-Christian religions. According to James Beilby, it "analyzes the basic concepts and themes in religious traditions as well as the arguments for and against the claims made by adherents of those religious traditions."[256] In the process, Christianity is shown to be far superior.

Classical apologists use philosophy to construct proofs for the existence of God. They often use the arguments of ancient philosophers, especially Plato and Aristotle. Norman Geisler writes, "One task of Christian philosophy, then, is to work on a pre-evangelistic level to get the outsider to look around the edges or through the cracks of his glasses, or to take them off and *try a set of 'theistic glasses' on* for size."[257]

Boa and Bowman say that apologists who focus on questions of creation and evolution, on the historical evidence for the truth of the scriptural accounts, or on evidence for the reliability of the text of Scripture must also use philosophy. "They see philosophy as an essential tool for clarifying concepts and presuppositions and for analyzing the methods used in science or other disciplines, including theology."[258]

John Frame wants to base faith on Scripture alone. But he admits that Scripture benefits from philosophy and is confident that problems arising from this can be avoided. He writes,

> Theology is not a mere reading of Scripture, but an application of Scripture to human need. Theology, therefore, always faces the danger of elevating the theologian's own conception of human need to a position of equal authority to, or even greater authority than, the Scripture. But through prayer and meditation on God's Word, that danger can be avoided.[259]

Nevertheless, some apologists offer a stern warning, like the early church father Tertullian did. Boa and Bowman quote Gordon Clark's warning, "When

---

[256] Beilby, *Thinking About Christian Apologetics*, p. 31.

[257] Kenneth D. Boa, and Robert M. Bowman Jr., *Faith Has its Reasons*, quoting Norman Geisler and Paul Feinberg, *Introduction to Philosophy,* p. 78 (emphasis added).

[258] Kenneth D. Boa, and Robert M. Bowman Jr., *Faith Has its Reasons*, pp. 316.

[259] Frame, *Apologetics to the Glory of God*, pp. 18-19.

evangelicals articulate their faith in terms of worldview, they make philosophy foundational to their theology, and this philosophy prevents them from grasping the literal message of Scripture."[260]

A conversion experience makes Christianity reasonable

Throughout the history of the Christian Church, many believers have sought and found a personal conversion experience. Augustine's conversion experience is viewed as a prototype. For years Augustine tried to put off his troublesome sins. All his efforts were in vain until God intervened and through a powerful experience enabled Augustine to give up his sins.

The experience found in association with the Catholic Church satisfies most. There the people have access to an infusion of power by which they can live God-pleasing lives. But others yearned for a more profound experience through which they can achieve a higher communion with God and a deeper commitment to the Christian life.

After the Reformation, various movements arose that featured a conversion experience. Having such an experience was a mark that one's faith was true. Calvin taught that one became a Christian by being united with Christ. This teaching moved the assurance of Christianity beyond simple faith and into the realm of experience. This teaching would be the theological foundation for the many experiential religious groups that spun off from him and from Jacob Arminius. Methodists also were considered genuine Christians only if they could relate a conversion experience of some sort.

Conversion experiences differ in nature and intensity. An experience can be described as a quiet moment when a person receives Christ into their life. It can happen at the finale of an evangelism meeting. It can be the anticipated outcome of a youth camp, where the day ends with a devotion and if they haven't done so, campers are invited to give their lives to Christ. Or it can be a high-level Pentecostal/charismatic experience accompanied by sign gifts and other phenomena.

---

[260]Boa and Bowman Jr., *Faith Has Its Reasons*, p. 369, quoting Gordon Clark, "The Nature of Conversion: How the Rhetoric of Worldview Philosophy Can Betray Evangelicals," in *The Nature of Conversion: Evangelicals and Postliberals in Conversation*, ed. Timothy R. Phillips and Dennis L. Ockholm (Downer's Grove, IL: InterVarsity Press, 1996), pp. 201-218.

Those who have one kind of experience don't always acknowledge the experience of others. Traditional Baptists, whose milder experience is a result of asking Christ into their lives, might consider the Pentecostal/charismatic experience with its accompanying gifts to be false, even demonic. And the latter might consider a milder Baptist experience to be less than what God intends Christians to have.

Having a conversion experience is more difficult than simply rejoicing in Christ's forgiveness. Parents who belong to a traditional evangelical church and want their children to have an experience know they cannot force their children to take that step. So they pray. They ask God to let their children see how much they need God and accept him into their lives. Those in Pentecostal/charismatic churches do the same. But not all have the experience. So they wait, seek advice from others who have experienced the same problem, and avail themselves of opportunities and venues where they *might* catch the spirit. But being in venues where everyone has the spirit except them makes this very uncomfortable.

Lutherans find this difficult to understand, but it is real. In many Lutheran churches there are members who came out of churches that stressed a conversion experience, and they understand this quite well.

Many Lutherans, even Lutheran pastors, label the experience as nothing more than emotionalism. But it is far from emotionalism. Typical is one of the conversion experiences described by Lee Strobel in his book *The Case for Christ*. He describes the conversion of a Jewish boy who was struggling with addiction and trying to figure out who Jesus was. One time, when he and his friends decided to get away into the desert, God spoke to him. He relates the event: "He convinced me, experientially, that he exists. And at that point, out in the desert, in my heart I said, 'God, I accept Jesus into my life. I don't understand what I'm supposed to do with him, but I want him. I've pretty much made a mess of my life; I need you to change me."[261]

Of the elements we have identified in Church history and in the modern apologetic movement, such an experience supplies the most certain proof of the truth of Christianity. One would imagine that apologists in the Evangelical/Reformed world would find their certainty in apologetic arguments. After all, that is the focus of their books and seminars. But it's not that simple. To many, the proof provided by a conversion experience trumps all the evidence and

---

[261]Strobel, *The Case for Christ,* p. 196.

arguments they have at their disposal. We'll let William Lane Craig, perhaps the greatest living apologist, explain this.[262]

Craig came to faith in high school "not through any careful consideration of the evidence," but because of the hope he saw in his Christian classmates.[263] As he explains, his increasing expertise in apologetics never became more important to him than his reception of the Holy Spirit.

He attended Wheaton College, which in the 1960s had become filled with skepticism and cynicism. Religious questions were answered by reason alone. Craig, however, refused to accept the arguments of reason against Christianity. "For me," he said, "Christ was so real and had invested my life with such significance" that if there was a conflict between the two, reason would have to take a back seat.[264] As he began to read books on Christian apologetics, he became convinced that "reason might be used to show the systematic consistency of Christian faith without thereby becoming the basis of that faith."[265] In simpler terms, Craig distinguishes between "*knowing* Christianity to be true and *showing* Christianity to be true."[266] He says that "rational arguments and evidence play an essential role in our *showing* Christianity to be true," but they "play a contingent and secondary role in our personally *knowing* Christianity to be true."[267]

According to Craig, a Christian's conversion is a dramatic experience that cannot be argued away. It happened; case closed. There is no rational proof against it.

Craig explains,

> I have elsewhere characterized the witness of the Holy Spirit as self-authenticating, and by that notion I mean that the experience of the Holy

---

[262]Craig, "Classical Apologetics," in *Five Views on Apologetics*, ed. Stephen Cowan, pp. 26ff.

[263]Craig, "Classical Apologetics," in *Five Views on Apologetics*, ed. Stephen Cowan, p. 26.

[264]Craig, "Classical Apologetics," in *Five Views on Apologetics*, ed. Stephen Cowan, p. 27.

[265]Craig, "Classical Apologetics," in *Five Views on Apologetics*, ed. Stephen Cowan, p. 27.

[266]Craig, "Classical Apologetics," in *Five Views on Apologetics*, ed. Stephen Cowan, p. 28 (emphasis original).

[267]Craig, "Classical Apologetics," in *Five Views on Apologetics*, ed. Stephen Cowan, p. 28 (emphasis added). This is Alvin Plantinga's point, and Craig credits him for developing it philosophically.

Spirit is (1) "unmistakable and truthful for the one who has it and attends to it;" (2) "that such a person does not need supplementary arguments or evidence in order to know and to know with confidence that he is in fact experiencing the Spirit of God;" (3) it is "an immediate experiencing of God' himself:" (4) *in certain contexts* the experience of the Holy Spirit will imply the apprehension of *certain truths* of the Christian religion, such as 'God exists,' 'I am reconciled to God,' 'Christ lives in me,' and so forth; (5) "that such an experience provides one *not only with a subjective assurance of Christianity's truth, but with objective knowledge of that truth;*" and (6) "that arguments and evidence incompatible with that truth are overwhelmed by the experience of the Holy Spirit for the one who attends fully to it."[268]

When it comes to knowing one's faith to be true, therefore, the Christian will not rely primarily on argument and evidence but on the gracious witness of God himself given to all his children by the indwelling Holy Spirit.[269]

Like most modern apologists, Craig gives the Holy Spirit final credit for bringing a Christian to faith and for sustaining that person's faith: "Conversion is exclusively the role of the Spirit." But like most apologists, he adds, "But we can rationally commend our faith to others in the confidence that some, whose hearts he has opened, will respond to the apologetic we present and place their faith in Christ."[270] He says that "in times of doubt, we should not only seek the face of the Lord, but strengthen ourselves by recalling these arguments and evidences."[271]

Apologetics in the Evangelical/Reformed context is intertwined with the "born again" conversion experience. Although the conversion and the resultant experience of the Holy Spirit is the most important element in their Christian faith, apologetics can play a key role in the process by which a person moves toward making his or her decision for Christ.

---

[268]Craig, "Classical Apologetics," in *Five Views on Apologetics*, ed. Stephen Cowan, pp. 29-30 (emphasis added, "veridical" changed to "truthful" in point 1, section slightly abridged).

[269]Craig, "Classical Apologetics," in *Five Views on Apologetics*, ed. Stephen Cowan, p. 36.

[270]Craig, "Classical Apologetics," in *Five Views on Apologetics*, ed. Stephen Cowan, p. 55.

[271]Craig, "Classical Apologetics," in *Five Views on Apologetics*, ed. Stephen Cowan, p. 54.

We will be returning to this point later in this book. But for now, please consider three points. First, in Scripture it's the message of God's grace in Christ that validates the Christian faith. That I am forgiven is the one message that is true for all and has the same result for all.

Second, in the longer quotation above, Craig says that a conversion experience "in certain contexts" will include various blessing, among others that "'God exists,' 'I am reconciled to God,' 'Christ lives in me,' and so forth."[272] Yet the phrase "in certain contexts" mitigates certainty. Conversion *always* results in knowing that in Christ God has reconciled me to himself, has forgiven my sins, and has established peace between him and us. In fact, it is these truths that the Spirit uses to lead a person to believe. It is not a conversion experience that is self-authenticating, but the word of the Gospel that is self-authenticating. If the conversion experience is the self-authenticating aspect of Christianity, then the door is open to authenticating Scripture and Christianity by using material not found in Scripture in order make Christianity reasonable and lead a person to have the experience of receiving Christ.

Third, the conversion experience always in some way involves the powers of the human will to cause it to happen.

Summary

Modern apologists want to make Christianity reasonable to unbelievers so it can be respectable to become a Christian. After the Reformation, the meaning of the Gospel again shifted from the message of forgiveness, to how people can best fulfill their natural yearnings for morality and the resultant blessings. Such yearnings are God-pleasing, it is said, because they stem from the image of God, which is supposed to remain in all people subsequent to the fall into sin. These natural desires are similar to the desires human philosophy attempts to address, creating an affinity between the two. These are among the cluster of ideas and emphases that together create a logical religion which can be promoted on the basis of rational arguments. In addition, the reception of Christ into one's life is the ultimate source of certainty in modern Calvinistic and Arminian churches. All of this makes Calvinism and its various offshoots a fertile seedbed for the apologetic movement.

---

[272]Craig, "Classical Apologetics," in *Five Views on Apologetics*, ed. Stephen Cowan, pp. 29-30.

Part 4
A Lutheran Looks at Apologetics

Chapter 9—By Grace Alone
Realize What Human Beings Are Like

Scripture describes human nature as having no power to contribute toward conversion. Modern apologetics assumes that people retain the image of God and for that reason have a desire to be in fellowship with him.

Chapter 10—By Scripture Alone
Embrace the Charge of Circular Reasoning

Scripture describes the role God's Word and the Holy Spirit play in how a person comes to faith. According to apologists, to be sure that Scripture and its message is true, they must be confirmed by information found outside of Scripture. The topic of *circular reasoning* is part of this chapter.

Chapter 11—Through Faith Alone
Never Settle for Less than 100 Percent Certainty

How Scripture describes the way a person comes to faith will shape how we use apologetics. Conversion is not a process leading to an experience. It is the point at which we realize sin and grace. The topic of certainty is found in this chapter.

Chapter 12—By Christ Alone
Give the Reason for Your Hope in Christ

Peter tells us to give a reason for our hope. This chapter is a study of 1 Peter 3:15.

Conclusion—Sin and Grace Apologetics

Chapter 9

By Grace Alone

Realize What Human Beings Are Like

Introduction

After the apostles died, the meaning of the Gospel changed. In our overview of Church history, we identified a cluster of teachings that are central to this change. We saw that the modern apologetic movement depends on this cluster of teachings.

The goal of Part 4 is to help Lutherans decide if modern apologetics ought to play a role in the Christian ministry. To organize this material, we'll use the traditional outline of Reformation teaching: (1) by grace alone, (2) by Scripture alone, (3) through faith alone, and (4) by Christ alone. We'll devote a chapter to each.

God's grace is his undeserved kindness to a world of sinners. He graciously sent his Son to take on himself the guilt of our sins and to bear God's punishment for sin in our place. He graciously made receiving the benefit of Jesus' life and death a matter of faith and not a matter of works. In Scripture, grace can also refer to the wide variety of gifts and blessings God gives to his people, especially gifts and motivation to serve God and each other.

Grace extends to our conversion. Our coming to faith is an undeserved gift, to which we contributed nothing: "For by grace you have been saved through faith. And this is not your own doing; it is the gift of God, not a result of works, so that no one may boast" (Ephesians 2:8,9). In this chapter we want to think about this facet of grace.

Modern apologetics depends on human spiritual ability

Over the years, the Christian Church adopted a relatively optimistic view about human spiritual abilities. They taught that people retain the image of God after they fell into sin, and for that reason they can participate in their conversion. Today's apologists do the same. To some degree, they say, people naturally resonate with the Gospel message—that is, with the Gospel message as they understand it.

Modern apologists assume it is reasonable to accept the Christian religion. The decision to accept Christianity may be hindered by sin, but it is still the logical thing to do. This assumption is based on the merger of several ideas.

First, they tend to view Christianity as a matter of piety. The focus is God's Law. Grace tends to become the power God gives people to keep the Law. Second, human beings retain the image of God, which creates an affinity between them and God and stimulates people to desire to become more like what God created them to be. Third, only Christianity resonates with what we know in our hearts by virtue of the image of God we possess, and satisfies our deepest yearnings.

Have people lost the image of God?

But do people retain the image of God? Did God send out his apostles to people influenced by the image of God within them, restless to be restored and reunited with God?

How a person uses apologetic arguments, particularly arguments from worldview apologetics, depends on whether people still possess the image of God or if people have lost the image of God. It depends on how much spiritual power human beings possess. And how one understands this issue will define the role of God's grace in conversion. So, in order to understand "by grace alone" we will look at what Scripture says about the image of God and about whether human beings retain it or not.

Scripture says that God created mankind "in his own image" (Genesis 1:27). Twice in Scripture God says that human beings must be respected because they were created in God's image. After the flood, God warned against murder. He told Noah, "Whoever sheds the blood of man, by man shall his blood be shed, *for God made man in his own image*" (Genesis 9:6). In the New Testament, James rebuked Christians for misusing their tongues, "With it we bless our

Lord and Father, and with it we curse people *who are made in the likeness of God*" (James 3:9).

Neither of the above passages lists characteristics of the image of God. And although they might imply that we retain the image of God, they don't necessarily say that.

Three other New Testament passages, however, help us understand what creation in the image of God means for us now. Those passage are Ephesians 4:23,24; Colossians 3:9,10; and 2 Corinthians 4:6. They are the only passages in Scripture that give us the information we are looking for.

In Ephesians 4:23,24, Paul urges Christians to "put off your old self, which belongs to your former manner of life and is corrupt through deceitful desires, and to be renewed in the spirit of your minds, and to put on the new self, *created after the likeness of God in true righteousness and holiness.*" Here Paul is addressing Christians, telling them to put off the old self—the sinful nature in which we were born—and put on the new self, which is characterized by "true righteousness and holiness." These qualities are defined as "the likeness of God." What is more, Paul says that the image of God is a characteristic of the new self—something we put on when we became Christians. And as new creations—made new through faith in Christ—we are being "renewed" in God's image.

Paul says much the same in Colossians 3:9,10: "Do not lie to one another, seeing that you have put off the old self with its practices and have put on the new self, which is being renewed in knowledge after the image of its creator." As God's people, we have put off the old self and its sinful practices and have put on the new self. The new self "is being renewed in knowledge," which is a characteristic of the image of God. We interpret this as a parallel to the "true righteousness and holiness" Paul spoke about in Ephesians 4:23,24. We might use Romans 12:2 as a parallel to these passages: "Do not be conformed to this world, but be transformed by the renewal of your mind, that by testing you may discern what is the will of God, what is good and acceptable and perfect."

In Colossians 3:9,10, Paul says that Christians are being "renewed" in knowledge. As in Ephesians 4:23,24, since we are being renewed in something, it means we have lost it. Nor is it a restoration of something we only lost in part. Scripture tells us what we were like before we came to faith. Paul describes what is going on in the hearts of unbelievers: "In their case the god of this world has blinded the minds of the unbelievers, to keep them from seeing the light of the gospel of the glory of Christ, who is the image of God" (2 Corinthians 4:4). Paul contrasts our natural blindness with the "sight" God is giving believers through the Holy Spirit: "And we all, with unveiled face, beholding the glory of the Lord, are being transformed into the same image from one degree of glory to another. For this comes from the Lord who is the Spirit" (2 Corinthians 3:18).

Paul also writes, "For God, who said, 'Let light shine out of darkness,' has shone in our hearts to give the light of the knowledge of the glory of God in the face of Jesus Christ" (2 Corinthians 4:6). Christ is the image of God. God has revealed to believers his glory, which is seen in the face of his Son. It is the glory of his forgiving love, the glory of his Son's sacrifice for us. As his children we reflect that glory.

These verses do not speak of the image of God as something we have by nature. Unbelievers do not have it. Believers are being transformed into it.

We can add to this Paul's contrast between faith and unbelief. It is much more radical than receiving the ability to do what deep down inside we want to do— much more radical than God giving us the power to satisfy our spiritual yearnings.

In Romans 3, quoting the Old Testament, Paul gives his commentary on the human condition. He wrote that "no one seeks for God," "no one does good, not even one," and "there is no fear of God before their eyes" (verses 11,12,18).

Paul describes the before and after of conversion like this.

Before:

> And you were dead in the trespasses and sins in which you once walked, following the course of this world, following the prince of the power of the air, the spirit that is now at work in the sons of disobedience— among whom we all once lived in the passions of our flesh, carrying out the desires of the body and the mind, and were by nature children of wrath, like the rest of mankind. (Ephesians 2:1-3)

And after:

> But God, being rich in mercy, because of the great love with which he loved us, even when we were dead in our trespasses, made us alive together with Christ. (Ephesians 2:1)

Therefore, if the image of God is the ability to do good and to serve God, and if by nature we can do nothing good, then it follows that we have lost the image of God in which we were created. And we begin to be *renewed* in God's image when we came to faith and as we mature in Christ.

What qualities are part of the image of God

The passages above contain all that Scripture tells us about the image of God. It is the ability to love God and serve him in holiness of life.

But throughout Church history, theologians have listed other qualities that are supposedly part of God's image and use this list to corroborate their view that people retain the image of God. They speculate that these characteristics must be part of the image of God because only human beings, created in God's image, have them. The most important of these qualities is the ability to engage in high level reasoning. Other qualities are self-consciousness, self-determinism, free will, the ability to sense the eternal, an awareness of God, a sense of right and wrong, and a sense of accountability for wrongdoing. But there is nothing like this list of qualities in Scripture; it is all speculation.

Some Lutheran theologians speak about the image of God in a wide sense and in a narrow sense. The narrow sense is the righteousness that all people lost but which believers are regaining in Christ. The wide sense is the qualities listed above. But this, too, is speculation. Scripture makes no such distinction.

Here's the point: Whenever theologians focus on the passages that specifically define the image of God and then view them in the light of passages that describe the depth of mankind's sin, they should conclude that human beings have lost the image of God.

True, human beings possess unique characteristics. We still have a sense of right and wrong. But these qualities are not necessarily part of the image of God. They can be viewed as gifts that God gave human beings to fulfill the work he assigned to them. In other words, mankind lost the image of God when they fell into sin, but God has allowed fallen mankind to keep certain gifts—tainted by sin as they are—to use for the good of society.

Whenever theologians focus on the qualities that *might be* included in the image of God, they conclude that people *have not lost* the image of God. The result is the idea that people still possess certain abilities that enable them to relate to God and provide a point of contact for a Christian witness. Some claim that people are dead in sin but still retain the image of God. In practice, however, this always ends up giving people some degree of spiritual life, and it provides a theological foundation for the argument that the Gospel is logical. This undermines the teaching of "by grace alone."

Scripture says only two things regarding the image of God. First, all people were created in the image of God, and this should shape how we treat our fellow human beings (Genesis 9:6 and James 3:9). And second, we were created in the image of God, we lost it, and in Christ we are renewed in the image of God and can live in righteousness and holiness once again. This takes the image of God off the table as a point of contact with an unbeliever and gives it a natural place as we describe sin and the need for God's grace.

Scripture and human yearnings

Worldview apologists assume that people retain the image of God, which generates God-pleasing yearnings. These yearnings serve as a touchpoint for doing apologetics.

But this is wrong for at least two reasons. First, for this form of apologetics to be valid, people *must be seeking* God and his blessings. Yet Scripture says that no one seeks God. Second, appealing to human needs and yearnings turns people inward and undermines true Christian service to God.

Christians praise God for many reasons, often because of a special blessing he has given them. But Christians serve God primarily because of what they have become in Christ. They serve God because they are free from the demands of the law and live in the freedom given them by Christ.

The apostles never tired of reminding their readers *why* they should hold on to their faith and battle against the sinful nature. And how creatively they did this, always relating it to what we are in Christ and never saying it is a way for people to satisfy their longings.

In Romans 6, Paul reminds his readers that when they were baptized, they died and rose with Christ. He tells Christians the implication of this for their lives:

> How can we who died to sin still live in it? Do you not know that all of us who have been baptized into Christ Jesus were baptized into his death? We were buried therefore with him by baptism into death, in order that, just as Christ was raised from the dead by the glory of the Father, we too might walk in newness of life. (verses 2-4)

Paul urged his readers to live God-pleasing lives because of the intimate connection that exists between them and the Savior:

> Now if we have died with Christ, we believe that we will also live with him. We know that Christ, being raised from the dead, will never die again; death no longer has dominion over him. For the death he died he died to sin, once for all, but the life he lives he lives to God. So you also must consider yourselves dead to sin and alive to God in Christ Jesus. Let not sin therefore reign in your mortal body, to make you obey its passions. (Romans 6:8-12)

Through faith in Christ's death—which was our own death—we came to life. And since we are dead to sin in Christ, as long as we live on earth we want to put to death the sin that remains in us.

Jesus and the apostles continued to make that point in other ways. We have believed the Gospel and "having been set free from sin, [we] have become slaves of righteousness" (Romans 6:18). Because we died to the law and rose with Christ, we now "serve in the new way of the Spirit and not in the old way of the written code" (Romans 7:6).

"We love," John wrote, "because he first loved us" (1 John 4:19). We wash each other's feet because "I . . . your Lord and Teacher, have washed your feet" (John 13:14). We give to others because, although Jesus was rich, "yet for your sake he became poor, so that you through his poverty might become rich" (2 Corinthians 8:9).

If we become lethargic in our service to God and others, we must wake up because our "salvation is nearer to us now than when we first believed. The night is far gone; the day is at hand. So then let us cast off the works of darkness and put on the armor of light" (Romans 13:11–12). If we carelessly encourage a brother or sister in Christ to do things that go against their conscience, we are in danger of destroying the faith of a person "for whom Christ died" (Romans 14:15).

God's grace, which guides and motivates us to serve others, has appeared. This grace brings

> salvation for all people, training us to renounce ungodliness and worldly passions, and to live self-controlled, upright, and godly lives in the present age, waiting for our blessed hope, the appearing of the glory of our great God and Savior Jesus Christ, who gave himself for us to re-

deem us from all lawlessness and to purify for himself a people for his own possession who are zealous for good works. (Titus 2:11-14)

Paul rebuked sin in no uncertain terms because a life of unrepentance and sin will end in Hell. He makes it clear that we have a sinful nature and will suffer its desire to control us until the day we enter Heaven. At the same time, he points us to the victory we have in Christ and to the Spirit at work within us: "But if by the Spirit you put to death the deeds of the body, you will live" (Romans 8:13).

In the heart of the book of Revelation, Christ gives us the big picture:

Now the salvation and the power and the kingdom of our God
and the authority of his Christ have come,
for the accuser of our brothers has been thrown down,
who accuses them day and night before our God.
And they have conquered him
by the blood of the Lamb
and by the word of their testimony,
for they loved not their lives even unto death.
Therefore, rejoice, O heavens and you who dwell in them!
But woe to you, O earth and sea,
for the devil has come down to you in great wrath,
because he knows that his time is short! (12:10-12)

This is the Christian worldview. Worldview apologetics requires a continual analysis of the culture in order to describe the Christian message in terms relevant to the current generation. True, workers in Christ's Church want to understand the culture in which they serve. Their work requires this. But the message of sin and grace is the same for all time and for all cultures. The kingdom of God, built on Christ's sacrifice, has come. All authority belongs to Christ because he died and rose. Satan has been robbed of his power because he can no longer argue that we are guilty of sin and deserve God's wrath. Satan has been conquered by the blood of Christ shed for all. He is conquered every day when the Gospel is proclaimed and people of all cultures come to realize that God is at peace with them.

This is our Christian culture. The specific place and time in which we live will shape our ministry at a limited level, relatively speaking. But people of all cultures can define the Christian Church and the Church's ministry as Peter defined it:

> Blessed be the God and Father of our Lord Jesus Christ! According to his great mercy, he has caused us to be born again to a living hope through the resurrection of Jesus Christ from the dead, to an inheritance that is imperishable, undefiled, and unfading, kept in heaven for you, who by God's power are being guarded through faith for a salvation ready to be revealed in the last time. (1 Peter 1:3-5)

None of this is possible if Christianity is centered on my wishes, my needs, my hopes, my yearnings. All of it is possible when Christianity is centered on God's unexpected yearning that all come to faith.

Scripture teaches election to faith

Scripture's teaching of election is a corollary to the teaching of "by grace alone." From beginning to end, Scripture tells us that a Christian's salvation begins with God's looking for us and finding us, not with our looking for God and finding him. In fact, Scripture takes God's intentions back into eternity past when he chose to bring us to faith.

The teaching of election comes up in many places of Scripture to comfort and give confidence to those who believe. When Peter confessed that Jesus was the coming Savior, Jesus pointed to God as the source of his faith: "Blessed are you, Simon Bar-Jonah! For flesh and blood has not revealed this to you, but my Father who is in heaven" (Matthew 16:17). And in his prayer for all Christians at the Last Supper, Jesus told Peter and the others that the choosing did not start with them but with him: "You did not choose me, but I chose you and appointed you to go and bear fruit—fruit that will last" (John 15:16 NIV84). And he thanked his Father for giving him those whom he, the Father, had chosen: "I have manifested your name to the people whom you gave me out of the world. Yours they were, and you gave them to me, and they have kept your word" (John 17:6).

When Elijah complained that he was the only believer left among the Israelites, God answered him, "*I have kept for myself* seven thousand men who have not bowed the knee to Baal" (1 Kings 19:18 quoted by Paul in Romans 11:4). Paul then applied this to the Jews of his day, "So too at the present time there is a remnant, chosen by grace" (Romans 11:5).

In Romans 8:29,30, Paul described each Christian in Rome as someone whom God predestined:

> For those whom he foreknew he also predestined to be conformed to the image of his Son, in order that he might be the firstborn among many brothers. And those whom he predestined he also called, and those whom he called he also justified, and those whom he justified he also glorified.

Ephesians 1 is a grand hymn of praise to God for his grace in electing us:

> Blessed be the God and Father of our Lord Jesus Christ, who has blessed us in Christ with every spiritual blessing in the heavenly places, even as he chose us in him before the foundation of the world, that we should be holy and blameless before him. In love he predestined us for adoption to himself as sons through Jesus Christ, according to the purpose of his will, to the praise of his glorious grace, with which he has blessed us in the Beloved. (1:3-6)

The good things Christians do are always the result of God's work within them: "For we are his workmanship, created in Christ Jesus for good works, which God prepared beforehand, that we should walk in them" (Ephesians 2:10).

When Paul thought about the reception the Thessalonian Christians had given him, he looked behind the scenes and came to this conclusion: "For we know, brothers loved by God, that he has chosen you, because our gospel came to you not only in word, but also in power and in the Holy Spirit and with full conviction" (1 Thessalonians 1:4-6).

Finally, Peter called the Christians to whom he wrote, "God's elect, strangers in the world" (1 Peter 1:1 NIV84). He reminded them that they were "a chosen race, a royal priesthood, a holy nation, a people for his own possession, that you may proclaim the excellencies of him who called you out of darkness into his marvelous light" (1 Peter 2:9).

The teaching of election should also temper one's use of apologetic arguments, just as it tempers all forms of talking to others about the Gospel. The desire to prove the Gospel true must always be abandoned in favor of speaking the Gospel, knowing that God will bring his elect to faith when they hear what his Son has done for them.

Methods that depend on God's grace

A discussion of apologetics must include another question, To what extent should Christians follow *the way* the New Testament witnesses proclaimed and defended the Gospel? In other words, what methods are God-pleasing when speaking to people who have lost the image of God, have no natural yearnings for the Gospel, but among whom we know there are people whom God has elected to come to faith?

Determining methods, tools, and approaches to use in the ministry can be complicated. Often, the discussion is set in the framework of "description and prescription." The argument goes like this: Things that Scripture "describes" the early Church as doing are not necessarily a "prescription" for how the Church should carry out its work today.

This is true at a certain level. How should the local parish be structured today? What musical instruments should Christians use? Scripture does not prescribe answers to those questions.

But there is a higher sense in which this discussion should be carried out. In Scripture, *description very often becomes prescription.* For example, Jesus said to his disciples, "Come, follow me, and I will make you fishers of men" (Matthew 4:19). So we listen to Jesus, watch how he gathered people into his kingdom, and take the description of his ministry—not the clothes he wore, not his mode of transportation from place to place, not the venue he used when he preached—but how he used the law, how he defined the kingdom of God, and how he urged people to live.

Paul did the same. He urged the Philippians to follow his pattern of ministry. Of course this meant that the Church should teach the same thing as he taught. But we should also imitate his life and ministry. He urged the Philippians, "Brothers, join in imitating me, and keep your eyes on those who walk according to the example you have in us" (3:17). Timothy was to use Paul's example as the pattern for his own ministry: "You, however, have followed my teaching, my conduct, my aim in life, my faith, my patience, my love, my steadfastness, my persecutions and sufferings" (2 Timothy 3:10,11). How Paul carried out his work of proclaiming and defending the Gospel left a pattern for Timothy to follow: "Follow the pattern of the sound words that you have heard from me, in the faith and love that are in Christ Jesus" (2 Timothy 1:13). Paul was confident that Timothy could pass on his, that is, Paul's example, to the next generation of believers: "Set the believers an example in speech, in conduct, in love, in faith, in purity. Until I come, devote yourself to the public reading of Scripture, to exhortation, to teaching" (1 Timothy 4:12,13). In short, by telling Timothy to watch what he said and did and to imitate him, Paul was turning descriptive elements of his ministry into "prescriptive elements" for Timothy and for us.

So what's the point? The point is that if we are to promote and defend the Gospel in a God-pleasing way, we must not only be clear about the Gospel we are defending, we must search out and follow the pattern of ministry laid down by Jesus and Paul. At the very least, we should watch Paul and ask if he would use the same methods we are planning to use. We should look closely at the content of Paul's letters and ask if our approach finds support there. Above all, we should ask if our Gospel is the same as his.

In regard to modern apologetics, we should ask if Paul used apologetics as it is defined and used today. Would arguments and evidence of modern apologetics have been on his mind when he said, "For the weapons of our warfare are not of the flesh but have divine power to destroy strongholds. We destroy arguments and every lofty opinion raised against the knowledge of God, and take every thought captive to obey Christ" (2 Corinthians 10:4,5)?

With that question in mind, we scour his letters in vain to find a hint of worldview apologetics or appealing to people's human yearnings as his springboard. His strategy was to proclaim the cross of Christ in a sinful world. His main "cultural" consideration was the worldview held by all people in all cultures, namely, a worldview in which idols replaced the true God and in which their worship life was completely overrun by the idea that people must earn the favor of the gods.

When one views culture and worldview in this way, it is clear why Paul had to depend on God's grace alone if his message was to produce fruit. If human beings have lost the image of God, which is what Scripture tells us, then there was nothing positive that Paul could latch on to and use as a touchpoint for the Gospel. We have outlined Paul's touchpoints above—the natural knowledge of God, of sin, and of God's judgment on sin. These facts, and not human yearnings, must guide the Church's methods and strategies for ministry.

Summary

Christians are saved by grace alone. This refers to the work Jesus did for us and to the work of the Holy Spirit in leading us to faith.

Modern apologists tend to depend on the logic of apologetic arguments to lead an unbeliever to faith. The apologetic touchpoint with an unbeliever is his or her yearnings that stem from the image of God.

Scripture, however, teaches that all people lost the image of God and have no true, God-pleasing yearnings. Scripture teaches that the Holy Spirit works through the message of sin and grace to lead a person to believe in the cross of Christ. That we are saved by God's grace is clearly shown through Scripture's teaching of election. Jesus' and the apostles' method of spreading the Gospel was simple. They preached the Gospel.

Chapter 10

By Scripture Alone

Embrace the Charge of Circular Reasoning

Introduction

Only people who know they were dead in sin can thank God for the new life they have in Jesus. In the last chapter, we saw how *worldview apologetics* casts a different light on what we are by nature. It depends on mankind's retention of the image of God, on natural yearnings that come from it, and on methods designed to appeal to those yearnings. Its goal is to prove that Christianity is true by demonstrating that it alone satisfies human yearnings for God and for meaning in life.

In this chapter we will look at *evidentialism*, another arm of the modern apologetics movement. Here the focus is the Word of God and how historical evidence affects its reliability.

Calvin taught that God gives his spirit directly, by implanting it in the hearts of God's elect. Arminius taught that people invite the Holy Spirit into their hearts and can do so only because people are endowed with prevenient grace. In both cases, the goal is to receive the Spirit, who imparts God's blessings.

For this reason, Reformed churches place little or no emphasis on what Lutherans call the "means of grace." For both Calvin and Arminius, the Spirit is something a person receives directly from God, either as a result of election (Calvin) or personal choice (Arminius). As we have seen, a person's receiving the Spirit directly fits better with a religion focusing on the yearning for an infusion of grace to be more pious.

Luther, on the other hand, was concerned with the question of forgiveness and how people can serve God willingly and without fear. These blessings come through the message of God's promises in Christ—facts written down for people to read and believe.

How we receive God's grace

The early apostles depended on the power of the Word they preached.

The apostles could have urged Christians struggling with sin to pray for and yield to a Spirit that would free them from temptation and the sins they commit. But they didn't. They relied on the power of God's Word, "the sword of the Spirit" (Ephesians 6:17).

God's Word has power

Apologetics focuses on arguments for the truth of Scripture found outside of Scripture—the massive number of Bible manuscripts in existence, the accuracy of its transmission, evidence from written history and archaeology, the rapid growth of the Christian Church, and even miracles recorded throughout Church history.

But God's Word does not need outside proofs. It can stand on its own. God's Word has power. When God spoke, things happened. In the beginning, God said, "Let there be . . ." Each time he spoke those words, a new part of creation came into being. The psalmist wrote, "By the word of the LORD the heavens were made, and by the breath of his mouth all their host" (Psalm 33:6). The writer to the Hebrews wrote the same: "By faith we understand that the universe was created by the word of God, so that what is seen was not made out of things that are visible" (11:3). And Peter writes, "The heavens existed long ago, and the earth was formed . . . by the word of God" (2 Peter 3:5).

Peter said that God sustains the world by the power of his Word: "By the same word the heavens and earth that now exist are . . . being kept until the day of judgment" (2 Peter 3:7). The Israelites ate in the wilderness because God spoke his Word and provided for them: "He fed you with manna . . . that he might make you know that man does not live by bread alone, but man lives by every word that comes from the mouth of the LORD" (Deuteronomy 8:3). Jesus quoted this passage when Satan tempted him to turn stones into bread (Matthew 4:4). God's Word, not bread, would sustain him.

John associated the Word of God with the Son of God, the source of all power: "All things were made through him, and without him was not any thing made that was made" (John 1:3). In Revelation John saw Jesus coming in judgment, "and the name by which he is called is The Word of God" (19:13).

The psalmist referred to certain people who rebelled against God and then repented and sought his favor: "Then they cried to the LORD in their trouble, and he delivered them from their distress. He sent out his word and healed them" (Psalm 107:19,20). In another psalm, the writer personified God's Word, giving it the power to accomplish God's will:

> He sends out his command to the earth; his word runs swiftly.
> He hurls down his crystals of ice like crumbs; who can stand before his cold?
> He sends out his word, and melts them; he makes his wind blow and the waters flow. (Psalm 147:15,17,18)

God's Word can reach into the deepest recesses of our being and inspect and judge every thought and intention. And note how the power of the Word is associated with God himself:

> For the word of God is living and active, sharper than any two-edged sword, piercing to the division of soul and of spirit, of joints and of marrow, and discerning the thoughts and intentions of the heart. And no creature is hidden from his sight, but all are naked and exposed to the eyes of him to whom we must give account. (Hebrews 4:12,13)

People are led to faith by the power of the Word

Apologists assume that the Holy Spirit uses apologetic arguments to bring people to faith. Scripture says that people come to faith through the power of the Word, specifically, through the Gospel of God's forgiveness.

Through the prophet Isaiah, God personified his Word as he described its power to bring people to faith:

> For as the rain and the snow come down from heaven
> and do not return there
> but water the earth, making it bring forth and sprout,
> giving seed to the sower and bread to the eater,
> so shall my word be that goes out from my mouth;
> it shall not return to me empty,
> but it shall accomplish that which I purpose,
> and shall succeed in the thing for which I sent it.
> (Isaiah 55:10,11)

God commanded the prophets to preach his Word faithfully; what he told them to preach had power:

> Let the prophet who has a dream tell the dream, but let him who has my word speak my word faithfully. What has straw in common with wheat? declares the Lord. Is not my word like fire, declares the Lord, and like a hammer that breaks the rock in pieces? (Jeremiah 23:28,29)

Jesus prayed to his Father on behalf of his disciples, who would spread his Word and bring people to faith:

> As you sent me into the world, so I have sent them into the world. And for their sake I consecrate myself, that they also may be sanctified in truth. I do not ask for these only, but also for those who will believe in me through their word. (John 17:18-20)

Paul spoke about what the Word has done for believers: "For the word of the cross is folly to those who are perishing, but to us who are being saved it is the power of God" (1 Corinthians 1:18).

Throughout the book of Acts, Luke repeatedly emphasized the power of the Word to lead people to faith. Although the apostles were arrested and thrown into prison, "many of those who had heard the word believed, and the number of the men came to about five thousand" (Acts 4:4). The Word was viewed as a living thing; it "increased." God's Word continued to expand its sphere of influence as an increasing number of people heard the Word and believed it. After the Church chose deacons to help the apostles, "The word of God continued to increase, and the number of the disciples multiplied greatly" (Acts 6:7). In Ephesus, Paul preached and drove out demons. Many gave up their magic arts, and "the word of the Lord continued to increase and prevail mightily" (Acts 19:20).

Paul personified the Word. It was spreading throughout the world: "In the whole world it is bearing fruit and increasing—as it also does among you, since the day you heard it and understood the grace of God in truth" (Colossians 1:6). And Paul was not afraid to be absent from the Thessalonian congregation because he knew they had God's Word, "which is at work in you believers" (1 Thessalonians 2:13).

The Word of God will never cease to exist:

> All flesh is like grass

and all its glory like the flower of grass.
The grass withers,
and the flower falls,
but the word of the Lord remains forever.
And this word is the good news that was preached to you.
(1 Peter 1:22-25)

The Lord creates faith. He does that through the message of sins forgiven through Jesus. Paul wrote to the Romans, "Faith comes from hearing, and hearing through the word of Christ" (10:17).

The apostles all relied on the power of the Word. Peter wrote, "You have been born again, not of perishable seed but of imperishable, through the living and abiding word of God" (1 Peter 1:23).

James wrote that God "brought us forth by the word of truth" (1:18).

When Paul departed from Ephesus, he left the church's leaders in good hands: "And now I commend you to God and to the word of his grace, which is able to build you up and to give you the inheritance among all those who are sanctified" (Acts 20:32).

He warned the Corinthians against ever giving up what he had preached to them: "Now I would remind you, brothers, of the gospel I preached to you, which you received, in which you stand, and by which you are being saved, if you hold fast to the word I preached to you—unless you believed in vain" (1 Corinthians 15:1,2).

The Word dwells within us

God's Word does not remain outside of us in the Bible. It resides within those who believe. Having God's Word within us is more than knowing it intellectually or striving to memorize it. It is a power at work within us. James wrote: "Therefore put away all filthiness and rampant wickedness and receive with meekness the implanted word, which is able to save your souls" (1:21).

Jesus rebuked the religious leaders for rejecting the words of his Father: "The Father who sent me has himself borne witness about me. His voice you have never heard, his form you have never seen, and you do not have his word abiding in you, for you do not believe the one whom he has sent" (John 5:37,38).

John says the opposite about those who believed:

I write to you, fathers, because you know him who is from the beginning.
I write to you, young men, because you are strong,
and the word of God abides in you,
and you have overcome the evil one." (1 John 2:14)

Scripture and the Holy Spirit do the same work

The Word and the Spirit are two different things. But the work of God's Word and the work of the Holy Spirit are the same. This comes out clearly in the following pair of passages:

Paul tells the Colossians:

Let the *word of Christ* dwell in you richly, teaching and admonishing one another in all wisdom, singing psalms and hymns and spiritual songs, with thankfulness in your hearts to God. (3:16)

And he tells the Ephesians to do the same thing. Only here he substitutes the Holy Spirit for the Word:

And do not get drunk with wine, for that is debauchery, but *be filled with the Spirit*, addressing one another in psalms and hymns and spiritual songs, singing and making melody to the Lord with your heart. (5:18,19)

From the very beginning, the Word and the Spirit have worked in tandem. In Genesis 1, God's Word (that is, Jesus) went into action to create the world, even as "the Spirit of God was hovering over the face of the waters" (verse 2).

People received God's Holy Spirit when they heard the Gospel: "While Peter was still saying these things, the Holy Spirit fell on all who heard the word" (Acts 10:44). And Paul reminded the Ephesians, "In him you also, when you heard the word of truth, the gospel of your salvation, and believed in him, were sealed with the promised Holy Spirit" (1:13).

The Spirit enables a person to reject idols and confess Christ as Lord. "Therefore I want you to understand that no one speaking in the Spirit of God ever says 'Jesus is accursed!' and no one can say 'Jesus is Lord' except in the Holy Spirit" (1 Corinthians 12:3). And the Word also enables a person to reject idols and confess Christ as Lord: "So faith comes from hearing, and hearing through the word of Christ" (Romans 10:17).

The Holy Spirit enables us to understand what God has given us in Christ. We have received "the Spirit who is from God, that we might understand the things freely given us by God" (1 Corinthians 2:12). And Paul could leave the Ephesian elders, trusting that the Word of God would do the same for them. Again quoting Acts 20:32: "And now I commend you to God and to the word of his grace, which is able to build you up and to give you the inheritance among all those who are sanctified."

The Holy Spirit leads us to know God as our Father in Christ: "For you did not receive the spirit of slavery to fall back into fear, but you have received the Spirit of adoption as sons, by whom we cry, 'Abba! Father!'" (Romans 8:15). And God's Word does the same: "Receive with meekness the implanted word, which is able to save your souls" (James 1:21).

Jesus told his disciples, "But the Helper, the Holy Spirit, whom the Father will send in my name, he will teach you all things and bring to your remembrance all that I have said to you" (John 14:26). Jesus also said, "When the Spirit of truth comes, he will guide you into all the truth" (John 16:13). And the record of what Jesus said and the truth into which the Spirit guides us is found in God's Word.

The Word is more than a record of teachings. It has a much closer relation to the Spirit than that. It is the Spirit's tool to advance and defend the Church. Paul encourages Christians to arm themselves for service: "Also, take up . . . the sword of the Spirit, which is the word of God" (Ephesians 6:17).

Does the Holy Spirit use apologetic arguments?

The writers of Scripture were conscious of the power of the Word and the Spirit. When the Word was taught, the Holy Spirit was at work. And where the Holy Spirit was at work, he was using his sword, the Word.

But how do apologetic arguments fit into this mix? Does the Holy Spirit use apologetic arguments to lead people to faith just like he uses the Word? If so, how would you express the relative importance of the Holy Spirit and the arguments and evidence of modern apologetics?

For example, R. C. Sproul speaks about how a Christian can know the Bible is true. He asks the question like this: "The question is not whether the Holy Spirit's assurance is the ultimate basis for certainty. That is granted by all. . . . The central question is whether the Holy Spirit works apart from or along with evidence for biblical inspiration in producing certainty in the heart of a believer."[273] In other words, does the Spirit work apart from arguments and evidence? Or does he use them in bringing people to faith?

Modern apologists do not provide a uniform answer to that question. Here are a few examples of their thinking:

Clark Pinnock presents a basic view: "Just as the Spirit can create comprehension in the reading of Scripture, so the Spirit can create comprehension in the reading of Christian evidences. Faith is created by the Holy Spirit acting upon good and sufficient evidences."[274] In this view, there is little difference between the power of Scripture and the power of apologetic arguments.

Boa and Bowman give less credit to apologetics by acknowledging a difference between the goal of apologetics and conversion itself:

> Logical argument in apologetics *does not produce faith*, nor is it the proper basis of Christian assurance or knowledge; these are the work of the Holy Spirit. Rather, the purpose of apologetic argument is to serve as means through which the Holy Spirit can lead *nonbelievers to acknowledge the truth of Christianity.*[275]

John Montgomery explains the relation like this: "As for the Holy Spirit, He works through that very Word to convince men of God's truth, so that in reality we bring men under His convicting aegis as we point them to the biblical evidences for Christ's truth."[276] He is saying that when apologetics convinces a person of the truth of Scripture, it is helping Scripture do its work. That is, people realize the Word is true and listen to it with greater confidence.

Nevertheless, not all see such a distinction, and they give more credit to apologetics. John Frame says that the apologist wants to be "a channel through whom God's Spirit can bring repentance (including intellectual repentance) and faith."[277] And William Craig also says that apologetics, with God's help, can lead a person to faith:

---

[273]Sproul, Gerstner, and Lindsley, *Classical Apologetics*, pp. 203-204.

[274]Clark Pinnock, "The Philosophy of Christian Evidences," in *Jerusalem and Athens: Critical Discussions on the Philosophy and Apologetics of Cornelius Van Til,* ed. E. R. Geehan, p. 424.

[275]Boa and Bowman Jr., *Faith Has Its Reasons*, p. 116.

[276]Montgomery, *Faith Founded on Fact*, pp. 34-35.

[277]Frame, "Presuppositional Apologetics," in *Five Views on Apologetics*, ed. Stephen Cowan, p. 219.

The Holy Spirit will then use such arguments and evidence to draw unbelievers to a knowledge of God by removing their sinful resistance to
the conclusion of our arguments. . . . Conversion is exclusively the role
of the Spirit. But we can rationally commend our faith to others in the
confidence that some, whose hearts he has opened, will respond to the
apologetic we present and place their faith in Christ.[278]

Once again, Greg Koukl's words are refreshing by contrast:

I came to believe that the Bible is God's Word in the same way I suspect
you did. I read it and was moved by it. I encountered the truth firsthand
and found it compelling. If you want skeptics to believe in the Bible,
don't get into a tug-of-war with them about inspiration. Instead, invite
them to engage Jesus' words firsthand, then let the Spirit do the heavy
lifting for you.[279]

Although John Frame in the quotation above says that apologetics is the Spirit's
tool to bringing a person to faith, in another place he echoes Koukl's words:
"Often the most effective thing is for the inquirer simply to read the Bible.
God's Word is powerful as the Spirit drives it into the heart."[280]

We still have not found a definite answer: Does the Holy Spirit use apologetic
arguments to lead a person to faith? And if so, how does he use them? These
quotations offer a variety of answers. One apologist puts greater emphasis on
the Spirit but claims that his tool is apologetic arguments. Another puts the
Word and apologetic arguments on the same level and says the Spirit is working through both. Another says that apologetic arguments show the Bible to be
reliable, which in turn helps the Spirit use the Bible to bring a person to conversion. Others put greater emphasis on the message of Scripture. In the end,
apologists do not give a definitive answer.

If this is confusing, remember that we are in the world of Calvinism and Arminianism. God's work in conversion and mankind's work in conversion is
not clearly defined in either of these systems, as it is in Scripture where God
alone gives his grace through his Spirit who is working through the message of
Scripture.

---

[278]Craig, "Classical Apologetics," in *Five Views on Apologetics*, ed. Stephen Cowan, pp.
54-55.
[279]Koukl, *Tactics*, p. 73.
[280]Frame, *Apologetics to the Glory of God*, p. 66.

Another attempt: Apologetics starts the work, and the Spirit takes over

Explanation of this argument

There is still another way of viewing the relation of apologetic arguments to the Word. Some apologists attempt to live in two worlds. They consider apologetics to be indispensable, but believe that it can go only so far. At a certain point, faith and conversion lie entirely in God's hands.

Alister McGrath writes, "God is the one who will convert; we have the privilege of bringing people to a point at which God takes over."[281] He explains what he means: "God is the one who converts people, while at the same time reaffirming we can aid this process by helping remove barriers and obstacles to the grace of God."[282]

This argument is particularly appealing to Lutherans. They divide the obstacles to conversion into two groups. In the first group of obstacles are those which apologetic arguments can overcome—challenges to the reliability of Scripture, the idea that all religions lead to God, the question about God's existence, etc. In the second group there is only one obstacle, which only the Holy Spirit can overcome. This is the offense of the cross, which Paul talks about in 1 Corinthians 1 and 3.

Lutheran apologists attempt to supply Christians with the apologetic tools they need to break down the pseudo-obstacles so that they can get on with the real work of telling people about the forgiveness they have through the cross of Christ. Their apologetics is about clearing a path for the Gospel, or getting a hearing for the Gospel, or putting on the brakes to human arguments long enough to begin sharing the Gospel of God's forgiveness.

John Montgomery puts it like this: "The non-Christian must . . . be offered the factually compelling evidence for the Christian truth-claim."[283] He writes, "Apologetics fulfills its function only when it brings the unbeliever to the 'offense of the cross.'"[284] People should be brought to the point where they see

---

[281] McGrath, *Mere Apologetics,* p. 44.

[282] McGrath, *Mere Apologetics,* p. 129.

[283] Montgomery, *Faith Founded on Fact,* p. 125.

[284] Montgomery, *Faith Founded on Fact,* p. 123.

"the cross as evidentially compelling and able to be resisted only by a deliberate act of egocentric will."[285]

Craig Parton says the same when he describes the challenges faced by missionaries. Mission work is done in various cultures, each of which "will present unique obstacles to the Gospel—obstacles that must be dismantled by effective apologetical work so that the unbeliever in that culture is faced with the only true offense: the offense of the cross."[286]

All obstacles to Christianity are spiritual obstacles

This approach to apologetics is faulty for a number of reasons. First, this way of thinking considers all of people's questions and doubts, except the offense of the cross, to be relatively benign and can be overcome by using apologetic arguments and evidence. Considering the scope of apologetics, the array of doubts and questions would also seem to include the challenges of humanism and atheism. It is almost arrogant to think that these challenges can be overcome by the intellectual arguments of apologists.

But Scripture never speaks like that. In addition to being intellectual, the world's roadblocks are deeply spiritual. By nature we are held in a sinful captivity and must ask if human arguments and evidence can clear away such roadblocks and create a clear path to the offense of the cross.

Paul describes what we were like before we came to faith, which explains why we reject God and allow our thoughts to be filled with obstacles to the Gospel:

> And you were dead in the trespasses and sins in which you once walked, following the course of this world, following the prince of the power of the air, the spirit that is now at work in the sons of disobedience— among whom we all once lived in the passions of our flesh, carrying out the desires of the body and the mind, and were by nature children of wrath, like the rest of mankind. (Ephesians 2:1-3)

The "ruler of the domain of the air" is behind all the "desires of the sinful flesh and its thoughts." Every false philosophy, wrong scientific interpretation, and errant worldview is nothing less than an idea Satan has put into people's minds to keep them from acknowledging their sin. These arguments are not benign. Only the Word and the Spirit can ultimately overcome them: "For the weapons

[285]Montgomery, *Faith Founded on Fact*, p. 123.
[286]Parton, *The Defense Never Rests*, p. 74.

of our warfare are not of the flesh but have divine power to destroy strongholds. We destroy arguments and every lofty opinion raised against the knowledge of God, and take every thought captive to obey Christ" (2 Corinthians 10:4,5). Anyone who wants to claim that the weapons Paul is referring to are rational apologetic arguments instead of God's Word has their work cut out for them.

We are not smart enough to understand all the obstacles

There is another fault with this approach to apologetics. We are told to use apologetics to overcome obstacles to the offense of the cross. But I must confess, I'm not smart enough to understand every doubt or skeptical thought a person might have so as to find a reasonable argument against it. Nor am I clever enough to anticipate Satan's next move in order to head off Satan with a well-placed piece of evidence.

Overcoming obstacles is the Spirit's work from start to finish. He alone can always anticipate Satan's next move, see through his lies, understand the tricks he is using—and intends to use,—and outsmart him. When we see evil strongholds that must be taken and arrogance that raises itself up above God, we ought to stick with the arguments the Spirit uses, which are found in Scripture. There may be a time and place to use apologetic arguments to show the foolishness of an unbeliever's argument and increase their guilt. But we can never depend on these arguments to supply the spiritual power necessary to overcome them.

Paul does not use modern apologetic arguments and evidence

Scripture tells us what people know by nature. People know that God exists, that they do wrong, and that God punishes the wrongs they do. People sense there is a God who takes care of them. They sense that events in their lives do not happen aimlessly but that someone is directing them. These truths are rational. They can be argued.

But Scripture never says that human argumentation will convince unbelievers to believe these things and live their lives accordingly. The problem does not lie in their natural ignorance, but in their attempt to suppress what they know to be true. This is the main problem; it is the essence of irrationality.

Only the Holy Spirit can break through this irrationality, just like he is the only one who can break through the offense of the cross. All apologetics should be used as Paul uses argumentation in Romans 1-3, *to expose sin.*

After Paul had exposed the sin of willful ignorance and said that God was punishing that sin, he revealed the righteousness of God's Son, who gives complete forgiveness. He did not use apologetics to give the Spirit a chance to work. Rather, he depended on the Holy Spirit working through both the Law—which admittedly can in certain cases come in the form of an apologetic argument—and through the Gospel message.

Sadly, this is not how apologists usually work. Some apologists focus on why Christianity is superior to other world religions: Unlike other world religions, it can be verified by history. But they rarely focus on the single most important difference: Christianity is the message of sins forgiven. In the process, the heart of Christianity—sin and grace—receives little attention. It doesn't help the apologetic goal of giving proof.

Other apologists try to prove the existence of God, going to great philosophical lengths to do this. But is it right to try to prove something that Scripture says needs no proving? Paul says that all people "knew God" and for this reason they are "without excuse" in denying him. God is "clearly perceived," yet people worship elements of his creation instead (Romans 1:20,21). Paul's way of talking about the existence of God is the path to the message of sin and grace, while apologetic argumentation for the existence of God is merely the path to a theistic worldview.

Some use as their touchpoint human yearnings that originate from the image of God (which they claim all people still have). Yet Paul centered his "apologetics" on the fact that "no one seeks for God" (Romans 3:11) and that "the whole world [is] held accountable to God" (Romans 3:19). Again, Paul's evaluation of human nature leads people to know their sin and receive God's forgiveness, which can be lost when the focus is on human yearnings.

To begin with apologetics necessitates ending with apologetics

There is another reason why apologetics cannot lead to a point where the Holy Spirit takes over. The doubts and questions that apologetic arguments are meant to overcome do not simply go away when a person comes to faith in Christ. Those doubts and questions may even intensify as the forces of evil try to take a person away from Christ. Scripture says we will never shake our sinful nature this side of Heaven. The temptation to reject the faith remains within us.

This temptation can be handled in one of two ways. Either the Christians is told, "Remember that you came to faith through the power of the Word and the Spirit. The Spirit will help you overcome your doubts and questions. He will strengthen you by his grace as you contemplate the Gospel message." Or the Christian is told, "Remember the reasons why your doubts and questions were resolved in the first place. Rethink those arguments and evidences. They will put your questions and doubts to rest like they did before you came to faith." The first is the way of Scripture. The second is the way of apologetics.

For those who came to faith in the context of apologetic arguments and evidence, apologetics will play a major role in their remaining Christians. But for those who came to faith through the message of Scripture, Scripture will play the most important role of supporting their faith. They will know what to do when plagued by questions and doubts. They will return to what brought them to faith in the first place—their knowledge of the cross of Christ. After that, they might seek out a wise counselor who will affirm their faith in Christ and then—perhaps by using an apologetic argument—will expose the foolishness of those who are leading them away from Christ.

In short, we should depend on the Holy Spirit to rebut all obstacles and challenges to the faith—those that come before faith and those that come afterward. All human obstacles are obstacles to the cross because in some way they attempt to make the cross foolish. For this reason, all obstacles can be decisively overcome only by the message of sin and grace and the power of the Spirit in that message.

The charge of circular reasoning

What is circular reasoning?

Modern apologists are intensely aware of circular reasoning, especially in regard to Scripture. John Frame writes, "Apologists typically *try to avoid* making their case depend on faith, because faith is what they are arguing for. They don't want to argue in a circle."[287]

Circular reasoning is a no-no in philosophical circles, and this includes modern apologetics. You can sense why from the following conversation.

Q: Why do you believe in Christ? A: Let me answer in the words of Martin Luther: "The Holy Spirit has called me by the gospel, enlightened me with his gifts, and kept me in the one truth faith."

[287]Frame, "Presuppositional Apologetics," in *Five Views on Apologetics*, ed. Stephen Cowan, pp. 310-311 (emphasis added).

Q: But how can you be sure the Gospel is true? A: Because it's what I have learned from the Bible.

Q: How can you be sure the Bible is telling you the truth? A: Because it has led me to Jesus. Jesus and the other Bible writers tell me that their words are true.

Q: But you're reasoning in a circle. Give me some proof that the Bible is true. A: OK, consider the fact that all the prophecies in the Old Testament about the Messiah were fulfilled by Jesus. Or that Jesus did so many miracles that the people of his day were forced to take notice of him. Or that Scripture offers many proofs that Jesus rose from the dead.

Q: But that doesn't answer my question. How can you be sure those prophecies and miracles are true? A: Because the Bible tells me they are true.

This argument could go on forever because it is circular. In a secular debate, you cannot prove something to be true simply because you believe that its source is true. You must also prove that your source is true. In other words, for your argument to be valid, the circle must somehow be broken. Much of modern apologetics—specifically, evidentialist apologetics—wants to supply the proof necessary to break the circle.

How apologetics breaks the circle

The question about circular reasoning is related to all the questions about the relation between the Holy Spirit and apologetics: Does the Holy Spirit work through Scripture alone, or does he rely on evidence from outside Scripture to prove that Scripture and its message are true?

Boa and Bowman construct a dialogue that illustrates evidentialist apologetics. Two people are accusing a believer of circular reasoning. The believer, an apologist, responds: "You're right, Sarah, but I won't ask you or Murali to take the Bible's word for anything. In fact, I encourage you to examine the evidence to see whether what the Bible writers say about Jesus is true or not."[288]

One example from a modern apologist will help us understand how the concept is applied. Gary Habermas is an evidentialist apologist. His specialty is the resurrection of Jesus. He contends that to be sure Jesus rose from the dead, one only has to know a minimal number of facts. Then, once a person is sure that

---

[288]Boa and Bowman Jr., *Faith Has Its Reasons,* p. 208.

Jesus rose, that person can also be certain about the wide range of truths Jesus taught.

Habermas sticks with truths that are accepted by both believers and skeptics alike. They are facts all New Testament unbelieving scholars accept, or at least admit are as well attested as any fact of history can be. Here are the minimal facts: (1) Jesus died by crucifixion. (2) Very soon afterward, his followers had real experiences that they believed were actual appearances of the risen Jesus. (3) The disciples' lives were transformed as a result, even to the point of being willing to die specifically for their faith in the resurrection message. (4) The disciples began teaching about the resurrection immediately after Jesus rose. (5) James, Jesus' unbelieving brother, became a Christian because he believed Jesus was the resurrected Christ. (6) The persecutor Paul became a believer after a similar experience.[289] Once the minimal facts argument is accepted, then Jesus being the Son of God must be accepted too. Once that is accepted, then one must accept everything he said and ultimately all of Christian teaching.

All of Habermas' minimal facts are proven by material outside of Scripture, which is why they are even accepted by unbelieving skeptics. None of them are accepted because it's what the Bible teaches. There is no circular reasoning in Habermas' beliefs.

William Craig says the same:

> In this chapter I want to summarize the crucial elements in a historical case for Jesus' resurrection, so that you can share it with anyone who asks you why you believe in the biblical God. . . . If the three facts mentioned above—the empty tomb, the postmortem appearances, the origin of the belief in Jesus' resurrection—can be established, and if no plausible, natural explanation can account for them as well as the resurrection hypothesis, then we're justified in inferring Jesus' resurrection as the best explanation of the facts."[290]

An interesting twist is that the minimal facts argument is said to prove the inspiration of the Old Testament. This is important because there is no way to demonstrate the divine nature of the Old Testament historically, like one can do with the New Testament. But, Habermas says, if Jesus accepted the Old Tes-

---

[289]See a short paper by Gary Habermas, "Minimal Facts on the Resurrection That Even Skeptics Accept," https://ses.edu/minimal-facts-on-the-resurrection-that-even-skeptics-accept/, accessed June 2023. The list in this article is by Gary Habermas. Other lists add the empty tomb.

[290]Craig, *On Guard*, pp. 229-230.

tament as true and Jesus is the Son of God, then we too should accept the Old Testament as true.

John Montgomery says the same about Jesus' stamp of approval on the Old Testament: "External confirmations touch only a portion of the entire content of the Old Testament books; and thus, without a transcendent Word establishing their revelational authority, one cannot make definitive revelational claims on their behalf."[291] He continues, "We do not argue that the Bible must be a divine revelation because it is inerrant; we argue, rather, that it must be a divine revelation because Jesus, who proves himself to be God, declares that it is such—and *he* regarded it as inerrant."[292]

This argument overlooks the fact that the Old Testament claims its own divine origin and inspiration. Also, the New Testament authors treated it as God's Word, no differently than the whole Jewish community did. We are never told that they believed the Old Testament was true based on what Jesus said about it.

Apologists assert that the validity of the Bible should be determined in the same way as any other historic document. Tests, like the tests applied to texts in a court of law, should determine whether Scripture can be used reliably. There are three tests it must past: (1) The text itself must be beyond reproach. How many different copies exist, and how do those copies compare with each other? How much time elapsed between when the document claims to have been written and the first available copy? (2) Does the document contradict itself? (3) Are there obvious historical errors within the document itself? Or does it find full support from contemporary documents and from archaeological research?

Apologetic material proves that Scripture passes all those tests with flying colors. Once Scripture is shown to be reliable, one's study of Scripture can begin.

Apologists claim they can successfully defend the Bible before the unbelieving, skeptical world. But at what cost to Scripture? Human reason becomes the judge of whether Scripture is true or not. Scripture's power is made subservient to human reason.

John Frame, however, seems more willing to let the Scripture work without human proofs. Although his religious background does not connect the work

---

[291]Montgomery, *Tractatus Logico-Theologicus,* p. 142.
[292]Montgomery, *Tractatus Logico-Theologicus,* p. 146.

of the Spirit with the work of the Word as clearly as Scripture does, he writes, "Scripture gives us faithful hearts. As indicated earlier, the Word of God is powerful to save (Romans 1:16-17). As the Holy Spirit speaks in the Scriptures, he turns our skepticism into faith. Our hearts are warmed as we hear the gospel (Luke 24:32)."[293]

Did the Bible writers use proofs from outside the Bible?

A popular claim of apologetics is that Jesus and the Bible writers often used material from outside Scripture in their work of preaching the Gospel. This, it is claimed, justifies our use of arguments from philosophy, science, archaeological finds, the miraculous preservation of Scripture, etc.

But there is no comparison between the "outside" evidence found in Scripture and the outside proofs used in modern apologetics. A study of Scripture bears this out.

Jesus sometimes makes a point using proverbs in general use: "When it is evening, you say, 'It will be fair weather, for the sky is red.' And in the morning, 'It will be stormy today, for the sky is red and threatening.' You know how to interpret the appearance of the sky, but you cannot interpret the signs of the times" (Matthew 16:2,3). Jesus also said, "Doubtless you will quote to me this proverb, 'Physician, heal yourself. What we have heard you did at Capernaum, do here in your hometown as well'" (Luke 4:23). Jude refers to a prophecy of Enoch that is not recorded in Scripture (Jude 14,15).

We already noted that in his sermon in Athens Paul referred to a Greek poet as evidence that all people know there is a God who created us. Paul also quoted another Greek writer: "Do not be deceived: 'Bad company ruins good morals'" (1 Corinthians 15:33). Paul quoted the observation of a poet from Crete: "One of the Cretans, a prophet of their own, said, 'Cretans are always liars, evil beasts, lazy gluttons.' This testimony is true. Therefore rebuke them sharply, that they may be sound in the faith" (Titus 1:12,13). After defending himself in court, Paul told the governor, Festus, and King Agrippa: "I am not out of my mind, most excellent Festus, but I am speaking true and rational words. For the king knows about these things, and to him I speak boldly. For I am persuaded that none of these things has escaped his notice, for this has not been done in a corner" (Acts 26:25,26). This is called an example of Paul appealing to Agrippa's

---

[293]Frame, *Apologetics*, p. 189.

knowledge of current events, which is considered to be material from outside Scripture itself.

Even a cursory comparison of these examples and modern apologetics shows how dissimilar they are. An appeal to a commonly used phrase to express one's point, or even to corroborate one's point, is hardly the same as introducing proof that the idea itself is true. Reminding a person that they themselves had witnessed events recorded in Scripture is hardly the same as proving the truth of Scripture on evidence of contemporary history.

What is striking, however, is how little of this kind of material is found in the New Testament Scriptures and how relatively benign it is. Jesus, Paul, and the other writers could have introduced any number of proofs into their sermons and writings. But they didn't. They could have argued against the irrationality of unbelief in order to prepare their readers to listen to the Gospel. But they didn't.

Catholic writer, Avery Dulles, agrees with this analysis: "Unlike the apologists of the next centuries, the New Testament writers do not engage in arguments with unbelievers or vacillating believers as to why one should be a Christian."[294]

Miracles and prophecy

Many books on apologetics cite the many miracles performed in the Old Testament and especially in the New Testament. They also cite the many Old Testament prophecies that were fulfilled in the New Testament. Josh McDowell's book *Evidence That Demands a Verdict* contains a list of the miracles found in Scripture.

Using Scripture's record of miracles and fulfilled prophecies is, in fact, circular reasoning

We can be certain that the Spirit is active in any Scriptural argument drawn from the evidence of miracles and fulfilled prophecy.

However, Paul Feinberg makes a general statement that can also apply to miracles: "To make Scripture a test for truth in apologetics is to argue circularly. I find this to be a problem. . . . I would not establish the general reliability of

---

[294]Dulles, *A History of Apologetics*, p. 1.

Scripture on evidence internal to it. I think the reliability of the Bible rests on the fact that evidence external to it corroborates what it claims."[295]

Feinberg's position is that of modern apologists in general. In attempting to reach people who don't believe the Bible, they are compelled to do what Feinberg says—find "evidence external to it [that] corroborates what it claims."

Therefore, it makes little sense for modern apologists to list miracles and fulfilled prophecies to prove that Christianity is true and that one should pay attention to it. To argue this way is circular reasoning. To be consistent, one must first use outside evidence to prove Scripture reliable and then use miracles and fulfilled prophecy to prove that Christianity is true.

Miracles and fulfilled prophecies are part of the Gospel

Miracles and fulfilled prophecies are far more than simple proof that Christianity is true, however. They are part of the Gospel. They proved to people in the Old Testament that God would fulfill his promise of a Savior and that he has power to do so. They prove that Jesus is the Son of God, that he fulfilled everything that was predicted about the Messiah, and that he has power to defeat Satan. They prove that he has power to forgive. They prove that God's kingdom has come—that he has power over all things and uses that power for the good of the Church.

John described the convincing power of miracles: "But these are written [Christ's miracles] so that you may believe that Jesus is the Christ, the Son of God, and that by believing you may have life in his name" (John 20:31). The unbelieving Jewish people should accept Jesus' words, but if not, they should at least believe on account of his miracles (John 10:37,38; 14:11). Jesus showed he was the Christ by his miracles. Peter said: "Men of Israel, hear these words: Jesus of Nazareth, a man attested to you by God with mighty works and wonders and signs that God did through him in your midst, as you yourselves know. This Jesus . . . you crucified and killed by the hands of lawless men" (Acts 2:22,23).

---

[295]Paul Feinberg, "Cumulative Case Apologetics," in *Five Views on Apologetics*, ed. Stephen Cowan, p. 349.

The power of miracles is the power of the Word.

People are prone to claim that miracles have greater convincing power than God's Word. Scripture says the opposite. The power of miracles and fulfilled prophecies is no different from the power of the Word.

In the story of Lazarus and the rich man, the rich man was concerned about his brothers. He didn't want them to end up in Hell like him. So he asked Abraham to raise Lazarus and send him to his brothers to warn them. Abraham replied, "They have Moses and the Prophets; let them hear them." The rich man replied, "No, father Abraham, but if someone goes to them from the dead, they will repent." To this Abraham said, "If they do not hear Moses and the Prophets, neither will they be convinced if someone should rise from the dead" (Luke 16:29-31).

Miracles are just as much a matter of faith as the record of Christ's victory over sin is a matter of faith. After Jesus rose from the dead, Thomas refused to believe. He wanted proof it was really Jesus who had appeared to them. Jesus gave Thomas the proof he wanted, not because Jesus normally gave such signs but because Thomas doubted the words of the other disciples: "Then he said to Thomas, 'Put your finger here, and see my hands; and put out your hand, and place it in my side. Do not disbelieve, but believe.'" Thomas answered, "My Lord and my God!" Jesus said, "Have you believed because you have seen me? Blessed are those who have not seen and yet have believed" (John 20:27-29).

There were times when a miracle was performed *because* someone believed: "Now at Lystra there was a man sitting who could not use his feet. He was crippled from birth and had never walked. He listened to Paul speaking. And Paul, looking intently at him and seeing that he had faith to be made well, said in a loud voice, 'Stand upright on your feet.' And he sprang up and began walking" (Acts 14:8-10).

In some cases, lack of faith in God's Word kept Jesus from doing miracles. When he preached at Nazareth, the people rejected him. Matthew tells us, "And he did not do many mighty works there, because of their unbelief" (Matthew 13:58). One time, the Pharisees asked Jesus for a sign to prove he was the Messiah. Jesus rebuked their request as an example of unbelief, "An evil and adulterous generation seeks for a sign, but no sign will be given to it except the sign of the prophet Jonah" (Matthew 12:39).

Miracles are proof, but they are never proof as the world looks at it. They are proof in the context of faith or lack of faith in the Word.

Summary

To address modern unbelievers, modern apologists claim that a person cannot say the Bible is true simply because the Bible says it is true. That's called circular reasoning.

To be certain that Scripture is true, it must be subjected to tests for reliability just like any other book. Apologists claim that the Bible cannot be judged by internal information. Rather, it must be judged by material outside of it.

But submitting Scripture to human analysis sets human judgment over Scripture. It breaks circular reasoning to be sure, but it does so at the expense of denying what Scripture says about itself, namely, that it is powerful and lives within us. The Word does the same work as the Holy Spirit and is called the sword of the Spirit. We confess that the Spirit can use anything he wants to lead people to faith. But Scripture gives no indication that the Spirit uses anything other than the Word of God itself to bring a person to faith.

Miracles and fulfilled prophecy prove that Christianity is true. But they are also part of the Gospel, and, like God's Word in general, can be accepted or rejected.

Chapter 11

Through Faith Alone

Never Settle for Less than 100 Percent Certainty

Certainty in Scripture

Scripture teaches that God's Word and faith in God's Word give Christians complete certainty in a world where doubt and skepticism rule.

Faith makes Christians certain

All believers in the Old and New Testaments shared this certainty. The author of the Hebrews made a list of Old Testament people who put their faith in God's promise of a Savior long before that promise was fulfilled. He begins his list with a definition of faith. He wrote, "Now faith is the assurance of things hoped for, the conviction of things not seen. For by it the people of old received their commendation" (Hebrews 11:1,2). The King James translation puts it this way: "Now faith is the *substance* of things hoped for, the *evidence* of things not seen." Faith in what God reveals in his Word is a "substance"—a genuine, firm, and tangible confidence in what God promises. Faith in God's promises is the "evidence" that convinces us that what we look forward to is real.

God gave the Old Testament people certainty by taking an oath. It was an unusual oath, for God swore by himself to fulfill his promise. The writer to the Hebrews described the oath and the effect this oath had on the Old Testament people—the same effect it should have on us.

> For people swear by something greater than themselves, and in all their disputes an oath is final for confirmation. So when God desired to show more convincingly to the heirs of the promise the unchangeable character of his purpose, he guaranteed it with an oath, so that by two unchangeable things, in which it is impossible for God to lie, we who have fled for refuge might have strong encouragement to hold fast to the

hope set before us. We have this as a sure and steadfast anchor of the soul, a hope that enters into the inner place behind the curtain, where Jesus has gone as a forerunner on our behalf, having become a high priest forever after the order of Melchizedek. (Hebrews 6:16–7:1)

Such certainty was also characteristic of all the New Testament believers. Paul was in a long line of those who believed in God's promise: "I stand here on trial because of my hope in the promise made by God to our fathers, to which our twelve tribes hope to attain, as they earnestly worship night and day. And for this hope I am accused by Jews, O king!" (Acts 26:6,7). For Paul and other believers, the resurrection of Christ was the foundation of their complete certainty. Quoting Psalm 16, Paul spoke about what God's resurrection of his son accomplished: "And as for the fact that he raised him from the dead, no more to return to corruption, he has spoken in this way, 'I will give you the holy and sure blessings of David'" (Acts 13:34). The blessings of David were a shepherd who died for the sheep and an internal kingdom of mercy and glory to which all would be invited.

Perfect certainty comes through Christ

Paul expressed his certainty like this: "For I am sure that neither death nor life, nor angels nor rulers, nor things present nor things to come, nor powers, nor height nor depth, nor anything else in all creation, will be able to separate us from the love of God in Christ Jesus our Lord" (Romans 8:38,39).

Complete certainty is instantaneous when we come to faith in Christ, and we lack nothing to keep our certainty at the 100 percent level. Peter writes,

His divine power has granted to us all things that pertain to life and godliness, through the knowledge of him who called us to his own glory and excellence, by which he has granted to us his precious and very great promises, so that through them you may become partakers of the divine nature, having escaped from the corruption that is in the world because of sinful desire. (2 Peter 1:3,4)

The writer to the Hebrews wanted his readers to abandon the Old Testament laws because they offered no certainty. He pointed them to Christ, in whom they would find complete certainty. He urged them to remain in Christ lest they lose their certainty. He wrote,

Therefore, brothers, since we have confidence to enter the holy places by the blood of Jesus, by the new and living way that he opened for us through the curtain, that is, through his flesh, and since we have a great priest over the house of God, let us draw near with a true heart in full assurance of faith, with our hearts sprinkled clean from an evil conscience and our bodies washed with pure water. Let us hold fast the confession of our hope without wavering, for he who promised is faithful. (Hebrews 10:19-23)

In Christ we can approach God without fear: "We have boldness and access with confidence through our faith in him" (Ephesians 3:12). Paul put his life in Jesus' hands. Even in suffering he remained confident of God's love: This "is why I suffer as I do. But I am not ashamed, for I know whom I have believed, and I am convinced that he is able to guard until that day what has been entrusted to me" (2 Timothy 1:12).

We can be completely confident that God wants each of us to be saved because Scripture tells us so. God "desires all people to be saved and to come to the knowledge of the truth. For there is one God, and there is one mediator between God and men, the man Christ Jesus, who gave himself as a ransom for all" (1 Timothy 2:3-6).

Certainty comes through the chosen witnesses of Jesus' resurrection. Their teachings and example are the foundation of the Christian Church. God confirmed the truth of their message by enabling them to perform miracles: "The signs of a true apostle were performed among you with utmost patience, with signs and wonders and mighty works" (2 Corinthians 12:12).

The twelve witnesses or apostles were chosen by Jesus himself,

So Jesus said to the twelve, "Do you want to go away as well?" Simon Peter answered him, "Lord, to whom shall we go? You have the words of eternal life, and we have believed, and have come to know, that you are the Holy One of God." Jesus answered them, "Did I not choose you, the twelve?" (John 6:67-70)

After Jesus died and rose, he spent 40 days with his followers. During that time, he gave "commands through the Holy Spirit to the apostles whom he had chosen" (Acts 1:2). Jesus explained their coming task: "You will be my witnesses in Jerusalem and in all Judea and Samaria, and to the end of the earth" (Acts 1:8).

The 12 men Jesus had chosen were to spearhead the advance of the Gospel. The apostles understood their mission. Shortly after Jesus rose from the dead, Peter led the group in choosing an apostle to replace Judas. He said,

> So one of the men who have accompanied us during all the time that the Lord Jesus went in and out among us, beginning from the baptism of John until the day when he was taken up from us— one of these men must become with us a witness to his resurrection. (Acts 1:21,22)

Sometime later, God added Paul to the Twelve. A leader in the church, Ananias, commissioned Paul and described his work: "The God of our fathers appointed you to know his will, to see the Righteous One and to hear a voice from his mouth; for you will be a witness for him to everyone of what you have seen and heard" (Acts 22:14,15).

The New Testament writer Luke, who accompanied the apostle Paul, wanted his friend Theophilus to be certain of what he had come to believe. Luke, who traveled with the apostle Paul, interviewed those who knew Jesus and had been part of the Church from the beginning:

> Inasmuch as many have undertaken to compile a narrative of the things that have been accomplished among us, just as those who from the beginning were eyewitnesses and ministers of the word have delivered them to us, it seemed good to me also, having followed all things closely for some time past, to write an orderly account for you, most excellent Theophilus, that you may have certainty concerning the things you have been taught. (Luke 1:1-4)

Certainty for Theophilus came through the research and writing of Luke, whose books, *Luke* and *Acts*, were added to the Scriptures.

We are certain of our election

We are certain, for we have been elected to come to faith. Simon Peter confessed, "You are the Christ, the Son of the living God." And Jesus answered him, "Blessed are you, Simon Bar-Jonah! For flesh and blood has not revealed this to you, but my Father who is in heaven" (Matthew 16:16,17).

Paul made the same point in several places. For example, the Ephesians had perfect certainty of their election and eternal life with God:

He predestined us for adoption to himself as sons through Jesus Christ, according to the purpose of his will. . . . In him you also, when you heard the word of truth, the gospel of your salvation, and believed in him, were sealed with the promised Holy Spirit, who is the guarantee of our inheritance until we acquire possession of it, to the praise of his glory. (Ephesians 1:5,13,14)

And Paul told the Thessalonians that he was certain of their election: "For we *know*, brothers loved by God, that he has chosen you, because our gospel came to you not only in word, but also in power and in the Holy Spirit and with full conviction" (1 Thessalonians 1:4,5).

We are certain that God will bless us

The apostle John wrote, "And this is the confidence that we have toward him, that if we ask anything according to his will he hears us" (1 John 5:14).

And through faith in Christ, we lack nothing. Paul wrote words that give all Christians certainty: "He who did not spare his own Son but gave him up for us all, how will he not also with him graciously give us all things?" (Romans 8:32).

Certainty and good works

Our works play a role in our certainty; they are a sign of our faith. John wrote, "If you know that he is righteous, *you may be sure* that everyone who practices righteousness has been born of him" (1 John 2:29). On the other hand, a life of willful sin robs us of the confidence we have in Christ's forgiveness of sin. Paul wrote: "Or *do you not know* that the unrighteous will not inherit the kingdom of God?" (1 Corinthians 6:9).

The author of Hebrews encouraged his readers to imitate the Old Testament saints who were certain of the promises of God. If his readers did the same, they too would be certain. He wrote, "And we desire each one of you to show the same earnestness to have the full assurance of hope until the end, so that you may not be sluggish, but imitators of those who through faith and patience inherit the promises" (Hebrews 6:11,12).

Certainty is found in Christ. Peter told the people: "God exalted him at his right hand as Leader and Savior, to give repentance to Israel and forgiveness of sins" (Acts 5:31). Because of him we can repent of our sins without fear, for the forgiving arms of God are there to receive us.

Only 100 percent certainty

In Scripture there is no probability. We are certain of God's existence from the evidence we find in his creation; from what God has written in our hearts we are certain of what is right and wrong; from the testimony of our conscience we are certain that God will punish sin. From Scripture we are certain that on the cross Christ was punished for the sins of every person in the world. We are confident that God wants everyone to be saved. We are confident that we are among the elect.

We are sinners and are in trouble with God. That is the only apologetic argumnt that is 100 percent true. No counter argument can defeat that fact. Only this argument leads directly to the need for Christ, who died for all sin and reconciled God and us.

Certainty among the apologists

Apologetics falls short of 100 percent certainty

Modern apologetics does not lead to certainty about one's salvation. It has grown out of what we are calling a shifted Gospel. In other words, it has grown out of a Gospel of infused grace rather than the Gospel of sin and grace.

To state it in another, very broadstroke way, Scripture says there is a point of time at which a person comes to realize his or her sin and comes to faith in God's forgiveness through Christ. At that point certainty is complete. The Gospel of infused grace, on the other hand, posits a period of time during which a person becomes more and more convinced that Christianity is true and that they need God in their life. This process is moved forward by various life events or by a mounting conviction that God is real. At some point the person has a conversion experience.

The first kind of Christianity is centered on sin and grace. It is based on a 100 percent certain need and a 100 percent certain solution. The second is more general. It is a realm of human needs and yearnings, a realm of religious thoughts and opinions, a realm of growing conviction and experiences. Apologetic arguments and evidence fit well with the second kind of Christianity but not with the first. The first depends on the truth of Scripture. The second depends on both Scripture and human philosophy, including apologetics.

The limited certainty of apologetic arguments and evidence

Because apologetic argument are human arguments, they are not 100 percent certain. They are only probable. Boa and Bowman discusse one of the first apologists, Joseph Buttler (1692–1752): "Buttler's dictum that 'probability is the very guide of life' is a classical expression of the evidentialist perspective. Finite human beings cannot expect to gain absolutely certain knowledge of the past, of the course of nature, or of any empirical reality."[296]

Most apologists admit the same. Lawyer and apologist, Craig Parton, writes,

> Is the factual case for Christianity 100 percent certain? We have already seen how this cannot in principle be the required standard to prove any issue of fact. We operate in everyday life on the basis of probabilistic reasoning. . . . But can we base ultimate concerns (Jesus' death, resurrection, deity, and claim to be the sole and exclusive door into heaven) on such probabilistic reasoning? As the analytical philosophers have shown, we have no other choice."[297]

But we should not worry, Parton adds, for "the evidence for the central claim of Christianity—that God was 'in Christ reconciling the world unto Himself'—is overwhelmingly solid."[298]

Tim Keller writes about his method of worldview apologetics:

> The approach I will take in the rest of this volume is called "critical rationality." . . . It assumes that some systems of belief are more reasonable than others, but that all arguments are rationally avoidable in the end. That is, you can always find reason to escape it that is not sheer bias or stubbornness. . . Nevertheless, this doesn't mean that we can't evaluate beliefs, only that we should not expect conclusive proof, and to demand it is unfair.[299]

Gary Habermas writes about a Christian who says, "I can't be a self-respecting person and base my life on something I can't be 100 percent certain is true. That would be a violation of who I am." Habermas answers that objection: "No

---

[296]Boa and Bowman Jr., *Faith Has Its Reasons,* p. 144.
[297]Parton, *The Defense Never Rests, Second Edition,* pp. 127-128.
[298]Parton, *The Defense Never Rests,* p. 128.
[299]Keller, *The Reason for God,* p. 125.

one makes decisions based on 100 percent certainty. The wise person chooses probabilities."[300]

We find another problem in modern apologetics. The certainty of faith invariably comes from scholars. A good example is Gary Habermas, who uses a small number of "minimal facts" for the truth of the resurrection. His argument depends on the approval of scholars. To qualify as a minimal fact, he says, a fact must be accepted by "a large body of historians from both liberal and conservative perspectives alike."[301]

Apologists want facts an unbeliever can't easily debate. Even facts found within Scripture *must be accepted by scholars* if they are to be useful in apologetics. A short quotation from William Lane Craig illustrates this point. Lee Strobel is quoting from his interview with Craig. Craig said,

> "Only Matthew reports that the guards were placed around the tomb," he replied. "But in any event, I don't think the guard story is an important facet of the evidence for the resurrection. For one thing, it's too disputed by contemporary scholarship. I find it's prudent to base my arguments on evidence that's most widely accepted by the majority of scholars, so the guard story is better left aside."[302]

The certainty of experience

This approach—reliance on the convictions of scholars—never leads to certainty. Another kind of evidence is needed, and as we saw above in chapter 8, Craig would agree wholeheartedly. Bernard Ramm makes a distinction:

> Most apologists settle for some sort of distinction between certainty and certitude. By certainty they mean the amount of evidence of all kinds *for Christianity*. This can never be absolutely conclusive but it can be very convincing. With reference to certainty then, the Christian faith possesses a high degree of probability.
>
> Certitude is our inward attitude. Here the Christian has complete assurance that Christianity is true. The witness of the Holy Spirit confirms him in the reality of his faith. It is very prudent to say in a lecture

---

[300]Habermas and Licona, *The Case for the Resurrection of Jesus*, p. 217.
[301]Chilton, *The Layman's Manual on Christian Apologetics*, p. 92.
[302]Strobel, *The Case for Christ*, p. 230.

on Christian evidences that Christianity is true—probably. But in one's prayers one would not say, "The Lord is my shepherd—probably."[303]

As mentioned previously, Evangelical/Reformed churches view coming to faith in Christ as a process. For the sake of convenience, we'll use a term employed by some in the Reformed church to describe the process: the "resistance/receptivity" axis. This refers to the idea that people are somewhere along the line of being resistant to Christianity and being receptive of it. Coming to faith is the *process* of moving closer and closer to the point of receptivity.

Although they don't use the term, Boa and Bowman explain the idea in the modern apologetic context:

> The validity of the apologetic does not depend on its success, but on its utility in facilitating success through the hidden illuminating work of the Holy Spirit within non-Christians. On this premise, we favor the view that an apologetic is valid and valuable if it provides the basis for a non-Christian moving at all closer to embracing the Christian faith. People are indeed either dead in sins or born again, lost or found, unjustified or justified. But they may be closer or further away from crossing over from life to death, depending on what they believe or do not believe. People are typically not standing still: they are generally either moving toward faith or toward unbelief.[304]

We see a good illustration of this movement in Augustine's description of his life in *The Confessions.* We also see good illustrations in the stories Christians tell of moving from sin and unbelief to the Christian life. Radio programs, Christian novels, and movies serve as venues for Christians to tell their stories—to describe the *process*, the road along which God moved them to faith. The end of the process is the point at which they receive grace—an infusion of grace—which convinces them of the truth of God, and they begin to live for him.

Apologists admit that apologetics may have an important role in the movement along the road of resistance/receptivity. But they admit that apologetic arguments and evidence are not required. Any number of forces may be the catalyst that leads a person to make the decision to become a Christian. But apologetics often plays that role. Apologetics is particularly important in an intellectual context where many *logical* roadblocks exist. The claim is that once a thinking

---

[303]Ramm, *Varieties of Christian Apologetics,* p. 23.
[304]Boa and Bowman Jr., *Faith Has Its Reasons,* p. 516.

person realizes that Christianity is reasonable, they are willing to make the decision to become a Christian.

This is in contrast to the *point* at which Luther realized that God had given him the gift of righteousness through the life and death of his Son—when he realized that salvation came by faith and not by works. He certainly went through a time of doubt, struggle, and fear. But he was never closer to faith than when the Holy Spirit led him to the wisdom of the cross. A person, like the scribe in Mark 12:32-34, might have profound ideas from God's Word that puts him or her "not far from the kingdom of God." But the realization that Christ was his Savior would come when he came to faith *in that fact.*

For most in the Evangelical/Reformed world, the resistance/receptivity road ends in a conversion experience. In many cases it ends when a youngster or teenager reports to their parents that they have accepted Christ into their lives and want to be baptized. They can subsequently tell the story of their conversion and usually the date when it happened. For young people, the story is usually uncomplicated. For others, though—especially for those who come to faith later in life—it is more complicated, drawn out, and filled with turmoil.

The certainty of experience

At this point we arrive at an important juncture in our evaluation of apologetics. In chapter 8 we looked at the Evangelical/Reformed conversion experience. We heard William Lane Craig tell us, "When it comes to knowing one's faith to be true, therefore, the Christian will not rely primarily on argument and evidence but on the gracious witness of God himself given to all his children by the indwelling Holy Spirit."[305] Craig was referring to the Evangelical/Reformed conversion experience.

Apologists may seem to be using apologetic arguments and evidence to create certainty. But we must remember that apologists usually have had their conversion experience. To them, apologetic arguments are merely leading a person down the Evangelical/Reformed path from resistance to receptivity and conversion. At that point, the conversion experience becomes what verifies Christianity, what gives it "certitude." A conversion experience is even more objectively real than the apologetic arguments that led to it. It is something felt, something real. Craig, for example, says that he cannot tell a person why

---

[305]Craig, "Classical Apologetics," in *Five Views on Apologetics,* ed. Stephen Cowan, p. 36.

he *knows* Christianity is real (through a real but unprovable experience), but he can *show* a person why he believes (that is, because apologetic arguments show Christianity to be true). Nevertheless, for him, experience is more important—more valid—than apologetic arguments. Without that, what is left? In one place he says, "the testimony of the Spirit is even greater than the apostolic testimony."[306]

What if a group does not promote a conversion experience?

If a group does not promote a conversion experience, they have a problem which apologetics cannot solve. If certainty comes through the witness of the Holy Spirit, and if one's conversion experience is the evidence that a person has received the Holy Spirit, then what is the source of certainty?

This is where many apologists, especially Lutheran apologists, have a problem. Most often, they came to faith through Baptism when they were young. Or they came to faith later in life when they heard about God's forgiving love in Christ and believed it. It was not a matter of being infused with power or of accepting the Spirit. It was a matter of hearing and believing.

Boa and Bowman say that the most common criticism of evidentialism by itself is the matter of probability. In other words, those who do not seek an experience at the end of a process, which includes apologetics, must simply say that *"it's the nature of the case"*[307] and then try and fit the probability of apologetic arguments with the certainty that only the Holy Spirit can give.

The Lutheran synthesis

Some Lutheran apologists attempt to merge their Lutheran teaching with the process language of Evangelical/Reformed apologists.

Think again of the expression that some Lutherans use to join apologetics and the work of the Spirit: Apologetics clears away the obstacles to the faith. When only the offense of the cross is left, the Holy Spirit must take over, for only he can lead a person to faith.

This way of trying to find a role for apologetics sounds simple enough. But as we have seen, this way of thinking overlooks many difficult questions. It disregards

---

[306]Craig, "Classical Apologetics," in *Five Views on Apologetics*, ed. Stephen Cowan, p. 32.
[307]Boa and Bowman Jr., *Faith Has Its Reasons,* p. 159.

the spiritual nature of human objections. It seems to posit a hypothetical point at which human objections are satisfied and when the only hurdle left is the offense of the cross, at which the Holy Spirit must take over. It fails to explain how a believer—one in whom the Holy Spirit is working—handles his or her doubts: Must a believer return to some pre-Spirit point in their life when apologetic arguments overcame their doubts? Must that person once again handle doubts with evidentialist arguments so they can get to some point when the Spirit will help them hold on to their faith in the cross? Can the Spirit be left out of the equation until the end? By nature people suppress the truth about God and sin which they know for certain. Can apologetics solve the sinful suppression of what people know is true? Is the Spirit not also needed for the spiritual step of ceasing to fight against the knowledge of God, against the knowledge of right and wrong, against the accusing voice of conscience?

There is no place in Scripture that says the Spirit needs a human-prepared path to access a person's heart; that is pure speculation. Any synthesis that attempts to merge the modern apologetic view of the Spirit's work with that of Scripture is wrong. The Scriptural position, as shown by the example of the apostles, is for a Christian to begin by leading an unbeliever—even one with a skeptic's attitude—down the path to Christianity with the message of sin and grace, knowing that the Holy Spirit is there building the path from beginning to end.

Arguments against Christianity will come up. When they do, Christians (as they are able) will have answers to expose the error of or the foolish thinking behind the unbeliever's objections—whether answers from Scripture or answers from outside Scripture. They should use them, if necessary, to keep themselves on the path of speaking about the hope they have in Christ. But they must never think that apologetic arguments build the path to faith. With that attitude, such arguments cease to be a part of conversion. Now they become ways you can show love to people by helping them put to rest things that trouble them.

The courtroom metaphor

The idea that apologetics paves the way and then the Holy Spirit takes over at the right time is a very weak position.

I think Lutherans sense this. The weakness of the position, the lack of Scriptural support, and the nature of conversion, lead Lutheran apologists to default to how Boa and Bowman say that some handle the problem of the lack of 100 percent certainty provided by apologetics: "It's the nature of the case."[308] In the face of this lack of certainty, some say, "But that's OK. That's life. All we need is proof beyond a reasonable doubt."

Craig Parton describes this attitude: "Apologetics also has a 'positive' role in establishing the affirmative case for Christianity, showing that the evidence for Christian commitment is, as we say in trial law, 'beyond a reasonable doubt.'"[309]

The idea of reasonable doubt brings us into a courtroom, which some apologists believe is a good place to be. Nowhere else, they say, are there as many rigorous techniques for uncovering the truth. Nowhere else can one find as many proven methods to uncover lies. The rules of testimony are in force. Manuscript and historical evidence can be properly evaluated. Expert witnesses can be called. There is be no circular reasoning allowed here.

But Lutherans, who believe that coming to faith is the point at which the Holy Spirit leads a person to believe in the Gospel, are hamstrung by probabilistic talk. They can find no words to clearly express the connection between the less than certain arguments of apologetics and that certainty that the Holy Spirit wants to give us. They hold on to their apologetic arguments and evidence at the expense of the Word, the sword of the Spirit.

But that's how it is in life, isn't is? There is no 100 percent. Perhaps that's true in some areas of life. But when, on the eve of her wedding, the bride asks her groom: "Do you really want to live with me the rest of your life?," he should have a better answer than: "Yes. I am 96 percent certain."

Scripture and conversion

As we have seen, there is no lack of certainty in Scripture. Neither is there any place in Scripture where coming to faith is described as a process. Nor is there any place in Scripture where probabilistic statements served as a path to the cross. People simply heard the Gospel, came to faith, and lived in 100 percent hope.

The crisis of Scripture is the crisis of sin—the feeling of having absolutely nowhere to flee from God's judgment. It's an absolute crisis that must be solved by the absolute statement of truth. Sins have been forgiven and guilt has been removed.

---

[308]Boa and Bowman Jr., *Faith Has Its Reasons*, p. 159..
[309]Parton, *The Defense Never Rests,* p. 62.

Frankly, the courtroom scene scares me. I don't want Christianity or Scripture put on trial. I don't want the credibility of evidence outside Scripture to have any role in my certainty. I don't want to hear that "modern scholars all agree" that a particular event really did take place or that such and such an artifact is almost certain evidence that a Bible event actually happened—even if that evidence is 99.9 percent certain.

Bad things happen when the truth of Scripture and Christianity are put on the witness stand. Trying to make Scripture more credible to an unbeliever with apologetic arguments actually lessens the credibility of Scripture. When Scripture is put on the witness stand, it becomes the object of human analysis and judgment. Scripture is not allowed to authenticate itself. One can almost hear Scripture cry out, "Get rid of all these witnesses to my truthfulness. I alone have the right to testify about myself."

The evidence of apologetics may go beyond the reasonable level of truth required in a court of law. But it cannot rise to the level of 100 percent proof required for true Christian faith. One hundred percent proof is found only in Scripture itself, even if that involves circular reasoning.

But actually, that last point should be put more strongly: *Only* if we practice circular reasoning can we find absolute certainty in the message of the cross. And only then can the words of Scripture serve their purpose.

There is only one argument that makes complete sense, only one "apologetic" that is certain and that all people will accept. Contrary to many, it does not lie in a religious experience. Rather, it come from what Scripture says. To repeat what we said previously, there is only one argument that is true for all: "Scripture says that you are a sinner. God is righteous and he will justly punish you for your sins." And there is only one argument that can defeat that accusation: "Scripture says that Christ died for your sins."

We do not deny that many people have a struggle before they came to faith. Paul did. But Jesus defined Paul's struggle as unbelief kicking against the goads of the conscience, as trying to find hope in the Law of Moses and knowing it can never be found there. At one moment Paul was 100 percent engaged in his hostile struggle against God. In the next he was 100 percent at peace with God. One moment he was 100 percent damned in his sin. In the next moment he was 100 percent an heir of heaven.[310] This is the pattern of conversion found

---

[310]Some Lutheran apologists make use of the ancient teaching that faith includes *notitia*, or "knowledge" of the truth; *assensus*, or "assent" that Christianity is true; and *fiducia*,

throughout the Scriptures. The wind blew and people become sure that Christ had freed them from sin.

Summary

Scripture says that believers are 100 percent certain of God's love in Christ. God gave the Church apostles, whose teaching is the sure foundation of faith. All Christians can be sure they have been elected by God, for God has called them to believe in Christ. Christians can be certain of all God's blessings because God has given them the best blessing of all.

Modern apologetics, which is based on evidence and arguments outside of Scripture, does not produce 100 percent certainty. Most modern apologists view apologetics as a tool to make a person more receptive to the Christian faith and closer to a direct experience of God. Lutherans, however, cannot express the relationship between apologetics and faith in that way. They either claim that the work of apologetics must at some point yield to the power of the Holy Spirit. Or they are content to base their faith on evidence that is less than 100 percent. There is no record in Scripture that Jesus and the apostles held either of these positions.

---

or "trust" that it is true for *me*. That is to say, faith entails a progression that ends when the Spirit leads people to faith. It is claimed that the two lower rungs, *knowledge* and *ascent,* can be accomplished with the help of apologetics. But only the Holy Spirit can engender *trust*, which is true faith.

That may be true of Roman Catholic theology or a shifted form of Christianity that minimizes the forgiveness of sins. But it is hard to envision apologetics leading someone to know and believe God has forgiven their sins. Even more so, it is hard to envision someone knowing and believing that God has forgiven them, yet be told they are still on the first two rungs of faith and need the Holy Spirit to finish it. Nevertheless, in Scripture there is no example of someone arriving at the second step who has still not also arrived at the third. This teaching was accepted by many older Lutherans who perhaps used it to describe three aspects of faith. But when used by apologists, it certainly refers to a progression.

Chapter 12

By Christ Alone

Give the Reason for Your Hope in Christ

Introduction

Nearly all modern apologists base their use of apologetics on 1 Peter 3:15. They claim this is Scripture's mandate to engage in the apologetic task.[311] In this chapter we will take a close look at that passage.

"Apologetics" in Scripture

The word apologetics is a transliteration of the Greek noun, *apologia*. The verb form is *apologeo*. The verb is commonly translated "defend," and the noun is

---

[311]This passage has become the apologetic movement's marching orders. Chatraw and Allen: "If ever there were one proof-text for apologetics, 1 Peter 3:15 would be it *(Apologetics at the Cross)*. Craig: *"This book is intended to be a sort of training manual to equip you to fulfill the command of 1 Peter 3:15" (On Guard)*. Craig: "Indeed, we are actually commanded by Scripture to have ready an *apologia* to present to any unbeliever who asks us the reason for our faith (1 Peter 3:15)" *(Five Views on Apologetics)*. Kreeft cites 1 Peter 3:15 and says, "Apologetics is the enterprise of obeying that command" *(Pocket Handbook of Christian Apologetics)*. Boa and Bowman, referring to 1 Peter 3:15: "Peter is definitely instructing believers to make a reasoned defense of their beliefs . . . requiring them to give reasons for faith in Christ" *(Faith Has Its Reasons)*. Sproul: "But there is a very good reason for reasoning with people. . . . That very good reason is this: God commands Christians to give a reasoned defense of the Christian religion. That is enough for any reasonable person" *(Classical Apologetics)*. Montgomery, regarding 1 Peter 3:15, "Note that his is not a pious suggestion; it is a command—and it is directed to all Christian believers" *(Always Be Ready)*. Beilby notes 1 Peter 3:15 as God's command. He says that the writers had modern apologetics in mind, not the use of Scripture itself *(Thinking About Christian Apologetics)*. Yet Boa and Bowman write: "The New Testament, then, does not use the word *apologia* and *apologeomai* in the technical sense of the modern world *apologetics*. . . . It was apparently not until 1794 that apologetics was used to designate a special theological discipline" *(Faith Has Its Reasons, pp. 3,4)*.

translated "defense." Depending on the context, translators sometimes use other words—"answer," "reply," or "explanation." But "defense" is the most common translation.

There is no place in Scripture that gives a formal definition of this word. From secular sources, we know it's the normal word the Greeks used for what a defense attorney does in a court of law. But the word is not restricted to that setting. It is used in a more general sense for what a person does when asked why he or she is doing something.

First Peter 3:15 is the only passage in Scripture that can be interpreted as God's command to use apologetic type arguments to spread Christianity. However, the word appears in other contexts, often followed by an example of a person giving a defense of his faith and life. Our first goal in this chapter is to get a feel for how the word *apologia* is used in Scripture. We will trace the use of this word, either in its verb or noun form, in the order it occurs in the New Testament. This background will help us interpret 1 Peter 3:15.

Luke 12:8,11,12

> "And I tell you, everyone who acknowledges me before men, the Son of Man also will acknowledge before the angels of God. . . . And when they bring you before the synagogues and the rulers and the authorities, do not be anxious about how you should *defend* yourself or what you should say, for the Holy Spirit will teach you in that very hour what you ought to say."

The *apologia* Jesus spoke about might refer to rational proof for the reasonableness of the Christian faith. In that case, Jesus would be promising that on the spot the Spirit would teach them how to use philosophical or evidential proofs to defend the truth of Christianity. But if we factor in the parallel between our witness to God on earth and Jesus' witness to our faith in Heaven, it is clear that Jesus is talking about our taking a stand and confessing our faith in him.

Luke 21:12-15

> "They will lay their hands on you and persecute you, delivering you up to the synagogues and prisons, and you will be brought before kings and governors for my name's sake. This will be your opportunity to bear witness. Settle it therefore in your minds not to meditate beforehand

how to *answer*, for I will give you a mouth and wisdom, which none of your adversaries will be able to withstand or contradict."

Although the setting in the verses above is a courtroom, a number of translations use the word "answer" instead of "defend," as the ESV does there.[312] Jesus said the disciples should not think beforehand about what they should say; God would give them the wisdom they needed. This does not rule out an "apologetic" response (in the modern sense). But it more likely refers to their testimony about Christ and what he has done for them, which is the nature of the defenses we have record of.

Acts 19:32,33

> Now some cried out one thing, some another, for the assembly was in confusion, and most of them did not know why they had come together. Some of the crowd prompted Alexander, whom the Jews had put forward. And Alexander, motioning with his hand, wanted to make a *defense* to the crowd.

Paul had preached the Gospel in Ephesus. He had pointed out that the true God was not made by hands. The silversmiths, who made money by hand-making silver images of Diana, accused Paul of undermining the honor of the goddess. The city was in confusion. A riot started, and most of the crowd didn't know why they were there.

A Jew named Alexander was placed before the crowd "to make a *defense*." Therefore, since the crowd did not know what was going on, Alexander's *apologia* (his defense) would not have been comprised of modern apologetic arguments against skeptics. If he had been allowed to make a defense, it would likely have been an explanation of Paul's motives or a statement about what Paul was actually teaching.

Acts 22:1

> "Brothers and fathers, hear the *defense* that I now make before you."

This begins a series of events in which *apologia* and *apologeo* are used frequently. The form of Paul's *apologia* would change. On this occasion, Paul's *apologia*

---

[312]Other examples are the King James Version and the New Living Translation.

took the form of a testimony. He explained the great change that had taken place in his life—from persecutor to proclaimer.

If Paul had primarily wanted to be released, he would have stuck to answering the charges brought against him by the Jews from Antioch. He could have easily proven that he was innocent of those charges. He chose, rather, to testify to Christ—to the same message God had earlier said the Jews would not accept.

Afterward, the Lord appeared to Paul and assured him of his safety. What Paul had done in Jerusalem he would also do in Rome, namely, bear witness that Christ was alive: "The following night the Lord stood near Paul and said, 'Take courage! As you have testified about me in Jerusalem, so you must also testify in Rome'" (Acts 23:11 NIV84). The word "testify" defines Paul's "defense." Paul gave witness to the power and love of Christ, who had appeared to him even when he was persecuting Christians. He was fulfilling his role as an apostle, namely, to bear witness to the resurrection of Christ. He would do the same in Rome, where everyone would soon realize that he was in chains because he was witnessing to Christ.

Acts 24:10

> And when the governor had nodded to him to speak, Paul replied: "Knowing that for many years you have been a judge over this nation, I cheerfully make my *defense*."

Since Paul was a Roman citizen, the Roman authorities had a legal responsibility to explore the charges against him and make sure he got a fair trial. The event at the temple in Jerusalem led to a series of appearances before Roman and Jewish officials in which Paul had an opportunity to make his defense.

The Roman tribune in Jerusalem sent Paul to Caesarea, to the Roman governor Felix. Paul's accusers came down from Jerusalem with their lawyer, Tertullus, and brought formal charges against Paul (Acts 24:1). Here it is clear that a formal trial was going on.

Tertullus accused Paul of outlandish crimes: "We have found this man to be a troublemaker, stirring up riots among the Jews . . . a ringleader of the Nazarene sect," and one who "tried to desecrate the temple" (Acts 24:5,6 NIV84).

Paul proceeded to make his defense. On this occasion, Paul did not report his conversion or testify to his faith. The Jews present had already heard that testimony and rejected it. Paul simply defended himself against the charges brought against him and proved they were all false.

Acts 25:8

> Paul argued in his *defense*, "Neither against the Law of the Jews, nor against the temple, nor against Caesar have I committed any offense."

Felix put off sentencing Paul and left him in prison until the new governor arrived. The new governor, Festus, held another formal trial in Caesarea. Jewish leaders came down from Jerusalem to press charges. We hear little about the trial. The Jews again charged Paul with crimes they could not prove. Paul defended himself: "Neither against the Law of the Jews, nor against the temple, nor against Caesar have I committed any offense" (Acts 25:8). This was a simple statement of his innocence.

Acts 25:16

> "I answered them that it was not the custom of the Romans to give up anyone before the accused met the accusers face to face and had opportunity to make his *defense* concerning the charge laid against him."

Acts 26:1,2

> So Agrippa said to Paul, "You have permission to speak for yourself." Then Paul stretched out his hand and made his *defense*: "I consider myself fortunate that it is before you, King Agrippa, I am going to make my defense today against all the accusations of the Jews."

Acts 26:24

> And as he was saying these things in his *defense*, Festus said with a loud voice, "Paul, you are out of your mind; your great learning is driving you out of your mind."

Festus was in a difficult position. In order to avoid a trial in Jerusalem, Paul had appealed to Caesar's court in Rome. Festus, however, didn't know what Paul had been charged with doing. A longtime regional official, King Agrippa, along with his Jewish wife, Bernice, came to visit Festus. Festus explained his predicament, and Agrippa said he was interested to hear what Paul had to say.

This would not be a formal trial, yet it was intended to find evidence to use in the formal trial in Rome.

Paul's defense consisted of confessing his faith with the intent of converting the people around him. Paul confessed his former sin of hostility against Jesus and his followers. Paul said that he had repented, and he explained that he would spend the rest of his life doing for others what the Lord had done for him, namely, open their eyes by leading them to repent and turn to God. He would bring them out of the darkness of Satan's power and into the light where they would receive the forgiveness of sins and a place among God's people. He would urge them to do the kind of works that were consistent with their changed attitude toward sin.

Paul spoke about his "hope," the same hope Peter referred to in 1 Peter 3:15. Paul explained that he was on trial for no other reason than that he had the same hope all believing Jews had and for which they worshiped God day and night. He looked forward to the resurrection of the dead. This hope was based on the promises God had made to their fathers. Paul testified that Jesus of Nazareth had fulfilled everything Moses and the prophets said would happen, namely, that God's chosen one would suffer death and rise again and then proclaim light to the Jews and non-Jews alike. What Paul said that day is called an *apologia*, a defense. This is a perfect example of doing what Peter urged his readers to do.

Festus and Agrippa saw through what Paul was trying to do. Festus rejected Paul's "sermon." He interrupted Paul and shouted, "Paul, you are out of your mind; your great learning is driving you out of your mind" (Acts 26:24). Paul then turned his attention to Agrippa. Paul had been trying to make Agrippa confess that the prophecies Agrippa knew—and perhaps believed in—spoke about Jesus. Agrippa asked Paul, "In a short time would you persuade me to be a Christian?" (Acts 26:28). Of course, that's what Paul was trying to do, namely, to tell Agrippa about his hope in Christ.

Romans 2:15 NIV 84

> They show that the requirements of the law are written on their hearts, their consciences also bearing witness, and their thoughts now accusing, now even *defending* them.

A person's conscience works in concert with the law written in that person's heart. The person's thoughts either accuse him of going against the law or defend him for keeping the law. This is clearly a trial scene.

1 Corinthians 9:1-3

> Am I not free? Am I not an apostle? Have I not seen Jesus our Lord? Are not you my workmanship in the Lord? If to others I am not an apostle, at least I am to you, for you are the seal of my apostleship in the Lord. This is my *defense* to those who would examine me.

In these verses Paul was defending himself against false charges. He had a courtroom setting in mind.

2 Corinthians 7:11

> For see what earnestness this godly grief has produced in you, but also what *eagerness to clear yourselves*, what indignation, what fear, what longing, what zeal, what punishment! At every point you have proved yourselves innocent in the matter.

This is not a courtroom, but the idea of proving one's innocence in the face of an accusation is certainly present.

2 Corinthians 12:19

> Have you been thinking all along that we have been *defending* ourselves to you? It is in the sight of God that we have been speaking in Christ, and all for your upbuilding, beloved.

This verse comes near the end of Paul's second letter to the Corinthians. Paul admitted to making a detailed defense of his apostleship. Paul's *defense* referred to clearing himself of charges that had been brought against him by false apostles, namely, that he was not a true apostle. His defense was to serve to strengthen the Corinthians' faith.

Philippians 1:7

> It is right for me to feel this way about you all, because I hold you in my heart, for you are all partakers with me of grace, both in my imprisonment and in the *defense* and confirmation of the gospel.

Philippians 1:16,17

> The latter do it out of love, knowing that I am put here for the *defense* of the gospel. The former proclaim Christ out of selfish ambition, not sincerely but thinking to afflict me in my imprisonment.

Paul was on trial in Rome. Paul would have to answer the formal charges brought against him. But notice that his concern was for defending and confirming the Gospel message he preached, not to gain his freedom.

We are not told what Paul said in court, but from his example before Festus and Agrippa, he probably said he had done nothing deserving arrest and imprisonment in Jerusalem but that he was being charged with preaching Christ. In the process he had a chance to proclaim the Gospel.

2 Timothy 4:16,17

> At my first *defense* no one came to stand by me, but all deserted me. May it not be charged against them! But the Lord stood by me and strengthened me, so that through me the message might be fully proclaimed and all the Gentiles might hear it.

Paul had been released from his first imprisonment in Rome. He had been arrested a second time. He was now in Rome standing trial again. Although everyone deserted Paul, God strengthened him. But once again, Paul was happy that the Gospel message had been "fully proclaimed" so that "all the Gentiles" would hear it. Paul would have addressed the formal charges against him, to be sure. But his concern was that the Gospel in all its truth be proclaimed to the Gentiles.

Summary

The word *apologia* is used enough times in the New Testament to give us a pretty good idea of what people in the New Testament would have thought when they heard it. An *apologia* was what happened in an ancient court of law when a defendant tried to prove his innocence. An ancient defense attorney would use every bit of evidence he could find to do his job.

But the word *apologia* cannot be strictly defined by what happens when a lawyer offers logical evidence for a person's guilt or innocence in a court of law. Men like Paul were not primarily concerned with defending themselves so they could gain their freedom. They were far more interested in using the opportunity to give a witness to Christ and their faith in him, which is what Jesus said the Spirit would help them do.

When defining *apologia,* Greek dictionaries make this distinction. They offer a technical definition for what is done in a courtroom, "to defend oneself against charges." And they offer more general definitions—to give an answer, to reply, or to offer a response.

A study of 1 Peter 3:15

The verse in context reads:

> But even if you should suffer for righteousness' sake, you will be blessed. Have no fear of them, nor be troubled, but in your hearts honor Christ the Lord as holy, always being prepared to make a *defense* to anyone who asks you for a reason for the hope that is in you; yet do it with gentleness and respect, having a good conscience, so that, when you are slandered, those who revile your good behavior in Christ may be put to shame. (1 Peter 3:14-16)

"honor Christ the Lord as holy"

Peter was writing to Christians who were being persecuted for their faith. In that context, his readers would have been asked to explain what was so important to them that they would endure such abuse. That explanation could be asked in a formal trial or in an informal hearing. If they were in prison, it might be questions from prison guards or fellow inmates—hostile or sympathetic. Non-Christian friends and neighbors would likely want to know why the Christian was in opposition to state required sacrifices and willing to suffer persecution for not offering them. Christians might be ridiculed by their friends for refusing to satisfy the sinful nature as they had in the past (1 Peter 4:3-5).

Peter begins this verse with an important reminder: "In your hearts honor Christ the Lord as holy." What does he mean by that? Isaiah 8:12,13 is a good explanation of what Peter means: "Do not call conspiracy all that this people calls conspiracy, and do not fear what they fear, nor be in dread. But the Lord of hosts, him you shall honor as holy. Let him be your fear, and let him be your dread."

In Isaiah's day, some Israelites were trying to make their fellow Israelites afraid of the difficulties the nation of Israel was soon going to experience. Isaiah told these Israelites not to worry about the plans of human beings. Rather, they should worry about God. They should set him apart as the one to respect, and they should seek to please him alone.

Jesus warned the disciples about the coming persecution and repeated what Isaiah had said: "Do not fear those who kill the body but cannot kill the soul. Rather fear him who can destroy both soul and body in hell" (Matthew 10:28).

Peter said the same. He had already urged wives who were vulnerable to the whims of unbelieving husbands to "do good and do not fear anything that is frightening" (1 Peter 3:6). And in the verse before the one we are studying, he urged those who were suffering persecution to see it as a source of blessing. He urged them: "But even if you should suffer for righteousness' sake, you will be blessed. Have no fear of them, nor be troubled" (1 Peter 3:14). After encouraging a spirit of the fear of God and boldness in his readers' hearts, Peter told them what to do when called on to give a reason for their hope.

"being prepared"

The word "prepared" is an important part of this verse. It is closely linked with the idea of setting Christ apart as holy. Many translations start a new sentence at this point. But the Greek literally says, "Make the Lord Christ holy in your hearts, always being prepared [or 'ready'] for a defense [or 'answer'] to everyone who asks you . . ." We might paraphrase it like this: "Out of honor and respect for the Lord Jesus, do not be afraid to defend or explain your hope, even if you must suffer for doing that."

In modern apologetics, the word "prepare" is interpreted as preparing to use apologetic arguments. But consider the different ways it is used in the New Testament. A wedding banquet was *prepared* (Matthew 22:8). Jesus urged us to be *prepared* for when he would return as judge (Matthew 24:44). Some of the young women in Jesus' parable were wise and were *prepared* to meet the bridegroom (Matthew 25:10). The room Jesus used for his last supper with the disciples was already *prepared* when the disciples came to arrange for its use (Mark 14:15). When Jesus warned his disciples that some would fall away, Peter said he was *prepared* to accompany Jesus to prison and death (Luke 22:33). The Jews set an ambush for Paul and were *prepared* to kill him when they had the opportunity (Acts 23:15). Paul was *prepared* to carry out church discipline in the Corinthian congregation, but only after the Corinthians' faith had matured

(2 Corinthians 10:6). Titus was to urge the Christians in Crete to be *prepared* (or ready) for every good work (Titus 3:1). Peter said that our salvation is *prepared* to be revealed in the last times (1 Peter 1:3).

When Christians are to prepare to give a defense or reason for their hope, it does not necessarily refer to a study of content, although that may be a part of the preparation. It can also refer to a posture of readiness, as when Paul was prepared to carry out church discipline or Peter was prepared to go with Jesus into prison and death.

In 1 Peter 3:15 there is no indication that Peter was telling the Christians to study evidence and arguments to defend Christianity. Christians were being encouraged to be ready when someone asked them about their hope. Every Christian will want to "grow in the grace and knowledge of our Lord and Savior Jesus Christ" (2 Peter 3:18 NIV84). And this can include the knowledge of Scripture as well as of other truths that might answer people's questions. But here Peter was primarily referring to having a posture of readiness rather than preparing to defend the faith with arguments and evidence.

"always"

The little word "always" supports the above interpretation of "prepared." It would be an impossible task always to be prepared to use modern apologetic arguments. People can spend years learning the arguments. Even after they have learned them, it is impossible to tailor the arguments to match perfectly the precise questions people have. What's more, one must master a method of presenting them logically and lovingly—which is perhaps the most difficult skill to master.

To interpret Peter as saying that everyone must become an apologist in the modern sense creates a burden that no Christian can carry. The push to adopt modern apologetics can actually hinder a Christian's confidence that he or she can *always* be prepared to share their faith as God wants them to. Anyone who has read a book or listened to a lecture on apologetics cannot but leave overwhelmed, and that includes pastors with a seminary training. If Peter had modern apologetic arguments in mind, the depth of specialized knowledge necessary to answer the objections of unbelievers even on a limited range of topics would be difficult or impossible for one person to acquire.

But being ready to give a witness to what gives us hope is a posture we can always have. To set Christ apart as holy and respect him alone, and then be ready to explain the reason for our hope in Christ—that we can always be ready to carry out.

"the hope"

The modern apologetic goal is to give logical reasons why a person can and should put their faith in the Christian religion. But Peter does not say that Christians should give a reason for *why* they believe. His focus is on *what* they believe, that is, the hope they have.

Today we use the word *hope* as a wish that may or may not be fulfilled: "I hope we are going fishing today" or, "I hope you get well." A Christian's hope, on the other hand, is a certainty. The only reason we *hope* for it is because we don't have it yet. A Christian has a sure *hope*, based on Christ's death and resurrection, which the Holy Spirit has led him or her to believe. Therefore, it is certain. A Christian can *hope* for eternal life in God's presence with absolute certainty because God promised it and made it as certain as his Son's death and resurrection.

A look at how the word is used in Scripture will bear this out. The *"hope* to which" God has called us is a synonym for "his glorious inheritance in the saints" (Ephesians 1:18). Our *hope* "is laid up for [us] in heaven." We heard about it "in the word of the truth, the gospel" (Colossians 1:5).

The *"hope* of salvation" was "a helmet," protecting the most vulnerable and strategic part of the body (1 Thessalonians 5:8). Christ Jesus himself is called "our *hope*" (1 Timothy 1:1). Our *hope* is something in which we boast (Hebrews 3:6).

The writer of Hebrews encourages us: "Let us hold on firmly to the confession of our *hope* without wavering, since he who promised is faithful" (10:23). Notice that the ESV translates "our hope." That gives it a subjective feel, something we do. But the Greek has "*the* hope," that is, the concrete, certain blessing that we have in Christ. That is how other translations, the NIV for example, translate.

We are focusing on Peter's use of *hope* in 1 Peter 3:15. Notice how Peter used this word earlier in this book. At the very beginning, he wrote: "Blessed be the God and Father of our Lord Jesus Christ! According to his great mercy, he has caused us to be born again to a living *hope* through the resurrection of Jesus Christ from the dead" (1 Peter 1:3).

1 Peter 3:15 and modern apologetics

There is nothing in 1 Peter 3:15 to support the idea that we are to offer arguments or present evidence that make the Christian faith reasonable to unbelievers. Rather, Peter is saying: "Fellow Christians, honor Christ. Seek to please him. If the people around you persecute you, don't be afraid of them. They will see you living and suffering as you are and can't imagine why. When they ask you to explain yourself, always be ready to tell them about the reason for your hope: Explain what Christ has done for you—and for them."

Even people who write on apologetics recognize this. Boa and Bowman write, "The New Testament, then, does not use the word *apologia* and *apologeomai* in the technical sense of the modern world *apologetics*. . . . It was apparently not until 1794 that apologetics was used to designate a special theological discipline."[313]

In effect, therefore, the word apologetics as it is used today is a made-up word. It is using a Greek word that in context means one thing and giving it meaning in terms of what many today are doing to prove that Christianity is rational.

Siegbert Becker writes about Luther's view of apologetics:

> Interesting in this connection is Luther's comment on Peter's admonition to be ready at all times to give an answer to anyone who asks a "reason for the hope" that is in us (1 Peter 3:15). This text is often used today as a call for a rational apologetic in defense of Christianity. It also was understood in this way by scholastic theology.[314]

Becker then quotes Luther, who criticizes the scholastics for how they used 1 Peter 3:15:

> The scholastics have twisted this text to the effect that one should overcome heretics with reason and out of the natural light of Aristotle, because it says here in the Latin, "rationem reddere" ("give a reason"), as though Peter meant that we should do it with human reason. Therefore they say that the Scriptures are far too weak to overcome heretics. It must be done with reason and must come out of the brain. From that

---

[313]Boa and Bowman Jr., *Faith Has Its Reasons*, pp. 3,4.
[314]Becker, *The Foolishness of God,* pp. 166-167.

source one must prove that faith is right. And yet our faith is above all reason and produced only by the power of God.[315]

Summary

The Greek word translated "to give a defense" or "to answer" can refer to one's defense in a court of law. However, it can refer to other activities, such as giving a report of something that happened or giving a reason for one's activities.

The context of 1 Peter 3:15, both the broader context of the book and the immediate context of the verse, defines the word. It refers to what a Christian might say when asked about why he or she has hope. The reason why a Christian has hope is because of Christ alone, specifically his work of suffering and dying for our sins. There is no indication of—in fact the words rule out—any connection between this verse and modern apologetics.

---

[315]Becker, *The Foolishness of God*, p. 167. "Rationem reddere" is translated "to give an account."

Conclusion
Sin and Grace Apologetics

Introduction

In this chapter we will do a number of things. We'll look at what Luther thought about apologetics. Then we'll summarize the cluster of teachings that are foundation for modern apologetics. We'll follow that with a list of questions that should be asked by anyone using modern apologetics. Finally, we'll look at how apologetic arguments can be properly used in our work with unbelievers.

Luther's use of apologetics

Catholic theologian Avery Dulles understood Luther well: "To draw up a set of preambles of faith that would demonstrate the antecedent possibility or probability of revelation was for Luther an act of works-righteousness, smacking of Semi-Pelagianism. Thus apologetics, conceived as a natural preparation for faith, stood condemned by his doctrine of the sole efficacy of grace."[316]

Siegbert Becker's chapter "Luther's Apologetics" in *The Foolishness of God* warrants careful study. Luther believed that human learning provides insights into how the world works and is a great blessing as it helps us carry out day-to-day tasks. For example, Luther valued Aristotle's *Logic* and said it should be used as a university textbook.

But according to Luther, human reason "can teach the hand and foot what to do, but only God can teach the heart of man to believe."[317] Human learning "does not understand holy things." One must "use it with care" and "limit philosophy to its own sphere."[318]

---

[316]Dulles, *A History of Apologetics*, p. 147.

[317]Becker, *The Foolishness of God*, p. 151. This book is about the place of reason in Luther's theology. Please note: Becker included references to Luther quotations in the Weimar Edition of Luther's Works. These references can be found in his book.

[318]Becker, *The Foolishness of God*, p. 141.

Becker wrote, "Luther, who saw reason as an enemy of faith, would have been horrified at the very thought of reason coming to the defense of the Christian religion."[319] And again, "When men seek proofs for the truths of Christianity, it is already too late."[320] God expects us to search out his Word to find answers to our questions, whatever they may be. But "whenever and wherever the Word of God has spoken, then and there we are not to ask for additional proof or to demand a rational explanation of what has been clearly revealed by God in the Holy Scripture."[321]

Becker quotes Roland Bainton, who describes Luther's understanding of faith:

> Neither is faith the final stage to which a man comes after a long, drawn-out reasoning process by which he is persuaded to rest his heart in the sufficiency of logical evidence. It is much rather a stepping-out into the darkness, where there is no "proof" in the ordinary sense of the term, but only a word of the Lord, which is infinitely better and more certain than all the rational proofs in the whole world. Faith is something done to us rather than by us.[322]

Luther found his hope in God's Word: "It is the very nature of the Christian faith that it seeks no foundation on which to rest except the bare word of Scripture."[323] And Luther says, "Such faith also does not come out of our own preparation, but when God's Word is preached openly and clearly, then such faith and hope, such a firm confidence in Christ begins to spring up."[324]

Luther believed there was a good use for logical argumentation. He used it against all his opponents to show the foolishness of their position or of a point they were making. Becker explains the difference: "It is also significant that Luther was willing to use against the position of his opponents an argument which he was not willing to use or to allow against Scripture."[325]

---

[319]Becker, *The Foolishness of God,* p. 141.

[320]Becker, *The Foolishness of God,* p. 148.

[321]Becker, *The Foolishness of God,* p. 148.

[322]Becker, *The Foolishness of God,* p. 148, quoting Roland Bainton, *Here I Stand,* 1950, p. 65. The bibliography does not state who published which edition of Bainton Becker was using.

[323]Becker, *The Foolishness of God,* p. 163.

[324]Becker, *The Foolishness of God,* p. 149.

[325]Becker, *The Foolishness of God,* p. 171.

Luther used arguments against the Catholic scholar Erasmus and against the Anabaptists, who denied infant baptism, and against the Lutheran teacher Andreas Carlstadt. Yet, as Becker points out: "It must be noted throughout that Luther is not seeking to establish the truth by reason, but to show that the arguments of Carlstadt are weak."[326]

Would Luther have written a book on apologetics? Becker answers:

> While [Luther] would never have written a book on the reasonableness of Christianity, he might conceivably have been the author of one with the title, "The Irrationalism of Unbelief." Philosophy will fulfill its proper role in the church when it serves to destroy the "pretensions of speculative reason."[327]

> "Whenever you must, outside of this doctrine of justification, debate with Jews, Turks, and sectarians about the wisdom, or the power, or the attributes of God, then use all your skill, and be as subtle and sharp a debater as you can be, for then you are in a different kind of argument." [328]

Someone might say that Luther was talking about polemics (arguing against false teachings) rather than apologetics. But Luther would not have seen a difference between the two. Unbelief is unbelief, whether in the mind of the unbeliever or in the mind of a Christian who denies some part of Scripture.[329]

Luther's apologetics goes no farther than God's Word. Becker states Luther's attitude:

> If we find people, therefore, who deny that the Scriptures are the Word of God we are to be silent and not speak a word to them. We should be ready at all times to give them proof out of the Scripture. If they believe it, well and good. But if they will not believe it, we need to give them nothing more. If men are afraid that by such a course of action the Scriptures will be ridiculed or that the Word of God will suffer shame, let them remember that this is God's concern and not ours. In other words, it is blasphemous to imagine that our reason can provide an

---

[326]Becker, *The Foolishness of God*, p. 173.
[327]Becker, *The Foolishness of God*, p. 175.
[328]Becker, *The Foolishness of God*, p. 176.
[329]See Becker, *The Foolishness of God*, p. 173

adequate defense for God's Word. The gospel stands in need of proclamation, not of defense.[330]

Luther's words encourage us to learn the arguments, and modern apologetic literature can be a good source for that. But the use of that information takes place outside the discussion of the truth of Scripture and outside proclaiming the Gospel of justification, and, we might add, outside the work of evangelism per se. Luther's purpose was to give a reason for his hope. And when he did point out that unbelief is irrational, it was not to prove that faith is rational but to expose the sin of unbelief. This, we might add, is the very thing Paul did in Romans 1.[331]

The problems with modern apologetics

Becker writes, "Luther did not believe that the gospel was reasonable, nor that it could be made reasonable and still remain the gospel."[332] He adds, "To judge according to reason and our understanding is a certain way to destroy and to lose the gospel entirely."

This is the premise of this book on apologetics. However, once the gospel message shifted to something other than how it is described in Scripture, it can be promoted and defended rationally. In this section we'll review some of the problems with modern apologetics we have uncovered.

The shifted Gospel, but not the true Gospel, can be dealt with rationally

When the Gospel shifts, a cluster of teachings arise that naturally fit with the shifted gospel. And, we maintain, these teachings are foundational to modern apologetics. The ministry of sin and grace also has a cluster of teachings that are integral to it. The first set of teachings is not found in Scripture. The second set of teachings is. We'll summarize these two clusters of teachings

God's favor versus the power to overcome sin. The shifted Gospel is less about the favor of God in Christ than about finding power to overcome sin. It is more about piety than forgiveness. It centers—sometimes more, sometimes less—on

---

[330]Becker, *The Foolishness of God*, p. 167.

[331]It is said that 17th century Lutheran theologians began to develop apologetic arguments similar to modern arguments. Supposedly modern Lutherans failed to continue that work and should imitate what their forefather started. This claim is only partially true and it is somewhat misleading. See the Appendix for more information.

[332]Becker, *The Foolishness of God*, p. 154.

the natural human idea that God's blessings come through by keeping the law. When shifted in this direction, the Gospel fits with the way people naturally think, and in the process it becomes rational.

Scripture, however, says that God's way of finding his favor and blessings comes because his Son sacrificed himself on a cross. This method of finding God is inherently foolish to human beings and cannot be proven by argument and evidence.

The image of God lost versus the image of God retained. The shifted Gospel grows out of the idea that people retain the image of God. Because people have the image of God, they have positive yearnings—to know God, to keep the law, to escape judgment, and to find righteousness and wholeness in life. In short, they yearn for the godliness they know they have lost.

But Scripture says that the image of God has been lost and is renewed when people come to know and believe God's love in Christ. It says that no one searches for God (at least not as he wants to be found) and no one yearns for him (at least not for what he has to offer). Human yearnings may provide an opportunity to tell about sin and grace, but they don't provide a natural touch-point for the ministry of forgiveness and reconciliation.

Philosophical verses Scriptural reasons to serve God. Scriptural reasons to serve God have nothing in common with human philosophical thoughts about morality. Philosophy can do nothing more than reinforce people's natural knowledge of God and their sense of right and wrong, and it can only use these truths as its motivation for people to become more moral. It cannot fathom God's method of salvation or the true Gospel.

In Scripture, reasons for serving God always center on the righteousness and freedom from the Law believers have in Christ. This is foreign to human philosophy, whose basic purpose is to help people do what leads to a fulfilled life.

Different levels of certainty. A rational gospel demands rational proof. Modern apologists admit that its arguments and evidence cannot provide 100 percent certainty that Christianity is true. They also believe that Scripture must be proven true before it can be believed. According to many apologists, ultimate certainty comes through one's conversion experience.

But Scripture says that its words and promises stand on their own. Scripture is the channel through which God's message of forgiveness comes to us. It comes with the power of the Spirit, who uses it to enable people to believe it. As such it is self-authenticating and does not need to be authenticated by apologetics.

Problems with arguments proving that Christianity is the only true religion

Apologetics is a vast field with many different approaches. Beside the general problem just described, some forms of apologetics have individual problems.

As religious pluralism increases, so does the need to prove that Christianity is more reasonable than the other world religions. In apologetics, this is proven historically.

Most other religions developed long after their founders died. There is often little information on how and when their sacred books were written. Christianity, on the other hand, is closely linked to history. Jesus is a real person, and the books of the Bible, the New Testament at least, can be traced to their origins.

These differences are true. But no matter how many historical differences exist between Christianity and non-Christian religions, the most obvious and important difference is often overlooked or given a back seat. Only Christianity has a Savior from sin. All non-Christian religions lay the burden of finding salvation, however they define salvation, on the worshiper.

This is the only important difference between Christianity and other religions. Noting other differences can be helpful, and Christians who are living among people of another religion want to understand their history and teachings. But at heart it's a matter of forgiveness. As we have seen, a shifted Gospel focuses less on forgiveness than it does on other matters, and this area of apologetics is a case in point.

Problems with arguments to prove the existence of God

In classical apologetics the goal is to prove the existence of God, lead a person to be a theist, and then prove that God has revealed himself in Christ. In general, the classical arguments for the existence of God are valid. If you believe these arguments, you cannot help but believe in God.

But the use of those arguments damages evangelism efforts. It implies that people don't necessarily know that God exists. This blunts the point Paul is making in Romans 1. There Paul is accusing people of the sin of suppressing the knowledge of God, whom all people know. This is why God is revealing his wrath,

Paul says. Paul then uses the revelation of God's wrath on the sin of idolatry that Paul uses as his springboard to reveal God's gift of righteousness in Christ.

This fact should prompt several questions. Most important, if we try to prove the existence of God, are we undermining Paul's message that people are sinfully suppressing the truth about God, which they already know? If we turn the discussion into a rational, philosophical argument for the existence of God, are we giving tacit permission for the unbeliever to reject it because his or her reason might find it not to be rational? If we use human philosophical arguments for the existence of God, are we misleading people into thinking that Christianity is inherently reasonable? If we can prove that God exists, are we inadvertently implying that we will be able to prove the Gospel?

But that is the point of his book. Modern apologists are most often working with a shifted Gospel, which can be proven because it contains teachings that fit with people's natural way of thinking about salvation.

Problems with trying to prove that Christianity satisfies human longings

Many modern apologists contrast the blessings of Christianity with the fruitlessness of secular humanism. Their argument is that only the Christian world view provides a framework that can lead to a full and satisfying life. They find a point of contact with various human yearnings that they claim are reflections of the image of God.

Who can disagree that secular humanism is fruitless? The disastrous philosophies of the Enlightenment, a view of the world through the glasses of evolution, and the idolatry of Eastern religions, all exact a toll. The Bible's worldview, however, is unique. From beginning to end, Scripture focuses on human sin and blessings of Christ.

This type of apologetics prompts questions. Are human beings able to yearn for what pleases God? Have all people lost the image of God, which apologists credit for such pious human yearnings? Does this lead to the implication that Christianity is primarily the way to a new worldview leading to a God-pleasing and happy life? Could that undermine the real ministry of the Christian Church, namely, leading people to the forgiveness of sins?

Problem with arguments for the truth of Scripture and Christianity

This type of apologetics tries to prove from evidence and argument that Scripture and Scripture's message are true. No one denies that the evidence points to the truth of Scripture and Christianity. But how necessary is this, especially since the evidence does not produce 100 percent certainty.

This prompts important questions. Is partial certainty all we can expect? How does the partial certainty of apologetic arguments relate to the complete certainty Scripture says we have in the Gospel message? How does the Holy Spirit use apologetic arguments to lead a person to faith? What is the nature of the gospel to which these apologetic arguments lead? When do arguments cease being servants of the things they are trying to prove and become judges of whether those things are true? Are we willing to say that a lack of certainty is OK? Or is a conversion experience necessary to arrive at complete certainty?

Apologetics can be detrimental to the faith

Apologetics can take one's attention away from Christ

Speaking to others about what Christ did to remove the guilt of sin is not complicated. No philosophical arguments are needed, no lifelong study. Tell them that your hope is found in Christ. Let people know they can live in hope in spite of their sin.

As I read various books on apologetics, I watched for how prominent Christ was. Were the apologetic arguments presented in those books chosen because they led directly to a witness to Christ? With few exceptions, they did not.[333] They led, rather, to the bare conclusion that God exists, that Christianity is true, and that Scripture deserves to be viewed as divine. Each type of modern apologetics led to an undefined Christianity, or at least failed to lead to the foolishness of the cross.

Apologetics puts a burden on Christians

Although the term *apologetics* is used in the singular—as a single, agreed upon body of knowledge that all apologists use—it is more accurate to speak of apologetics in the plural—as a cluster of apologetic approaches and techniques.

---

[333]Note the books by Gregory Koukl, *Tactics*, and Voddie Baucham, *Expository Apologetics*.

Anyone who says, "I want to learn apologetics" faces a daunting task. Apologetics is highly philosophical, especially arguments that prove the existence of God, that pit the benefits of Christianity against the damage of secularism, and even the use of evidence and arguments to prove that Christianity is true. All demand at least some understanding of philosophy and much study of fairly technical material. Even learning a single type of apologetics, like creation science, can take a lifetime.

It is impossible to understand the full range of the arguments against Christianity and master how they can be countered. One person said that Christians attend apologetic lectures as a source of Christian entertainment. They want to hear someone skilled enough in apologetics defeat the arguments of unbelievers. When they see it can be done, they clap their hands and thank the apologist. But they leave the auditorium thinking that such a level of knowledge and skill is beyond them. It would consume all their time—time that might be better used in learning about Scripture and the Christian's hope in Christ.

Worst of all, modern apologists imply—some actually say it—that 1 Peter 3:15 makes it God's will that they become versed in apologetic argumentation. Intended or not, this idea leads to the guilt of a hopeless task.

The proper use of apologetic arguments

The role of apologetics

When I was a senior in a Christian high school, I began to think about evolution. I believed the Genesis creation account, but like all Christians, I wondered about the claims of evolutionary science. Our library had two fairly recent books by creation scientists. They were among the first: *Genes, Genesis, and Evolution* by John Klotz and *The Genesis Flood* by Henry Morris and John Whitcomb. I read them. They were helpful. I didn't take everything as "gospel truth." But they helped me see that there were other ways of looking at the data and that evolution was not as conclusive as it was claimed to be.

What role did these books play? Frankly, I can't define it doctrinally. Did they sustain my faith? increase my faith? No. Were they tools of the Holy Spirit? I don't think so. At least they were not means of grace; they did nothing to lead me to Christ. Still, the information was good to know. It satisfied my need to know certain things about the claims of evolution, and I was thankful to the authors of the books.

For others, books like these may play a more important role. They may have helped the person overcome genuine doubts which were directly conflicting with the teachings of Scripture or the truth about Christ.

God can certainly use apologetic arguments to show the foolishness of unbelief. But, as Luther said, they don't create faith. We might say that he gives them to us for the same reasons he gives us everything else in life—a great blessing as we interact with a sinful world, a way of helping us suppress our reason, appropriate advice from a fellow Christian. We might say they are acts of providence—ways he is working in all things for the good of those who love him.

Use apologetic evidences and arguments to show love

For Christians to ignore the questions they are asked or to withhold their help from people who are in doubt, is nothing short of unloving. For that reason alone, Christians will want to know answers to the questions they may be asked.

At the same time, if we Christians see ourselves becoming wrapped up in apologetics, if we like their logic and rationality, if we find them replacing the ministry of sin and grace or overshadowing our joy in Christ, if we sense the Scriptural problems that exist with certain forms of evidence—then we are wise to carefully rethink what we are doing. We should think again of the power of the word and Scripture's way of spreading it.

Learn the evidence and arguments well

As I said at the beginning of this book, our task is not to reject the truth of apologetic arguments, but to use those arguments in a God-fearing way. What follows are some suggestions.

Realize that using the arguments used by modern apologists does not mean becoming a modern apologist. After all, you can give the reason for your hope without having to know anything more than that you are forgiven in Christ.

But you can show love by talking to Christians and non-Christians alike about questions that trouble them. Christians have been doing this for years. They study false teachings and religions so they can discuss them knowledgeably. They study the ideas of those who reject Scripture in order to show them to be incorrect and even foolish. To do this, you don't have to buy into the false teachings that come out of churches that have shifted the Gospel. You don't have to argue that Christianity is reasonable or link it together with natural human longings. You don't have to argue philosophically. You can abandon all this while still helping people find answers to what is troubling them.

We should always pray for the spirit Isaiah spoke about in Isaiah 65:2:

> All these things my hand has made, and so all these things came to be, declares the LORD. But this is the one to whom I will look: he who is humble and contrite in spirit and trembles at my word.

Ask God for wisdom about the world in which we live.

The world's secular, unbelieving culture rears its head and promotes any number of ideas that go against God's will. Christians will want to be aware of what's happening so we can speak intelligently with unbelievers and lead the conversation to the hope we have in Christ. We should study carefully the challenges fellow Christians face—challenges from false religions or from unbelieving scholars. This may sound like the opposite of what we have been saying in this book, but it isn't.

For example, no pastor should be ignorant of arguments for the divine nature of Scripture or have no grasp of its amazing transmission. If you live by a university, you know that Christian students are often troubled by what their unbelieving professors say about Scripture. Pastors and other church leaders must have specific answers to those challenges. Parents of those students would do well to prepare themselves also.

Evolution is considered a true account of the earth's origins. Many Christians have questions about it. Christian parents should have clear and unequivocal answers to the questions their children might ask. And they should be versed in how evolution ultimately undermines the work of Christ.

More and more mosques and temples are being built. Church members are rubbing elbows with members of these non-Christian churches. Christians should not be ignorant about what these churches are teaching.

Start where you are

It can take years to learn apologetic arguments and apply them in a conversation. Don't let that happen to you. One apologist, Voddie Baucham, recognized the problem. "Where should a person start?" he asked. "With the questions that come up" he answered. That's common sense. And it's all Christian love asks of us. Too often churches do studies on issues that their members are personally interested in. It is better to look outside and ask what might be troubling the people around them—Christians or non-Christians—and seek ways to use the information for the good of that person's eternal life.

If I live in a Mormon community, in love I'll want to understand the basics of Mormonism. I can talk intelligently when questions come up as I explain to a Mormon the reason for my hope.

If I live or serve near a college campus and after a few weeks of a "Bible as Literature" course, a freshman wants to talk about what he's hearing, I'll want to understand higher criticism, as best I can, so I can answer that person's question while rehearsing the reason for the hope we share.

If my Christian friend is toying with theistic evolution, I'll want to answer questions about evolution that come up as I tell that person about the hope I have. I'll explain what evolution does to my hope and that I don't want to sacrifice my hope on the altar of naturalism.

If my new college roommate rolls her eyes every time I leave for church and talks excitedly about the new philosophy she just learned that explains the world so well, I'll want to understand what she's referring to so I can tell her about my hope in a way that takes into account her way of thinking. In that context, I might want to do some research on why her philosophy is wrong. Regardless, as best I can, I will want to show why her philosophy runs counter to Christ. The very context implies a request to give a reason for my hope.

How do we know we're getting it right?

We're on the right track if we think carefully about problems associated with the modern apologetic movement. We ask questions about some of their assumptions. What role does proof play in answering objections to Christianity and in establishing the reliability of Scripture. Is it okay to settle for less than 100 percent certainty? Does Scripture verify itself or must it be verified by evidence from outside it? What is the relationship between the Holy Spirit and apologetic arguments? These and other questions asked in this book deserve careful attention. It is not right to jump on a bandwagon simply because it offers an easy way to communicate the truth.

We are on the right track if, in love, we help people who are troubled by the foolishness of arguments against Christianity. We are on the right track if we carefully cease to use evidence and arguments if we are falling into the temptation of using them to prove the truth of our faith.

We're on the right track if we focus on the power of God and his Word and always ask what we are trying to do with this or that argument and evidence? Is it leading the conversation to Christ or in some other direction.

We're on the right track if our goal is always to teach what gives us hope, not to prove why our faith is reasonable. Nothing says that *if I can* defend the faith with a reasonable argument, *I am obligated* to so do. It may be better to refrain from giving such an argument so that God will be glorified when a person comes to faith.

We're on the right track if we carefully distinguish which modern apologetic approaches are invalid and counterproductive. For example, proving the existence of God through rational arguments is proving what doesn't need to be proven. And trying to prove the rationality of God's method of salvation through Jesus' cross is trying to prove what that Scripture says is humanly foolish. We should avoid both.

Although we find pleasure in discussing the transmission of the text of Scripture, the witness of ancient archaeology and history, the findings of Christian anti-evolutionary scientists, etc., we're on the right track if we always find our source of power in Scripture itself.

We're on the right track if we find our hope in the witness of the apostles, Christ's appointed spokesmen.

We're on the right track if we don't have to make a "right turn" somewhere in our presentation about Christ. That is, if we make people's needs and yearnings our point of contact and then must lead them in another direction as we urge them to repent and escape eternal death through faith in Christ.

We're on the right track when we sufficiently appreciate the power of Satan's devilish logic and that if we use rational arguments to defeat him, he'll have us for lunch.

We're on the right track if we read the apostles' writings to learn not just their doctrine but also their pattern of ministry. Along this line, the apostles never refer to the office of "apologist" or to a spiritual gift of "doing apologetics." Rather, Scripture speaks of apostles, prophets, evangelists, teachers, witnesses, etc. We're on the right track when we align our ministry with the offices and spiritual gifts referred to in Scripture.

We're on the right track when we have made every attempt to lead a person to faith in Scripture's message of sin and grace without success, and can still find comfort in what Luther once said:

> If people will not accept the doctrines of the Christian faith on the authority of Scripture we should not even desire their assent on other grounds. . . . It is the very nature of the Christian faith that it seeks no foundation on which to rest except the bare word of Scripture.[334]

A Final Word

Preach the Word

Let me offer a few anecdotes. They illustrate an apologetics of sin and grace.

While working on the internet one day, I found this blog post by a man named Stephen Bedard. He related how he came to faith. This is not an acceptance of all Billy Graham's teachings. But Stephen Bedard is arguing for Graham's approach to spreading the Gospel and the effect it has on him in a world given increasingly to modern apologetic arguments:

> Few people would point to Billy Graham as one of the world's great apologists. I would like to argue that he is.
>
> It is true that Billy Graham does not have a PhD in the philosophy of religion, nor is he known for debating atheist professors. But that is a narrow definition of apologetics, one that most of us cannot attain to. I would suggest that Billy Graham is an apologist in the way that many of us could and should emulate.
>
> Let me turn the clock back twenty-five years. I was a former atheist, a recent theist and very much still the skeptic, not sure what to make of Christianity. I happened to be flipping through the channels and came across the Billy Graham Crusade. The only reason I gave him a moment was that even our liberal Anglican priest seemed to respect him. There was something about his preaching that kept me coming back. It was not that he was really funny or that he was flashy. It was pretty plain. But there was a confidence in his message. There is a fine line between confidence and cockiness and Graham came down on the right side. As I listened to Billy Graham, Christianity seemed to make sense; he

---

[334] Becker, *The Foolishness of God,* p. 163.

had a way of making the faith sound reasonable without going over my head. He dealt with the questions I was asking, not the questions people decided I should be asking. Each time I watched this program, I became more and more convinced that Christianity was true. Billy Graham may not have set out to be an apologist, but that is exactly the role he played in my life.

Billy Graham is an apologist in a way that we all can be. His apologetic is not based on his level of education but in his confidence in the gospel.[335]

Keep repentance and faith always in mind

Another time, I met a man at the coffee shop where I like to work. He saw a book on my table and noticed who wrote it. He said, "I studied apologetics under that guy!" We talked.

He asked me what I was writing. I gave him my title, *Sin and Grace Apologetics*. I explained that most apologists are trying to prove Christianity. I said I preferred that witnesses get right to the heart of the message of our need for a Savior.

We continued to talk. He told me about his conversion. At a point in life, he realized he was guilty before God. He heard someone tell him the message of Scripture—that God had forgiven him. And he came to faith. Then he said, "I'm interested in apologetics. And I'm good at talking with people. I really like to walk around college campuses and talk with students. I challenge them on what they're being taught. Usually, I use a few apologetic arguments. But my ultimate goal is to let them know they are forgiven."

I know nothing about this person's denomination and little about his approach to apologetics. But it was clear that he had Christianity straight in his own mind. I'm convinced that his approach led students to know the peace that he knew. God had put him on the right track.

---

[335]Stephen Bedard, "Billy Graham—Apologist," http://www.stephenjbedard.com/2013/11/07/billy-graham-apologist/ accessed May, 2023. (Slight shortening, no content change).

Don't major in the minors. Rely on God's way of leading people to faith

Lutheran minister, Rev. Paul Koester, wrote a senior paper at Wisconsin Lutheran Seminary about using apologetics among Mormons. He interviewed Rev. Mark Cares, a seasoned pastor who for many years has served a church in the heavily Mormon city of Boise, Idaho. Cares said that at first he used apologetic type arguments to prove that Mormonism is wrong. But after a while, he started simply talking about sin and grace. Koester writes, "Cares does not diminish the role of a reasoned defense against Mormon claims. Those conversations will come up; however, the goal is always to go back to the message of perfection through Christ alone."[336]

Koester speaks about his own experience interviewing ex-Mormons:

> Using apologetics in our witness to Mormons really is a case of majoring in minors. I had opportunity to speak with four Ex-Mormon Lutherans about their journey out of Mormonism. Not one of them pointed to a conversation about the nature of God, or the deity of Christ, or even the authority of Scripture as a reason why they came out of Mormonism into the Lutheran faith.[337]

Reflecting on Cares' approach, he wrote,

> Striking [the Mormon] heart is not done by using a sound reasoned defense against their teaching about the nature of God and the authority of Scripture. It's done by wielding the power of God for the salvation of all who believe. It's done by the message of sin and sin forgiven. It's done by giving them a message of how we actually become perfect: through the sacrifice of Jesus Christ.[338]

These three anecdotes prompt us to ask, "Do we need apologetic arguments to promote or defend Christianity?" If it can be shown from Scripture that in this skeptical world we must establish the existence of God and the credibility of Scripture before we can engage a skeptic, then the answer is yes. But if Scripture says it's OK to start point blank with the truths of Scripture and God's plan of salvation, then the answer is no.

---

[336]Paul M. Koester, "The Role of Apologetics in Witnessing to Mormons" 2018, http://essays.wisluthsem.org: 8080/handle/123456789/4372, accessed June, 2020, p. 35.

[337]Koester, "The Role of Apologetics in Witnessing to Mormons," p. 35.

[338]Koester, "The Role of Apologetics in Witnessing to Mormons," p. 38.

Modern apologetics is about arguments and evidence. But to repeat, there is only one piece of evidence that is 100 percent certain: We all sin. And there is only one solution that is 100 percent certain: Christ died for the sins of the whole world.

As stated previously, there is a role for evidence and arguments. But we make the best use of apologetic evidence and arguments if we

Understand Scripture's description of human nature.

Understand the message of sin and grace.

Understand the foolishness of the cross.

Understand the power of Scripture.

We're on the right track if we spread the message by spreading the message, if we defend Scripture by using Scripture, and if we defend the Gospel with the Gospel.

Bibliography

Allen, Diogenes. *Philosophy for Understanding Theology.* Atlanta: John Knox Press, 1985.

Aquinas, *Summa Contra Gentiles,* Book Three, Chapter 147.6. Translated by Vernon J. Bourke. https://isidore.co/aquinas/ContraGentiles3b.htm#147. Accessed January 2023.

Augustine. *Instructing Beginners in Faith.* Edited by Boniface Ramsey. Translated by Raymond Channing. Hyde Park, NY: New City Press, 2006.

_____. *The Confessions of Saint Augustine.* Translated by Rex Warner. New York: New American Library, 1963.

_____. *The Confessions, Revised.* Translated by Maria Boulding. New York: New York City Press, 2002.

_____. *The City of God: 2 Volumes.* Hyde Park, NY: New City Press, 2012.

Ayling, Stanley. *John Wesley.* New York: William Collins Publishers, Inc., 1979.

Bahnsen, Greg L. *Always Ready: Directions for Defending the Faith.* Edited by Robert Booth. Nacogdoches, TX: Covenant Media Press and Powder Springs, GA: American Vision Press, 1996.

_____. *Presuppositional Apologetics: Stated and Defended.* Edited by Joel McDurmon. Nacogdoches, TX: Covenant Media Press and Powder Springs, GA: American Vision Press, 2011.

Bainton, Roland. *Here I Stand.* Nashville: Abingdon, 1950.

Balge, Richard. *Acts,* of The People's Bible Series. Milwaukee: Northwestern Publishing House, 1988.

Battles, Ford Lewis and Walchenbach, John R. *Analysis of the Institutes of the Christian Religion of John Calvin.* Phillipsburg, NJ: P&R Publishing, 2001.

Baucham, Voddie, Jr. *Expository Apologetics: Answering Objections With the Power of the Word.* Wheaton: Crossway, 2015.

Becker, Siegbert W. *The Foolishness of God: The Place of Reason in the Theology of Martin Luther.* Milwaukee: Northwestern Publishing House, 1982.

Bedard, Stephen. "Billy Graham—Apologist." *Stephen J. Bedard* (blog). November 7,2013. http://www.stephenjbedard.com/2013/11/07/billy-graham-apologist/.

Beilby, James K. *Thinking About Christian Apologetics.* Downer's Grove: Intervarsity, 2011.

Bente, Fred. "Historical Introductions to the Symbolical Books of the Evangelical Lutheran Church." in *Concordia Triglotta.* St. Louis: Concordia, 1921.

Boa, Kenneth D. and Bowman, Robert M., Jr. *Faith Has Its Reasons,* Second Edition. Downer's Grove: Intervarsity, 2005.

Calvin, John. *Commentary on Romans,* Romans 6:2 https://www.studylight.org/commentaries/eng/cal/romans-6.html. Accessed April 2023.

_____. *Justification by Faith.* Edited by Nate Pickowicz. Translated by John Allen. Peterborough, Ontario, Canada: H&E Publishing, 2018.

_____. *The Institutes of the Christian Religion.* Translated by Henry Beveridge. 1559 Edition. Kindle file.

Campbell, Ted. The Religion of the Heart (Columbia, SC: University of South Carolina Press, 1991),

Chatraw, Joshua D. and Allen, Mark D. Apologetics at the Cross: An Introduction for Christian Witness. Grand Rapids: Zondervan, 2018.

Chesterton, G. K. *St. Thomas Aquinas.* Mansfield Centre, CT: Martino Publishing, 2011.

Chilton, Brian G. *The Layman's Manual on Christian Apologetics.* Eugene, OR: Wipf & Stock, 2019.

Christian Worship. Milwaukee: Northwestern Publishing House, 2021.

Christian Worship: A Lutheran Hymnal. Milwaukee, Northwestern, 1993.

Clendenin, Daniel. *Eastern Orthodox Christianity: A Western Perspective.* Grand Rapids: Baker, 1994.

Cowan, Steven B., ed. *Five Views on Apologetics.* Grand Rapids: Zondervan, 2000.

Craig, William Lane. *On Guard: Defending Your Faith With Reason and Precision.* Colorado Springs: David C. Cook, 2010.

Crook, Jason A. *The Rational Faith: A Review of the Evidence for Christianity.* 2020.

John Donne, "A Hymn to God the Father." https://www.poetryfoundation.org/poems/44115/a-hymn-to-god-the-father. Accessed May 2023.

Dulles, Avery Cardinal. *A History of Apologetics.* Eugene, OR: Wipf & Stock, 1999.

Edgar, William and Oliphint, K. Scott, eds. *Christian Apologetics Past & Present: A Primary Source Reader.* Two Volumes. Wheaton: Crossway, Vol. 1, 2009 and Vol. 2, 2011)

Eggert, Arthur A. and Kieta, Geoffrey A. *Clearing a Path for the Gospel: A Lutheran Approach to Apologetics.* Sun Prairie, WI: In Terra Pax Lutheran Publishing, 2019.

Feinberg, Paul. "Cumulative Case Apologetics." In *Five Views of Apologetics.* Grand Rapids: Zondervan, 2000.

Frame, John M. *Apologetics to the Glory of God: An Introduction.* Phillipsburg, NJ: P&R Publishing, 1994.

_____. *Apologetics: A Justification of Christian Belief.* Phillipsburg, NJ: P&R Publishing, 2015.

_____. *Cornelius Van Til: An Analysis of His Thought.* Phillipsburg, NJ: P&R Publishing, 1995.

Gatiss, Lee, "The Inexhaustible Fountain of All Good Things: Union With Christ in Calvin on Ephesians," Section 2.1, "Benefits Together," Themelios. Vol 34. No 2. https://www.thegospelcoalition.org/themelios/article/the-inexhaustible-fountain-of-all-good-things-union-with-christ-in-calvin-o/. Accessed April, 2023.

Geehan, E. R., ed. *Jerusalem and Athens: Critical Discussions on the Philosophy and Apologetics of Cornelius Van Til.* Phillipsburg, NJ: P&R Publishing, 1974.

Geisler, Norman. *Baker Encyclopedia of Christian Apologetics.* Grand Rapids: Baker, 1999.

Gerrish, B. A. *Grace and Reason: A Study in the Theology of Luther.* Eugene, OR: Wipf & Stock, 1962.

Gould, Paul M. and Davis, Richard, eds. Four Views on Christianity and Philosophy. Grand Rapids: Zondervan, 2016.

Habermas, Gary R. "Minimal Facts on the Resurrection That Even Skeptics Accept." SES https://ses.edu/minimal-facts-on-the-resurrection-that-even-skeptics-accept/. Accessed October, 2023

Habermas, Gary R. and Licona, Michael R. *The Case for the Resurrection of Jesus.* Grand Rapids: Kregel, 2004.

House, H. Wayne and Holden, Joseph M. *Charts of Apologetics and Christian Evidences.* Grand Rapids: Zondervan, 2006.

Hugh T. Kerr and John M. Mulder, *Conversions.* Grand Rapids: Eerdmans, 1983. Taken from *Grace Abounding to the Chief of Sinners* in *The Complete Words of John Bunyan.* Philadelphia, 1874.

Hunter, Braxton. *Evangelistic Apologetics: Compatibility and Integration.* Evansville, IN: Trinity Academic Press, 2014.

Keller, Timothy. *The Reason for God.* New York: Penguin Books, 2018.

Kenny, Anthony. *Aquinas.* Oxford: Oxford University Press, 1980.

Kerr, Hugh T. and Mulder, John M. *Conversions,* Grand Rapids: Eerdmans, 1983.

Koester, Paul M. "The Role of Apologetics in Witnessing to Mormons." 2018 http://essays.wisluthsem.org:8080/ handle/123456789/4372.

Koester, Robert, *The Spirit of Pietism.* Milwaukee: Northwestern Publishing House, 2013.

Koukl, Gregory. Tactics. Grand Rapids: Zondervan, 2019.

Kreeft, Peter and Tacelli, Ronald K. *Pocket Handbook of Christian Apologetics.* Downer's Grove: InterVarsity, 2003.

Luther, Martin. *Luther's Works.* Edited by Theodore G. Tappert. American Edition. Vol. 54. Philadelphia: Fortress Press, 1967.

_____. *Luther's Works*, ed. and trans. Philip S. Watson, American Edition, Vol. 33 (Philadelphia: Fortress Press, 1972)

McDowell, Josh. *Evidence That Demands a Verdict.* Revised Edition. San Bernadino, CA: Here's Life Publishers, 1979.

McGrath, Alister E. *Iustitia Dei: A History of the Christian Doctrine of Justification, Volume 1: Beginnings to 1500.* Cambridge: Cambridge University Press, 1986.

_____. *Mere Apologetics: How to Help Seekers & Skeptics Find Faith.* Grand Rapids: Baker, 2012.

McInerny, Ralph. *A First Glance at St. Thomas Aquinas.* Notre Dame, IN: University of Notre Dame Press, 1990.

McKim, Donald K., ed. *The Cambridge Companion to John Calvin.* Cambridge: Cambridge University Press, 2004.

Montgomery, John Warwick. *Always Be Ready: A Primer on Defending the Christian Faith.* Irvine, CA: 1517 Publishing, 2017.

_____. *Christ as Centre and Circumference: Essays Theological, Cultural and Polemic.* Bonn, Germany: Verlag fuer Kultur und Wissenschaft, 2009.

_____. *Faith Founded on Fact: Essays in Evidential Apologetics.* Irvine, CA: NRP Books, 2015.

_____. *Tractatus Logico-Theologicus.* Eugene, OR: Wipf & Stock, 2013.

Morley, Brian K. *Mapping Apologetics: Comparing Contemporary Approaches.* Downer's Grove, IL: Intervarsity Press, 2015.

Nicole, Roger. "John Calvin's View of Limited Atonement." *Westminster Theological Journal*, Vol. 47, No. 3 (Fall 1985), https://www.apuritansmind.com/arminianism/john-calvins-view-of-limited-atonement/. Accessed October 2023.

Parton, Craig. *The Defense Never Rests.* Second Edition. St. Louis: Concordia, 2015.

Peter Erb, Editor. *Pietists, Selected Writings*. New York, Paulist Press, 1983.

Peters, Paul. "Melanchthon the Humanist," *Wisconsin Lutheran Quarterly*, Vol. 44 (October, 1947).

Pieper, Francis. *Christian Dogmatics*. Volume II. St. Louis: Concordia, 1951.

Pinson, J. Matthew. *40 Questions About Arminianism*. Grand Rapids: Kregel, 2022.

Plantinga, Alvin. *Knowledge and Christian Belief*. Grand Rapids: Eerdmans, 2015.

Portalie, Eugene. *A Guide to the Thought of Saint Augustine*. Chicago: Henry Regnery Company, 1960.

Preus, Robert. *The Inspiration of Scripture: A Study of the Theology of the 17th-Century Lutheran Dogmaticians*. St. Louis: Concordia, 1955.

Quinn, Philip L. and Taliaferro, Charles, eds. *A Companion to Philosophy of Religion*. Malden, MA: Blackwell, 1999.

Quist, Allen. *The Reason I Believe: The Basics of Christian Apologetics*. St. Louis: Concordia, 2017.

Ramm, Bernard. *Varieties of Christian Apologetics*. Grand Rapids: Baker, 1973.

Shelton, W. Brian. *Prevenient Grace: God's Provision for Fallen Humanity*. Anderson, IN: Francis Asbury Press, 2014.

Sproul, R. C., Gerstner, John., and Lindsley, Arthur. *Classical Apologetics*. Grand Rapids: Zondervan, 1984.

Strobel, Lee. *The Case for Christ: A Journalist's Personal Investigation of the Evidence for Jesus*. Grand Rapids: Zondervan, 2016.

_____. *The Case for Grace: A Journalist Explores the Evidence of Transformed Lives*. Grand Rapids: Zondervan, 2015.

Sweeny, Jon M. *The Saint vs. the Scholar: The Fight Between Faith and Reason*. Cincinnati, OH: Franciscan Media, 2017.

Tertullian, "Prescription Against Heretics," Chapter 7. In *Early Latin Theology*, Library of Christian Classics V (1956). Translated and Edited by S. L. Greenslade. https://www.tertullian.org/articles/betty_prae/betty_prae.htm. Accessed October 2023.

Thorsen, Don. *Calvin vs. Wesley: Bringing Belief in Line with Practice*. Nashville: Abingdon, 2013.

Van Til, Cornelius, Why I Believe in God. Phillipsburg, NJ: P&R, 1975. Kindle file, Fig-books, 2012.

Williams, Thomas. "Reason & Faith: Philosophy in the Middle Ages, Lecture 7." In *The Great Courses*, Chantilly, VA: The Teaching Company, 2007.

Wynkoop, Midred Bangs. *Foundations of Wesleyan-Arminian Theology*. Kansas City: Beacon Hill, 1967.

Zachman, Randall C. *John Calvin as Teacher, Pastor, and Theologian: The Shape of His Writings and Thought.* Grand Rapids: Baker, 2006.

Appendix
Apologetics and the 17th-Century Lutheran Theologians

Some have complained that the early Lutheran theologians of the 17th-century developed apologetic arguments similar to those used in modern apologetics. At some point, they say, Lutherans dropped the ball, failed to continue that work, and should do so now.

Apologetics and theology

The Lutheran dogmaticians did, in fact, include what we call apologetic arguments in their theology books. But can we use their example as an encouragement for modern Lutherans to join in the modern apologetic movement?

A complete answer to that question is beyond the scope of this book. Anyone who might want to explore the topic, however, should be encouraged by the fact that many of the original works have been scanned and are available.[339]

---

[339]If you are not familiar with material available, the following information was supplied by Rev. Andrew Hussman and will get you started:

There are a few ways you can search for these writings. The main places they're stored online are either on Google Books (make sure to set it to "full view only"), Internet Archive, or directly on the websites of German universities. Typically the German universities have the highest quality copies, but sometimes you can find those same copies posted on Google Books and Internet Archive, but I'd say these two usually still have good copies of books. I think the Google Books and Internet Archive are pretty self-explanatory.

Rather than search each individual university library database separately, there are places you can go to search all of them. The most comprehensive place to check are the VD websites (See https://www.bsb-muenchen.de/en/competence-centers-and-state-wide-services/competence-centers/vd-16/ for more information on VD websites.) You go to VD 16 for 16th century writings, VD 17 for 17th century, and VD 18 for 18th century. Searching on these lets you find nearly everything written by an author that's found in a German university library. But since it's so inclusive, you'll still have to narrow your search as to whether a particular volume has been digitized yet (many volumes are listed but when you click on them you can only find bibliographic information and it turns out the volume hasn't been digitized or is still in the process of being digitized). You can set the settings to search only for volumes that are digitized

Here are some thoughts on using their material as an example.

First, the Enlightenment began at the end of the 17th-century and became and gathered momentum as the 18th-century progressed. Except for the very latest Lutheran dogmaticians who lived at the beginning of the 18th century, most of the dogmaticians did not live when the existence of God, the truth of Scripture, or the six twenty-four-hour day creation were being challenged. Therefore, it's not fair to strictly compare them to modern apologists. Nor is it fair to say that their use of apologetics was merely an initial foray into the field, and that we ought to continue what they started.

Second, modern apologetics includes far more than arguments and evidence. It also contains theological assumptions that determine how the augments and evidence should used. Even modern apologists admit this. The most important question is what role apologetics has in creating and sustaining faith.

Lutheran theologians were just that, Lutheran. They understood Martin Luther well and believed his teachings reflected those of Scripture and they considered it their job to uphold his teachings. As we have seen from his own writings, the Word and its power was tantamount to Luther. Anything that competed with the place of the Word in a Christian's life would injure their faith.

It would be odd for them to offer a view different from Luther's. And they didn't. Perhaps the greatest example of this—their teaching of the self-authenticating power of Scripture—directly opposes modern apologists' reliance on proofs from outside Scripture to prove that Scripture is true. They were not afraid of circular reasoning and the fact that it destroys the ability to be logical and makes it impossible to satisfy the skeptic.

---

and freely available. (Sometimes books have been digitized but you need a subscription or institutional access to view them.)

I go to VD if I want to see what an author has written and whether anyone has digitized it yet. Therefore, that's the place I'd recommend you looking if you're strictly looking for digital volumes of books. It's the easiest place to browse by author and in other ways too. PRDL stands for Post-Reformation Digital Library (www.prdl.org.) You can read more about them in their About section. This website doesn't store any of the books themselves, but directs you to where you can find them in Google Books, Internet Archive, or a university. I often like to use the advanced search settings because they let you search by title, author, and all the usual things, but also by genre, tradition (Lutheran, Catholic, Anglican, etc), and language.

My favorite German library is ULBH (Universitäte-und Landesbibliothek Halle) because they usually do the best job of giving a table of contents that is hyperlinked, so it's very easy to navigate and explore.

Robert Preus, who has read all or most of what the Lutheran dogmaticians taught about Scripture, summarizes their position: "The dogmaticians all answer that Scripture itself has the power to made us divinely certain of its authority." The Spirit "moves and enlightens our hearts to faith in His Word and promises."[340] He quotes Abraham Calov as saying, "If rational or empirical investigation contributes anything toward strengthening the truthfulness or authority of Scripture, then Scripture is no longer [self-authenticating]; in fact, it is no longer authoritative, and, what is of infinitely greater concern, our Christian faith is undone."[341] If modern apologists followed the Lutheran dogmaticians on his point, it would have to reject the greater part of evidential apologetics.

Third, how much importance did the Lutheran dogmaticians give to apologetic arguments? We have already seen that their view of Scripture greatly limited their use of these arguments. Robert Preus, in speaking of the various apologetic type arguments used by the dogmaticians, writes that all the dogmaticians answer "that there are a great number of criteria, both external and internal, which powerfully speak for the authority and heavenly origin of Scripture. . . . These criteria are able to convince the unbeliever who is not incorrigible that Scripture is the inspired Word of God, but, however, convincing they may be, they can bring about only a human conviction and opinion."[342] However, Preus also says, "Markedly less emphasis is placed on these criteria by the later dogmaticians."[343]

Preus wonders why the dogmaticians emphasized criteria of Scripture that demonstrates their truth. He writes,

> The whole of this emphasis reveals a certain concession to rationalism which is inherent in their theological method unless carefully guarded against, and betrays a certain inconsistency with their rigid adherence to the *self-authenticating* nature of Scripture and to their principles of *by Scripture alone* and *by faith alone*. The witness of the Spirit which is

---

[340]Robert Preus, *The Inspiration of Scripture: A Study of the Theology of the 17th-Century Lutheran Dogmaticians* (St. Louis: Concordia, 1955), pp. 108–109.

[341]Robert Preus, *The Inspiration of Scripture*, p. 91 (English substituted for Greek autopistos).

[342]Robert Preus, *The Inspiration of Scripture*, p. 106.

[343]Robert Preus, *The Inspiration of Scripture*, p. 106.

by faith alone and which is the result of *by grace alone* simply rules out the necessity and the validity of any observable criteria.[344]

---

[344]Robert Preus, *The Inspiration of Scripture*, p. 114. (English substituted where there are italics.)

279

www.ingramcontent.com/pod-product-compliance
Lightning Source LLC
Chambersburg PA
CBHW070343090426
42733CB00009B/1268